West Turkey Hunting

Strategies For All Levels

Scott Haugen

H|E

Dedication

My most fond turkey hunting memories are those spent with my family. No other form of hunting I know of promotes family togetherness like turkey hunting. Watching the spring woods come to life, hearing thundering gobbles of distant toms and sharing it with family is what turkey hunting is all about.

Jerry Haugen   *Tiffany Haugen*   *Braxton Haugen*   *Kazden Haugen*

This book is dedicated to my dad, Jerry Haugen, who introduced me to turkey hunting. Also, to my wife, Tiffany, for the great times we've shared in the turkey woods and for allowing me to finish writing this book on the day of our 22nd wedding anniversary. I appreciate your understanding and continued support more than you know.

Finally, to my two sons, Braxton and Kazden, whom I've been blessed to experience many fond memories with, including all those great turkey hunting adventures.

I look forward to more unforgettable times with you all.

Published in 2013 by Haugen Enterprises

All photographs taken by the author unless otherwise noted.

SB ISBN-13: 978-0-9819423-4-6   UPC: 0-81127-00351-8
Printed in China

Table Of Contents

Acknowledgements 4

Introduction 5

Chapter 1:

Meet The Wild Turkey 10

Chapter 2:

Gearing Up For The Hunt 49

Chapter 3:

Spring Hunting Season 112

Chapter 4:

Fall Hunting Season 144

Chapter 5:

Youth Turkey Hunting 165

Chapter 6:

Conclusion 177

Appendix I:

Field To Table 184

Appendix II:

Favorite Recipes 193

Index 202

Acknowledgments

Jody Smith, one of the West's top turkey guides and one of my favorite people.

I'd like to thank the many people over the past decades who've made it possible and allowed me to hunt turkeys. From land owners to wildlife personnel to guides who are too many to mention, and more, it goes to show that the number of people who impact a turkey hunter's life is great, and should never be taken for granted.

I would like to extend a special thanks to Jody Smith, one of the West's top turkey guides, a man who has been so gracious both as a guide and a friend over the years; a man I'd be proud to have my sons grow up to be like.

Introduction

Not until I was in junior high, in the late 1970s, did talk begin to stir about the possibilities of turkey hunting in my home state of Oregon. Transplanting efforts had been going on for years, and though we were seeing a growing number of turkeys while spending time in the deer hunting woods, there was no season.

That all changed in 1986. That year, the first year turkey hunting came to Oregon, both my dad and I held prized spring tags which were awarded in a lottery. The hunt took place only an hour's drive from our home, near the town of Roseburg, but in anticipation of the hunt we drove down the afternoon prior so we could try and locate birds as they went to roost.

During the final hour of daylight we heard numerous gobbles echoing throughout the oak-covered, rolling hills and grassy meadows along the pristine North Umpqua River. It was the first time either Dad or I had heard wild turkeys gobble. The sounds were even sweeter than we'd imagined and invigorated our sprits with bursts of adrenaline every time a gobbler fired off.

The power with which the gobbles reverberated up and down the valleys left us speechless. Every little owl hoot we let out, multiple toms replied. Sleep was almost impossible that night.

Opening morning we were up well before daylight. Parking the truck along a country road, we got out and listened for gobbles. Nearly an hour passed before we heard our first gobble in the distance. As daylight broke on the horizon, birds grew more vocal.

Unable to resist any longer, dad let out a soft yelp on his diaphragm call. Instantly three different groups of toms fired-back. Dad and I just looked at each other and smiled. Originally, our plan was to hunt together, but when we heard so many birds gobbling in different places, we split up. Dad headed east to the creek bottom while I hiked west, into the rolling hills.

Nearly 30 minutes later I heard Dad shoot. I'd yet to call in a tom, though I kept chasing distant gobbles. An hour later I sat against a skinny oak tree, resting, trying to figure out what I could do differently. Setting my box call aside, I put a diaphragm call in my mouth and let loose with some aggressive yelps.

No sooner had the sounds passed my lips when two toms gobbled back. A few soft yelps brought more gobbling, and before I knew it, three big toms rounded the knoll, fans fully spread, walking right at me. Instantly my mouth dried-up, and I dared not call again for fear of screwing something up. Fortunately, I didn't need to call anymore, for the toms were locked-in.

When the strutting toms broke into the tiny opening in front of me, they stopped, pirouetted and gobbled at one another. Daring not to move a muscle, I nervously sat, gun balanced on my knee, heart racing. When the tom on the left came out of a strut and extended his head, I covered it with the bead of my waterfowling shotgun and pulled the trigger. The hand loaded #4 shot hit the mark, dropping the tom on the spot, inside 30 yards.

My dad, Jerry Haugen, and I with our first Oregon turkeys. It was on this hunt where I fell in love with turkey hunting, a passion I carry to this day.

Walking up on that tom, his brightly colored, patriotic head at rest amid lush green grass and a sea of purple and yellow wildflowers, he was more striking than I imagined. I couldn't get off the hill fast enough, eager to show Dad.

For days, Dad and I relived our hunts to anyone who'd listen. It was fun sharing our stories, but what meant the most to us was that we'd found another way to spend time together as a father and son, doing what we love. We were blessed to be among the first of a handful of hunters lucky enough to kickoff turkey hunting in Oregon. The fact the hunt took place on a beautiful spring day made it even more special.

Dad and I have shared many memorable days in the turkey woods. We have this grand bird to thank for creating such unforgettable moments.

Since that glorious day, Dad and I have shared many great hunts in the spring, and fall, turkey woods. We never take these hunts, or our time together, for granted.

Today, Oregon is one of the greatest conservation success

stories in the country in terms of wild turkey management. At the time of this writing, turkeys could be hunted in every county of the state, and with over 35,000 birds estimated to be roaming within state boundaries, hunters can get three toms in the spring, two birds in the fall.

In a relatively short time Oregon went from having few birds to supporting a hunting season, then allowing five birds a year per-hunter with a comprehensive four months of hunting. Oregon is just one of the prime examples of how adaptive turkeys are, and how biologists, hunters, hunting organizations, landowners and volunteers can all work together to promote the perpetuation and conservation of wildlife.

Other western states have followed suit, creating more turkey hunting opportunities than ever before. Today, turkey hunting–not only out West, but nationwide–continues to be one of the fastest growing segments within the world of hunting. It's hard to believe that a century ago, fewer than 30,000 turkeys remained in the United States. Today, more than 7 million turkeys roam the country, with huntable populations in every state except Alaska.

Without the dedicated efforts of hunters, volunteer groups and fish and wildlife agencies, turkey hunting would not exist to the level it does throughout the West.

Because turkey populations continue to thrive and expand so rapidly, the intent of this book is not to share where to go hunting, but how to successfully hunt for turkeys in the variety of habitats they occupy throughout the West. Be it Merriam's in the high-country, eastern birds in isolated pockets where they've been successfully introduced, or Rio's in wet climates of the Pacific Northwest, this book will help you fill tags.

In terms of finding a place to go turkey hunting, I encourage you to start with local wildlife agencies, namely the offices in charge of wild turkey management. These folks know where bird populations are solid, growing or suffering from poor nesting success or predation on both public and private land. They are a great resource, as are landowners, Forest Service personnel and timber companies.

Because turkeys continue to adapt and expand their range, to try and pinpoint the best hunting locales in each state would be futile, and could be obsolete in a short time. True, some specific locales in multiple western states have been consistently producing good numbers of birds for three decades or more, but relatively speaking, turkey hunting is fairly new to the West. Birds continue taking up residence in places they've never before been seen, yet sometimes leave places they've historically frequented. Such population shifts mean prime hunting destinations can change over time.

*Turkey populations throughout the West continue to grow,
as a result their range is steadily expanding.*

In terms of western turkey hunting, it's the Merriam's and Rio Grande subspecies that are pursued most by hunters. There are some isolated pockets where eastern subspecies of birds exist, thanks to past transplanting efforts. But for the most part, where eastern birds have been introduced, they either perished due to an inability to adapt to harsh, wet weather, or crossbred with Rio's.

Within the pages that follow, it is my intent to share valuable information I've personally learned through trial and error during my brief, 26 years of turkey hunting around the West. More important than focusing on the species themselves, or where to hunt them, my success has come by focusing more on how to best use my hunting skills to meet the demanding terrain, current conditions and bird behavior being faced on any given day.

Turkey hunting the West can find you in a wide range of habitats and conditions. Being mentally and physically prepared will greatly increase the odds of success.

Perhaps the most important lesson I've learned while turkey hunting out West is to be flexible. The habitat and broken terrain that makes up the West is big and varied. At the same time, it can be simple, flat farmland. One day you may be hunting spring turkey in 80° temperatures, the next it may be snowing. One hunt may find you pursuing Merriam's at 4,000 feet in elevation, the next chasing Rios at near sea-level.

Mind you, I don't have all the answers and don't pretend to. In fact, I have a lot to learn and I'm reminded of that just about every time I set foot in the turkey woods. That's what I love so much about turkey hunting, and hunting in general; the learning never stops. For these reasons, I encourage you to approach turkey hunting with an open mind and a willingness to adapt. A dose of patience and persistence will help, too.

No matter where or when you hunt wild turkeys, their behavior can change from one day to the next, one hour to the next, even from minute to minute. Flexibility, seeing the whole pictures and never giving up, those are the key ingredients to building a solid foundation for hunting turkeys, western style.

Chapter 1:

MEET THE WILD TURKEY

No matter what animal we pursue, it best serves us to know all we can about the species we hunt, and the wild turkey is no exception. Of all the hunts I've been blessed to experience around the world, I can honestly say turkey hunting can be one of the most frustrating, thus one of the most rewarding when everything comes together.

Turkeys are North America's largest game bird. Adult toms can tip the scales to 30 pounds and stand four feet tall. In the fall, turkeys weigh 10% to 15% more than in the spring, when they're focussed on breeding. Their stunning beauty and susceptibility to the call explains why more than four million turkey hunters take to the field each year, and why turkey hunting is one of our country's fastest growing segments within the hunting community. But these big, beautiful, cunning birds are far from easy to hunt.

With brains no larger than a walnut, you'd think the wild turkey would be easy to consistently outwit. True, there are hunts that end after just a few minutes of effort, but things don't usually come together that quickly. Turkeys are high strung, always moving, fidgeting and nervously looking around. All this on-edge behavior sometimes makes it tough to close the deal.

Their innate, nervous demeanor begins early in life and becomes more prevalent with age. Bagging an old tom can be tough, seemingly impossible at times. But if you stop and analyze why a tom behaves the way he does, and what his goals in life are at the time of the hunt, it becomes more apparent how to best go about hunting him.

Given my formal education background in the sciences, my hunting approach is based more on animal behavior, geography and current weather conditions, rather than blindly stepping into the woods, hoping to fill a tag. Gaining a full understanding of the life a wild turkey leads is enlightening as to why they behave the way they do. It will also help to figure out how to hunt them on their terms, not yours.

Contrary to belief, Benjamin Franklin did not rally for the wild turkey to become our national bird, but he did compare it's beauty to that of the bald eagle. Many hunters consider the turkey to be our most striking bird, and one look tells why.

Wild Turkey Lifecycle

No matter what the subspecies, the lifecycle of the wild turkey is similar across the country. Though seasonal shifts and brooding times can vary throughout the West's vast and varied habitat—much of which can be weather dependent, especially at higher elevations—overall the behavior of all birds share common and consistent threads: to reproduce at a certain time, move to the most productive food sources during the changing seasons and survive by avoiding bad weather and dodging predators.

Since spring is the most mesmerizing time to be in the turkey woods, let's start there. Most spring turkey seasons throughout the West are meant to start after the peak of the breeding season. Many hunters are surprised when they learn that by the time spring season has commenced in their area, most hens have been bred. That's not to say all the hen's have

been serviced, or are setting on a full clutch of eggs, as some hens have not been bred by the time hunting season rolls around.

Throughout many western states the average peak of the breeding season runs from mid-March to mid-April. In higher elevations east of the Cascade Mountains, the breeding season can be delayed a week or two, even more, depending on the amount of snow, cold temperatures and a lack of food.

During a single mating session with one tom, up to 50 eggs are capable of developing inside the hen. When her body says it's time to start laying, the hen will build a nest and lay one egg every 24 to 32 hours. The average size of a clutch is 11 to 12 eggs. The hen waits until the final eggs is laid prior to setting on the clutch, or incubating the eggs. Some 28 days after incubation began, the eggs start to hatch.

Sometimes a hen may lay up to 17 eggs, but not all will develop. On rare occasions a hen's nest may be subject to dump nesting, where one or more hens lays their eggs in another hen's nest. If you come across a nest that has 18 or more eggs, dump nesting may explain it. If a young, first-time laying hen can't find suitable nesting habitat, she may lay her eggs in another hen's nest; or if she wasn't bred, she may also dump nest, though those eggs will be infertile. If a nest gets destroyed amid the laying process, that hen may abandon the site and finish laying her eggs in another hen's nest.

Upon hatching, turkey chicks are precocious, meaning they can walk soon after hatching, usually leaving the nest 12 to 24 hours after hatching. They are more fully developed in the egg, versus a songbird that hatches and develops while in a nest high up in a tree; ground-nesting birds need to move fast after hatching if they want to escape predators. After spending 8 to 14 days on the ground, the developing young are able to fly short distances and roost in trees. If weather is favorable at this time, their chances of surviving greatly improve.

Predators like ravens, crows, hawks, skunks, raccoon, fox, coyote, bobcats and stray cats claim many nests and young turkey broods.

A turkey's most vulnerable time is the first two weeks of its life. Escaping predators and wet weather are crucial.

The sperm which is deposited in a hen is viable for more than 30 days. This means that if a hen loses a clutch or two within 30 or so days of mating, she can re-nest without having to breed again. Not only is this nature's way of helping the hen have a successful nesting season, but it raises some misconceptions among hunters.

12

Upon seeing a newly hatched brood of turkeys in late August or September, many people believe it's the hen's second or third clutch. What really happened is the hen lost a brood or two and simply re-nested. Wet, cold spring weather is the leading cause of lost broods. Foul weather and predators are leading causes of lost broods in the summer.

If you see a hen with her brood in late summer or early fall, chances are she bred with a tom more than once that mating season as the sperm which entered her reproductive organs became infertile. Rio grande turkeys have been observed re-nesting up to four times while Merriam's don't re-nest very often. This explains why Rios are more prevalent in many western states.

When chicks and poults are seen in summer, it's not the result of a hen raising a second brood; it's because she lost an earlier clutch.

How active a hen is while tending a nest depends on temperature and weather conditions. Typically, hens will come off a nest around the middle of the afternoon to defecate and feed, then they'll get right back to setting. If temperatures are warm and there's no rain, hens will leave their nest in the morning, too. Likewise, if the weather is colder and more wet than normal, the hen will stay on the nest to protect her eggs as long as she can.

It's the setting hens that wander away from their nest that can give hunters fits. Toms usually latch on to these hens, making it tough for hunters to pull them away. This is where it pays to watch the hen. If she's on a mission to feed, not slowing down for the puffed-

up tom who wants to breed, chances are she'll feed, water and soon return to her nest. The worse the conditions, the closer to her nest she'll stick and the quicker she'll return to it. Once she returns to set, that's the time to get after the tom that was courting her.

Another reason the Rio Grande subspecies of turkey has done so well, not only in the West but nationwide, is the fact they tend to nest and contribute to the overall population as yearlings. Though few jakes (one year-old males), will mate, most jennies (one year-old hens), will. This is not the case for Merriam's, as their first mating season takes place at the age of two.

Have you ever stopped to think about how, upon stumbling on a lone turkey egg in the field, that egg got there? This is usually where a newly expectant mother didn't understand what her biological clock was telling her and she failed to make it to the nest before her body expelled the egg. This is not uncommon among one-year old Rio hens. It's not unlike finding a songbird egg laying in the backyard.

The biggest threat to a turkey's survival is within its first 10 days of life. If their down gets wet from rain, hypothermia is likely, and this is when they're most vulnerable to predation. Should they make it past that time, under ideal conditions toms can live up to five years, hens six to eight years. A hen that survives to eight years of age is rare and could be compared to a 100-year-old person. Typically, a tom that lives two or three years is the norm given the rigors they encounter throughout life.

The number one killer of adult birds are prolonged winter storms where crusted ice keeps them from accessing food. But turkeys are tough, too, being able to survive some very nasty storms. They can stay in a tree for several days, losing a good bit of body fat but still surviving.

Turkeys are survivors, now living in every state but Alaska. When I lived in Alaska, a buddy north of Fairbanks raised five Rio Grand turkeys. He turned them loose early one

winter because he got tired of tending them. Not only did the birds overwinter, but they did it on their own, with no help from the man who brought them there. This part of Alaska has some of the harshest weather on the planet, and with temperatures dipping to more than 50° below zero that winter, amid days of total darkness, the fact all five of these jakes survived is amazing and goes to show how hardy turkeys really are.

While jakes can breed at one year of age, most don't because they have to overcome mature toms in the area. But if jakes are willing to travel–and they have been known to do so over long distances–they will successfully mate. In fact, many transplanting efforts have centered around jakes that are willing to travel and breed with more hens. Most old toms are home bodies, having about a one-square mile range, and don't commonly travel far in search of hens. The older the tom, the less they tend to move during breeding season, and the rough country of the West plays a big part in that for some populations. This is why nature has programmed hens to go to the strutting grounds of toms during breeding season.

Hens, on the other hand, will travel long distances to find a tom and seek a secluded nesting site. In some western states, hens have been known to travel more than 15 miles to nest from where they were bred. I've seen hens with young broods in some of the highest, most secluded logged units around, several miles from the nearest turkey meadow. It always surprises me to see how far these hens will travel to nest, but solidifies how adaptable they are and how such movements play a big part in spreading wild turkey populations.

Because jakes are willing to follow hens great distances in the spring, they can play a big part in the breeding and natural expansion of turkey populations throughout the West.

Though some hens may travel 15 miles to nest in seclusion, they will often return to where they were bred to raise their brood. Some hens, however, stay within a 1/4-mile of where they were bred, to nest. Some hens will travel back to the same exact breeding, nesting and brooding sites year after year. Once a hen finds an optimal nesting location, she may use it for life, as long as the habitat and surroundings remain constant.

It's the willingness of hens and jakes to travel great distances that have lead to the explosion of turkey populations throughout the West. Knowing this, biologists make conscious efforts to transplant birds between existing populations of already established flocks, so they can fill in the gaps.

As summer progresses, hens and their developing young will join with others of their own kind. By fall, it's not uncommon to see three or more hens with their young of the year. At the same time, mature toms form bachelor flocks, often of like ages.

Sometimes, depending on the habitat, weather conditions and lifestyle of the birds, winter flocks of 200 birds or more are not uncommon. This is one of the best times of the year to not only hunt, but to also find places to hunt in the spring.

This hen was spotted in thick brush and heavy timber amid Oregon's Coast Range, 12 miles from the nearest private property. Out West, hen's have been known to travel 15 miles in search of prime nesting grounds.

I've secured many great spring hunting spots over the years by knocking on the doors of landowners who were overrun with big flocks of winter turkeys. Tired of having the birds defecating on their property all winter long, they were eager to have some birds removed. When I explain that these are the same birds that live in the area during the spring months, I often get an invitation to return. It's a classic example of how hunting really does serve as a tool of game management and wildlife conservation.

In low elevation habitats like valley floors, turkeys throughout the West don't undergo any type of migration. The weather is mild enough at these elevations, turkeys don't have to move far, if at all, to survive.

However, at higher elevations and where severe winter weather can put birds at risk, turkeys will migrate. That is, they move to lower elevations in the winter, higher elevations in spring. It's not a migration as you might think of deer or elk migrating, rather a shift in elevation to more comfortable habitats with ample food and shelter.

Turkey Anatomy

As with any wild animal, turkeys are equipped with physical characteristics that help them attract mates and escape predators. While hens are camouflaged and low-profile for nesting and raising young, toms are built to be seen and attract mates.

The head of the male wild turkey is one of the most impressive, whimsical features in the hunting woods. Consisting of skin from the base of the neck, up to the base of the beak, there's more to a tom's head than you might realize.

At the base of the tom's neck are the caruncles, often called waddles. These bumps and folds of skin hang from the base of the neck, over the adjoining feathers and the bumpy adornments continue all the way to the tom's face. Beneath the chin is a flap of skin known as the dewlap. Hanging over the beak, or when constricted, sitting atop the beak and in front of the eyes, is the snood.

All of these facial features can become bright red as the tom gets excited during breeding season. They can also turn white, almost instantly, when danger approaches or they get aggressive toward other toms. When the neck, dewlap and snood turn red, the sides of the turkey's face, around the eyes, can transform to a brilliant blue while the top of the head looses nearly all it's color and turns bright white. This patriotic red, white and blue head is one of the most stunning sights in the turkey hunting woods.

In the center of the tom's chest is a beard. The beard, like the head and its varied colorations, serves as a status symbol for both hens and competing toms. Like the antlers atop the head of a deer or elk, the beard of a mature tom gets him out of many potential conflicts just by confidently showing it off. The bigger the beard, usually the older and more dominant the tom, which puts him higher atop the pecking order.

The turkey beard is made of a rudimentary type of feather, or feathers, not hair like many people believe. The feather filaments, sometimes referred to as a mesofiloplume feather, correlates to the bristles of a beard having characteristics of two types of feathers. A tom's beard can grow at a rate of about four to five inches

Anatomy of a Tom Turkey Head

White Crown

Snood

Ear

Dewlap

Minor Caruncles

Caruncles or Waddles

a year. However, once a beard reaches about 10 to 12 inches, it starts dragging the ground and becomes worn down. This means a tom that's three year's old or older may only carry a beard of 10 to 12 inches in length. At this age, the beard becomes thicker in diameter, giving a good indication that the tom is older than three years of age.

Keep in mind, not all beards grow at the same rate or with the same durability. Some beards grow so fast, they don't get worn down by dragging on the ground. Some birds live in a more friendly habitat, meaning their beards don't wear down as quickly. For instance, a farmland Rio living in grassy pastures his whole life will likely sport a longer beard than a tom of the same age living in rugged, dry, rocky terrain 3,000 feet up in the mountains.

The filaments of some toms' beards are stronger than others, either due to genetics and/or diet, so they hold together longer. At the same time, toms living in more mild climates don't subject their beard to severe conditions like freezing, or dragging it over crusted snow, both of which can make it brittle which result in breakage.

Some beards appear rusty in color on the tips, or bent in certain parts with a reddish or even whitish line running horizontally across the beard. This is usually caused by a vitamin or mineral deficiency in the bird's diet. The melanin deficient part of the beard–the lighter colored part–sometimes breaks off and curls where it was broken, making for a tom with a shorter than normal beard. Sometimes the beard stays intact, faint stripe remaining, and continues growing as melanin production increases or as vitamins and minerals are acquired. Some beards–like other feathers on the bird–can be of different color, which can be explained by genetics.

Interestingly, about 15% of hens grow beards. The first fall turkey my son, Braxton, shot was a bearded hen. The first fall hen my wife, Tiffany got, sported three beards. Over the years I've observed several bearded hens, the longest being nearly 10 inches. In my personal experience, it seems bearded hens occur more in pockets than throughout random samplings of the population. There are areas we'll see bearded hens year after year, sometimes multiple ones in a day; other places we've never seen one.

18

Rounding out the physical features of toms are sharp spurs on the backs of their legs and their iridescent plumage. The older the bird, the longer, sharper and more curved the spurs become. Spurs are used to ward off predators and establish dominance among other birds. The longest spurred tom I've taken measured 1 7/8" and he carried a 12 inch beard. I've also shot toms with 10 and 11 inch beards, with short or no spurs. I've seen a good number of toms taken with only a spur on one leg, nothing on the other. Like all appendages, you never know how each and every one will turn out.

About 15% of hens grow beards.

A tom's breast feather (left) is tipped in black, while a hen's is buff to whitish color. Knowing this will tell you what birds are active in the areas you hunt.

As for a turkey's plumage, each bird carries between 5,000 and 6,000 feathers. The iridescent feathers of mature toms could be among the most stunning sights in all of nature. The way their red, green, bronze, gold and copper colorations reflect in the natural light is something that leaves the most experienced turkey hunter speechless every time he approaches a downed bird. But the purpose of these brightly colored feathers serves a great advantage when attracting a hen; the bigger, brighter and older the tom, the more likely he is to gain breeding rights to the hens.

The breast feathers of tom turkeys are edged in black, while the hen's breast feathers are edged in tan or white. This is a good identifying mark for hunters to know when looking at birds and also when running across such feathers while afield.

While on the topic of identifying features that differentiate toms from hens, their droppings are another clue. The droppings of toms are usually in the shape of a J. Though this is not always the case, normally they have one, elongated end. A hen's droppings are usually coiled or more spiral-shaped. A hen's droppings may also contain more white coloration.

Of course, diet and digestion play a part in the actual formation and appearance of droppings. When in the field, deciphering what type of droppings you're seeing–tom's or hen's–can offer valued clues to help filling a tag.

Tracks are another identifier hunters will want to pay attention to. If the tracks are surrounded by obvious drag marks left by the wings of a strutting tom, then it's clear you're looking at a tom. But if the drag marks aren't there, or you're trying to track down a tom in the fall, knowing what you're looking at can be important.

Generally, a mature tom's track will measure up to 5-inches from the back toe to the tip of the longest, middle toe. A hen's track will be about 4-inches. But not always is the dimple of the back toe visible in a track. When measuring a track from heel to toe, subtract about a half-inch of the overall length.

On a tom the middle toe will usually exceed 2 1/2-inches in length, while jake's and hen's will fall short of that mark. Of course, the size of a turkey's track changes with age and is also influenced by the type of ground it's left on. Tracks that are sunken in the muddy fringes of a pond or puddle may mislead you into thinking the bird is bigger than it actually is.

I've measured and collected many turkey feet over the years, from toms, jakes and hens. Overall, hen tracks are more slender than jakes or toms. As tom's grow older, their foot becomes bigger and thicker. The tracks of old toms often reveal swollen knuckles and thicker parts throughout.

As for a turkey's internal anatomy and skeletal structure, we'll take a closer look at that in Chapter 2, under the Bows section of that chapter.

A hen's droppings (left) are usually coiled, while a tom's is normally shaped like the letter J.

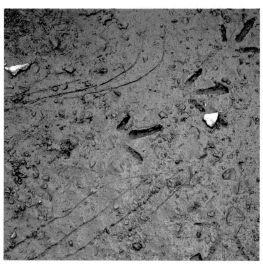

Tracks and wing drag marks reveal a tom recently strutted here.

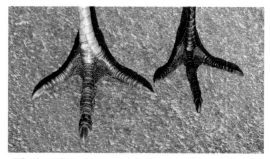

The foot of a mature tom (left), is considerably larger than that of a hen.

The coloration of a tom is key to establishing dominance and breeding rights.

Turkey Senses

Seasoned hunters agree that if the turkey had a sense of smell to match that of its vision and hearing, we'd be hard-pressed to ever fill a tag. In fact, it's the turkey's poor sense of smell that makes it so reliant upon its ears and eyes to help stay alive.

When it comes to vision, turkeys have some of the best and some of the worst eyes in the woods. It's believed that most birds, turkeys included, see in color, like humans. But the turkey is a bit unique in that its eyes are widely spaced on the side of its head. It's because of this wide spacing that turkeys struggle with depth perception. In reality, turkeys struggle to decipher all objects directly in front of them because they can't simultaneously focus on images with both eyes. Their less than ideal depth perception also makes it difficult for turkeys to accurately determine the size of objects. This explains why the hunter who sits stone-still will often encounter turkeys walking to within spitting distance of their gun barrel, or why turkeys have trouble landing in trees.

While a turkey's monocular vision creates challenges with depth perception, it's binocular-like power and 300° field of view make it tough to hunt.

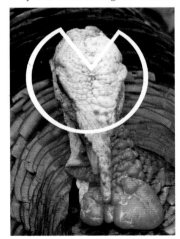

Conversely, turkeys can bust you from surprising distances with the slightest of movement. Think about how a turkey walks in relationship to how its eyes are set inside its skull. Their continual head bobbing when they walk, and the constant dipping, twisting and turning action of their head allows them to view objects from two different angles. This action will allow them to clearly see the object with both eyes and determine not only the distance to the object, but whether it's a potential threat or not.

In other words, turkeys have excellent monocular vision. This, combined with the fact they can see in a 300-degree arc without moving their head, gives them a complete view of their surroundings.

Often times hunters feel they are busted when a turkey looks right at them. In reality, the turkey is studying what he's looking at, and if no movement is detected, the bird usually goes about its business. However, if the hunter panics and moves ever so slightly, that's all the bird needs to confirm the threat and get out of there.

More than anything, the nervous nature of turkeys sets hunters on-edge. Don't perceive the turkeys nervous disposition as busting you. Just because they look at you, twisting their head and cranking their neck, doesn't mean they know what you are. Stay still, control the breathing and don't make a move until the turkey puts his head down and goes about his business.

As for hearing, as with most birds, the ears of the turkey are set on the sides of the head. They have no outer ear–of skin or feathers–which funnels the sound, so can detect sounds coming from all the way around them. This is another reason they constantly move their head, to pinpoint sound sources.

Turkeys have poor night vision and are continually preyed upon by predators from both the ground and sky. This, along with their eye and ear structure, explains why their hyper temperament is necessary in order to decipher exactly where potentially dangerous sounds are coming from. Should they not pinpoint where dangerous sounds are coming from, they might flee in the wrong direction. Wild animals usually only make one mistake, then they die.

Turkeys rely heavily on their speed and camouflage to keep them alive. When predators approach, turkeys either run off or fly away. Turkeys can run up to 25 miles per hour, and fly at speeds up to 55 miles per hour. This explains why so many hunters miss shots at spooked toms on the move.

Western Turkeys

When it came to introducing wild turkeys throughout the West, it wasn't easy. Wide-ranges of habitats, vast changes in elevation and severe seasonal shifts in weather had to be taken into consideration before figuring out what subspecies of birds might best survive in a particular place.

Throughout various western states, the initial introduction of the eastern turkey subspecies didn't go as hoped. Wet, cold springs and bad weather lasting into the summer months meant reproduction success rates were low, making it tough for the birds to perpetuate on their own. After many failed attempts in some regions, biologists shifted transplanting efforts to the Merriam's and Rio Grande subspecies.

There are still pockets of eastern turkeys in some western states, but in many of their original relocation sites, these birds have since crossbred with Rio Grande turkeys, creating a hybrid. Toms of these subspecies exhibit more of a cream coloration at the tips of their tail feathers and upper and lower tail coverts.

Today, Merriam's turkeys dominate states like Montana, Wyoming, Colorado, New Mexico and some of their neighboring states to the east. Arizona, Utah and Idaho also have their share of Merriam's, while Utah and Idaho are also home to Rios. California and Oregon consist primarily of Rio Grande turkeys or hybridized birds. Washington is the only state recognized in the entire country for having all three subspecies of turkeys in their pure form (Rio's, Merriam's and eastern's), though hunters do report taking birds that look very eastern-like in parts of Idaho, Oregon and northern California.

The Rio Grande turkey was first described by George B. Sennett in 1879, who noted it's appearance falling between the likes of the eastern and Merriam's turkeys. Native to the arid and semi-arid habitats of the Great Plains, this bird received its name from the Rio Grande River, which offered just the right conditions for it to thrive.

Today, the Rio Grande turkey has expanded its range from the Great Plains, and has been successfully introduced in several western states. What allows this subspecies of turkey to thrive in the West is that it can live in areas receiving between 16 to 32 inches of annual rainfall.

Originally, Rio Grande turkeys numbered into the millions. By the 1920s their numbers had plunged and in the 1930s trapping and transplanting efforts helped bring the bird back. Today, more than one million Rio Grande turkeys roam North America.

I've seen Rios at over 5,000 feet in elevation, all the way down to sea level. They occupy brushy areas near streams and rivers, thriving in lower elevation oak, Douglas fir and pine forests. These are gregarious birds, often seen in groups of 100 or more during the winter months.

The Rio usually has a distinct summer and winter range, and roosting sites can vary depending on the habitat they're found in. In the Douglas fir forests of the Cascade Range and continuing to the west, birds may roost high in big, mature trees. East of the Cascades and in their southwestern reaches, the Rio will seek out large pine trees. In areas with sparse tree growth, low growing oak trees may serve as primary roosting sites. In desolate regions, birds may simply roost in bushes surprisingly low to the ground.

I've seen the Rio Grande roost in some not so common places, too. From power lines to power line towers, barn roofs to inside abandoned barns, atop old buildings and even on fence posts and old gates, these birds can be opportunistic when it comes to finding a place to sleep. Sometimes these odd roost sites are used for weeks, other times only a few days. More natural roosts, like trees, may be used season after season, for years on end.

Rio Grande turkeys.

When fully mature, a male Rio Grande turkey stands about four feet tall and weighs up to 25 pounds. Birds over 30 pounds have been taken by spring hunters.

The tips of the tail and upper and lower tail covert feathers of a Rio are gold to semi-yellow in coloration. These feather parts may also appear tan or darker shades of brown. It's overall coloration is lighter than the eastern bird, darker than the Merriam's, making it easy to identify.

The Merriam's turkey was named in 1900 after the first chief of the U.S. Biological Survey, C. Hart Merriam. Its original range in the Southwest left it secluded from other turkey populations. Over the years the Merriam's has expanded its historic range from Colorado, New Mexico and Arizona, both naturally and through human efforts.

Merriam's turkeys.

Today, it's estimated that nearly 350,000 Merriam's roam the West, occupying all 11 western states. Very few Merriam's are found in Utah, and the ones living in Oregon and parts of Idaho have crossed with Rios and other turkeys, making for a hybrid. However, the northeast corner of Oregon does get the occasional pure strain of Merriam's that cross over from Idaho.

Merriam's turkeys are very adaptable birds, capable of living up to 10,000 feet in elevation, in areas with two feet of annual rainfall and in severe cold temperatures with excessive amounts of snowfall. Snow at higher elevations will push them to lower elevations in winter, where they congregate along habitat zones where deciduous and coniferous forests meet. Toms live in bachelor flocks at this time, not associating with hens until breeding season, which takes place at higher elevations than where they typically wintered.

Due to their black-tipped breast feathers, toms appear to be black when viewed straight-on. Once they turn to the side, however, the white-tipped coverts and tail feathers give them a unique appearance, one that conveys why so many hunters consider the Merriam's to be the most striking of all our wild turkeys.

The Merriam's turkey closely resembles another turkey subspecies of the American Southwest, the Gould's. The Gould's turkey is found in the extreme southern boundaries of Arizona and New Mexico, and thrives in old Mexico, where it is sought by serious turkey hunters.

One of the West's most accomplished hunters, outdoor writer, Bob Robb, with a Gould's turkey taken in Mexico. Efforts are being made to reintroduce the Gould's to parts of the southwestern U.S.

BOB ROBB PHOTO

Over the years I've hunted Merriam's in some of the biggest stands of ponderosa pine trees imaginable, and amid the brushy banks along some of the West's more popular rivers. In one area I hunt them in southeastern Montana, droppings are two feet thick beneath roost trees; here, ranchers tell me birds have been roosting in the same trees, year-round, for over 30 years.

Of the three main subspecies of western turkeys, the Merriam's can be among the most gullible to the call. Then again, they can prove the best of turkeys hunters, wrong, ignoring even the most alluring of sounds from time to time, for no apparent reason.

More than five million eastern turkeys roam the United States, making them the most wide-ranging of the five turkey subspecies (The Florida, or Osceola, turkey not being covered in this book). As the name implies, the eastern wild turkey inhabits the eastern part of the country, historically ranging as far west as Texas, Oklahoma, Kansas and Nebraska.

The eastern turkey was also successfully transplanted in Washington, Oregon and California, as well as in a few other isolated pockets west of the Rocky Mountains. However, their inability to thrive in wet habitats of the Northwest, and their ease of crossbreeding with other strains of turkeys, have left very few places where pure-strain eastern birds can be hunted in any of the 11 western states.

Eastern birds grow the biggest of all the turkey subspecies, with weights commonly being reported over 30 pounds in historic ranges where they are well fed. Out West, food and living conditions are not as friendly, so eastern birds are often surpassed in weight and height by the more adaptable Rio.

Eastern turkey.

Reddish-brown or chocolate-brown tail tips and coverts help identify the eastern turkey from the Rio and Merriam's. Without question, eastern birds are the toughest to bring to a call, especially in the ranges of western Washington, where the highest concentration of these birds are hunted out West.

There's another turkey subspecies worth noting; the Hybrid. During the Great Depression, many families around the Northwest went to raising turkeys, not only to sell but to feast on, themselves. When the depression ended, many farms were left with a surplus of turkeys. Not knowing what to do with them, many farms simply opened the gates and let the birds go.

Unfortunately, this happened about the time many wildlife agencies were trying to establish viable populations of wild birds (eastern, Rio and Merriam's). The result was crossbreeding between wild and feral stock. Though these birds did well, many of the turkeys hunters pursue today in the Northwest still carry the genetically expressed feral markings. These hybrid turkeys usually display dull, milky colored tail and covert tips, somewhat more pale than the creamy color of a Rio and not as reddish as those of eastern birds.

Crossbreeding between the Rio, Merriam's and eastern birds have occurred in many places where more than one subspecies was introduced. The result is a hybrid bird that, again, doesn't carry the distinct tail and covert tip colorations as the pure strain subspecies do. Because hybridization is never ending, it's difficult to pinpoint the precise locations where it takes place. If wanting to learn more about hybrids or feral turkey populations where you hunt, contact regional wildlife agencies for up-to-date facts.

Color Phase Turkeys

There are various color strains of wild turkeys worth noting. Color variations of any animal species–birds, fish, mammals or otherwise–are usually when a recessive trait becomes expressed, or visibly seen. Often times this requires the mating of a pair, both carrying the recessive trait. Though neither carrier may express the genes, they are both carriers, so their offspring will express the traits.

John Thomas with a smokey gray Rio Grande gobbler.

Eric Braaten with a partially melanistic tom taken in Washington's Lincoln County. Note the lack of pigmentation on both wings.

The most commonly perceived color variation among wild turkeys is the very rare albino. This is a bird that's completely white and has pink skin, feet and eyes. These birds lack any pigment in their plumage. Birds that express partial albinism–white feathers mixed in with the regular colored plumage–are fairly common, about 1/100, and are generally referred to as smokey gray turkeys. These are not to be confused with pure albinos. There are also all white birds, with normal colored eyes and feet which occur in about 1/10,000.

When birds have dominant dark pigmentation, they appear completely black and are called melanistic. Sometimes primary and tail feathers are black, carrying the melanistic trait. Melanism is also extremely rare among wild turkeys and very few hunters have reported every seeing one in the woods.

There exists another very rare color phase, one that stands out as perhaps the most stunning. It's called erythrocism, where red pigmentation dominates. These erythristic, or erythritic, birds are red and white. The primary and secondary flight feathers are pure white in erythristic birds, and the majority of the tail feathers are white with a smattering of rusty-red.

In the spring of 2010, while hunting with good friend and noted turkey guide, Jody Smith, I shot a mature Rio sporting the rare, erythristic color phase. I've never seen such a beautiful sight in the turkey woods. At the time, it was the first reported erythristic bird taken in the state of Oregon, and the odds of taking a bird like this were estimated to be about 1/300,000. What surprised me with this bird was the number of calls Jody received after our TV episode aired, looking to book hunts to shoot a big red and white tom. They didn't realize that in the wild, these birds truly are a once in lifetime prize, and that's only if you're really lucky.

Erythristic color phase wild turkey.

Jody Smith and I with our prized, 1/300,000 erythristic color phase Rio Grande tom.

There's another possibility for color variation birds, and that comes from domestic crossbreeding. Turkey breeders, in an effort to attain strikingly colored birds, have genetically bred turkeys to express the colors they desire. Sometimes these birds escape, explaining their place in the wild.

However, domestic birds don't live long in the wild turkey woods. Not only are they susceptible to predators, but their bodies aren't made for survival. Escaped domesticated birds usually travel alone, have trouble finding a mate and are easily identified by their thick legs and toes, a result of living high on the hog in the barnyard.

When the red and white bird I shot peeled away from two normal colored Rios, I knew he was a wild tom and not some feral stock. Fish and wildlife officials confirmed the wild nature of the erythristic tom with careful inspection and tarsal measurements.

Turkey Communication

For turkey hunters, it's the allure and challenge of calling birds to within shooting range that's most desired. While many western hunters pride themselves on spot-and-stalk turkey hunting–which can be every bit as challenging as stalking deer or elk–the truth is, most hunters thrive for the thrill of calling in toms.

I don't care what animal you call in, when they respond, it's exciting and rewarding. I've called in coyotes, bobcats, bears, multiple deer species, elk, moose and more, along with hundreds of turkeys over the years.

While calling in any wild animal is an accomplishment, and a rush, bringing in a turkey is different. I'm not going to pretend to make it something it's not. While calling in a turkey is a thrill, it's not on the same level as calling in a bugling bull elk, of which I often hear the comparison being made. Though both are exciting, bringing in a 700 pound, rut-crazed bull that's slobbering and bugling in your face, well, that's simply a different experience than fooling at 22 pound bird.

Don't get me wrong, calling turkeys is a true joy and offers an adrenaline rush unlike any form of

bird hunting I've experienced. Once that first bird comes to your call, you'll be hooked for life, no matter what your age.

As is the case with calling in any game animal–big game, predators or birds–the key lies in understanding a turkey's seasonal behaviors, food sources and what sounds they make, when and why. Turkeys make a wide range of sounds, many of which are different in spring and fall.

Though most hunters routinely fill tags by using only two or three sounds, it's good to know what sounds turkeys make, and why. This will help you dial-in to more effectively calling them, and will allow you to make the right sounds at the right time.

Keep in mind, when it comes to calling turkeys, we're defying nature. In the turkey woods, toms gather on strutting grounds, calling in an effort to bring hens to them. Hunters are doing just the opposite, making sounds of hens (or toms) to bring in the toms. Anytime hunters try to defy nature, there's no telling what the outcome will be.

Following is a listing of sounds made by both tom and hen turkeys. Because it's not easy describing sounds, in words, I encourage you to watch TV shows, DVDs and listen to on-line sites that have actual recorded sounds from wild turkeys. Of course, the best way to learn the sounds is to spend time in the woods, listening to turkeys talking, then figuring out why they're making the sounds they are. But before doing that, here's an offering of sounds to listen for and to try and emulate with the intent of helping to better understand bird behavior and recognize their sounds in the woods.

Hen Yelp: The most commonly heard sound in the turkey woods is made by the hen, and it's called a yelp. Toms also yelp, but it's louder, raspier and usually more drawn-out than that of hens.

A hen yelp is an easy call for hunters to make, and accounts for most turkeys that are called in.

The yelp is a basic call and the easiest sound to make. It's also the one that will bring in the most birds. I'd say about 80% of the toms I've called in, and seen called in over the years, have come to a hen yelp. When my boys were four years old, each were calling in turkeys with yelps made on a box call. When Braxton was nine, he called in a tom from nearly a mile away with yelps from a box call. These sounds are easy to make and they work in the spring, it's as simple as that.

The yelp is usually delivered in a series of one-note tunes. However, yelps can take on various forms. Specifically, there are three types of yelps hunters will want to be aware of, each of which carries different meaning.

The plain yelp usually occurs when turkeys are within sight of one another. It can range from three to seven notes, even up to nine or ten notes. On each note, the pitch and volume remain constant, with three to four notes being made per second, and each burst lasting up to 0.10 seconds. The sequence is simple, and resembles a *chirp, chirp, chirp* or a *yup, yup, yup* sound.

Yelps are easily made with box calls, slates, diaphragms, push-pull calls and more. The purpose is to send the message that all is safe and to let one another know where they're at. This is a good call to use when trying to bring birds to close-range, whether you can see them or not. Should birds appear edgy, plain yelps can help calm them.

Another type of yelp often heard in the turkey woods is what's called the lost yelp. The lost yelp is just what it sounds like, yelps made when birds get lost or separated from the flock. Usually younger birds and hens with broods make the lost call. This is a sound I like making when birds are split-up, feeding. It's also a good sound to offer when trying to pull in a hen, hoping a rut-crazed tom will follow.

Lost yelps are more intense than plain yelps, lasting up to 0.15 seconds. Lost yelps routinely consist of 20 or more notes, which also sets them apart from the more relaxed plain yelps. Lost yelps are more of a pleading sound that grows louder toward the end of each sequence. Because of the added intensity toward the end of the sequence, the bird's voice can crack in an effort to reach as high a volume as possible. Lost yelps can also be a bit raspier, and can be heard year-round, but predominantly in the spring and fall months.

Of even greater intensity are the assembly yelps. The intent of assembly yelps are just what the name implies; to bring together birds that have gotten separated from the flock. Though sometimes assembly yelps are heard in late spring, largely this is a sound heard in the fall, when adult hens try to gather poults that have become spread out, usually through feeding on the move in tall grass or brushy areas.

Assembly yelps sound much like plain yelps, but with much more intensity. Though the sequence is similar in terms of the number of yelps, the loud, stressing cries of the assembly yelp is easy to recognize. Young birds of fall usually respond quickly to these calls when made by hens. In the spring, toms often respond to the calls, and while I'm not sure if the sounds are intended for toms or other hens, toms do respond to them. I've brought in strutting toms as well as toms off the roost, to assembly yelps I've offered them.

The individual yelps can be twice as long, even more, than plain yelps. They drag out and escalate in intensity as they go, something like this: *Yuuup, yuuuuup, yuuuuuuup, yuuuuuuuup.*

All forms of yelps can greatly vary depending on the age and mood of the hen making the sounds. I think that's why they are so effective in the turkey woods, because hunters don't have to sound perfect when making yelps. In fact, some of the worst yelps I've heard have come from turkeys, themselves.

One word of caution, if you do mess up and make a bad yelp, don't stop. Instead, push through it and keep right on calling. When alarmed, birds may make a sporadic, out-of-tune yelp, then they'll stop. This is a red flag for other birds in the area. If you hit a bad note, don't stop, keep calling through it.

Cluck: The cluck is one of the most basic sounds in the turkey woods, but still carries strong meaning. The one to three note sound goes something like: *tuck...tuck,...tuck.* It's purpose is to get the attention of another bird or to reassure an approaching tom that a hen is waiting for him. It's an alluring, attention-grabbing sound that's simple yet powerful when it comes to bringing in a tom.

Clucks are made up of one to three single, staccato notes, usually separated by two to three seconds. The sharp, crisp sounds of a cluck are mainly used in close range calling situations. When an approaching tom hangs up in sight of your setup, a cluck made with a diaphragm call will often pull him the rest of the way in.

Often times hens are called in with clucks, and I think this is because when turkeys cluck, they like hearing others respond in the same way; it's their way of saying, "I'm here and all is safe." This is true with plain yelps, too. Though the sound is short, and sharp, it's not to be confused with a putt or cutts, which we'll soon look at. Clucks are not as intense or abrupt as putts, and they're not as fast paced as cutts.

Many times when birds are feeding, clucks are made in conjunction with

purrs. I've heard these sounds every month of the year, with the fall and winter months being the most vocal times. Clucks and purrs together send a message that all is safe and the birds content, especially when in a flock situation. Clucks and purrs, together, sound something like *tuck, tuck, errrrr.....tuck, errrrr...tuck, tuck, tuck, errrrr, tuck.* If looking to pull in wary toms or hens, using the cluck and purr, together, is about as real and convincing as it gets. They're also good, calm sounds to stop a tom for a shot.

Often times, no matter how good your call sounds, there's simply no pulling a tom away from a live hen.

Purr: As with the cluck, purrs can easily be made on slates and box calls as well as some push-pull calls. The sounds are tougher to make with diaphragm calls, but are worth mastering for the times you find yourself in the open and needing to bring a tom in closer or stop him for a shot.

Purrs are the most relaxing, most powerful reassurance call I know of. They send the simple message that birds are content and feel safe. When a flock of birds spread out feeding in early spring and fall, purrs can continually be heard. This is their way of keeping in touch with one another, especially when feeding in brushy country or broken terrain where they easily lose sight of one another.

Purrs are a soft sound that roll in a smooth, calming fashion, thus, are not very loud. The purr is a single, drawn-out note that sounds like, *errrr*. This is a great call to offer when toms are close, especially if they seem nervous, as it will convince them a hen is nearby and that she feels safe.

It's believed that hens have a variety of purring sounds they make, based on their breeding status and even when being bred, but I've not found these sounds to come into play when calling toms. Purrs can take on many forms, from low pitch at the beginning and low at the end, to high then low, to various pitch levels that remain constant from start to finish. As with yelps, if you make a mistake, don't worry about it and keep on calling. Often times the sequence and pace of the sounds being delivered are more important than their overall sound quality.

Purrs, clucks and even short putts are good to use when birds are flocked up. They're also effective when following a series of aggressive cuts or fly-down cackles. The soft purrs simply seem to calm even the most intense of calling situations, reaffirming all is well.

There's another form or purring sound turkeys make, and it's called the fighting purr. Both toms and hens make fighting purrs, and while it sounds like regular purrs, it's much more strung out and intense. Fighting purrs are a way of establishing social dominance within a flock, and I've seen it with hens just as often as with toms.

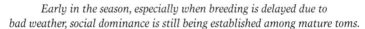

Early in the season, especially when breeding is delayed due to
bad weather, social dominance is still being established among mature toms.

Rather than short, sweet *errrr* sounds, fighting purrs are longer and more frequent, often with a putt occurring in the middle or at the end, something like; *errrrrrrrr, errrrrrrr, errrrrrrrrrrr, errrrrrrrrrrrr, putt, errrrrrrr, putt, putt, errrrrrrrrrrrr, errrrrrrrrr.*
Often times both birds that are battling, or displaying to establish dominance, will produce fighting purr

sounds. These can sometimes be heard from long distances and can be good sounds for hunters to make when talking to stubborn toms that think they're king of the hill. When mimicking a fight, toms often come running in to inspect, especially early in the season when a pecking order is being developed.

Cutts: Cutts, or cutting, are a series of loud, insistent, fast-paced, single-note sounds turkeys use to announce their presence, often in hopes of hearing a response from another turkey. It also sends the message that, "If you hear me, and are ready to breed, you'll need to come find me."

Cutts are easy sounds to make on a box or slate call, but diaphragm users may find it challenging due to the stop-start, hard, rapid pace. Cutts are made in fast bursts of two or three notes, usually followed a second or so later with more of the same. The sequence sounds like; *tut...tut....tut, tut, tut, tut...tut...tut...tut...tut. tut. tut, tut, tut.* The sequence can widely vary, so if offering these sounds, don't feel like they have to be exact.

Many hunters like using cutts to locate toms, or to get them to shock gobble in the early morning hours. Personally, I use cutts all day long for the simple reasons they are natural turkey sounds birds use to announce their presence and because they carry well in the big, timbered, often wet terrain of the West.

Following cold spells and during high winds, or when trying to penetrate wooded draws in deep canyons, aggressive cutts are one of my favorite sounds to get a tom to gobble. I've had more toms announce their presence to cutting sounds than any other sound, no matter what time of day. If looking to get birds fired-up and vocal, this is what

usually starts it off. It's also a good call to use when toms are hung-up, especially in brushy, wooded areas. When delivering this call, be ready, a nearby tom may quickly approach.

Putt: Putts are a single alarm note used to warn other birds of danger. So, why use them when trying to call birds in? I've had good success using putts in two situations. The first is in the fall, when breaking up a flock so I can later try calling them back in. The second is in the spring, when an approaching tom or hen comes to the call, senses something's not right and begins to putt.

In the fall, when looking to call birds in, a common approach is to rush into a flock, bust them up, then wait for them to start calling to reassemble. I've had the best success doing this when birds are in brush or feeding uphill along timbered edges, where I can approach without being seen. When making the rush to scare the birds, make a series of loud putts, to make them think another bird caused the commotion.

When using putts in the spring, often times a sharp-eyed bird senses something's not right, and begins to putt. There's no greater feeling of helplessness than when you've called in a bird and it begins putting, just out of shooting range. In a last effort to convince the bird everything is okay, make a putt and follow it up with some soft yelps and purrs.

One time I had an approaching tom hang-up at 60 yards. He started putting, and every time he putted, I putted right back, and followed it with some seductive yelps. That tom putted well over a dozen times, but I didn't give up, hammering right back with my own putts the moment he finished. Eventually the tom came in and I shot him. There's no doubt in my mind I wouldn't have been able to fool him were it not for my firing right back with my own putts and yelps. I simply was replying to him by saying, "Okay, maybe something isn't right, and I acknowledge that, but I'm a hot hen and I'm comfortable right where I am. I'm not coming to you; if you sense danger, you better come to me." It helps having a decoy in this situation.

Should an approaching bird begin to alarm putt, don't panic, there's a trick to try and calm them down.

A putt sounds exactly like it's spelled: *putt!* If I hear a single note *putt, putt!,* I don't worry. But if I hear a series of putts; *putt, putt, putt!..putt! putt! putt! put!,* then I get nervous. Once a birds reaches the point of nervousness where it's consistently and rapidly putting, I usually shut up, let the bird leave and come back another day. When frazzled to the point where a bird–tom or hen–won't stop putting, there's little I've been able to do to calm them down, and I've tried lots of calling tricks. This is still a work in progress.

The same holds true if the putts grow louder, but are still spaced out every few seconds. Even though they're not rapidly occurring in succession, they are loud and deliberate, which is an alarm sound that's tough for hunters to regain control of. You can try calling to calm birds that have turned putt-crazy, but it may be best to sit quietly and return another day. Then again, if hunting an area you'll not be back to any time soon, you don't have anything to lose, so offer sounds that might calm him down. That's the great thing about turkey hunting, you never know what will happen unless you try, and many times what happens is a big surprise.

Personally, I make my best putt sounds with a slate call, followed by a box call. Some of my hard-core turkey hunting buddies are great at making putts with their diaphragm calls, but that's something I strive to improve upon. Being able to make putts with a diaphragm call greatly broadens your calling spectrum and allows you to call hands-free and motion-free, should a bird be in sight.

Tree Call: When birds are on the roost early in the morning, they create a series of soft, muffled yelps and clucks. This serves as a sort of wakeup call to the rest of the birds in the area and marks the start to a new day. Sometimes tree talk commences an hour before birds actually fly out of the roost. Then again, there are some mornings I've only heard a handful of soft tree yelps before the birds hit the ground.

The tree call, or tree yelp as it's often called, is simply made to communicate with others in the flock. Yelps, clucks, purrs and gobbles are all part of tree communication and when birds start talking amongst themselves, it's a good time for hunters to slip in and start doing the same. Think of it as if you're trying to join the flock.

By offering soft yelps, muffled clucks and purrs, you're sending the message that you're a bird on the edge of the flock and you acknowledge that it's time to wake up. You're also sending a feeling that the woods are calm and safe, so when it comes time for your fly-down calling and hen yelps to be made, an approaching tom won't be as weary.

If you've roosted birds the night before, then get into calling position before the first hint of daylight, place a decoy in front of you and tree call when the birds start it off. Often times it only takes soft yelps, clucks and purrs to convince a tom there's something worth checking out.

I've had my best success with tree yelps early in the season in areas of high tom to hen ratios, and late in the season, when most hens have gone to nest. These are times of competition between mature toms, meaning this approach can be very effective.

Prior to leaving the roost, turkeys become quite vocal.

Fly-Down Cackle: A call that sounds like the cutt, with some clucks and yelps mixed in, is the fly-down cackle. Fly-down cackles can be made with box, mouth and pot calls. Fly-down cackles should have around 10-12 notes, the start of which are some soft clucks. From there, transition into making the cackle sounds which are nothing more than five or six sharp, quick cutts that slow down and soften toward the end of the sequence. After the cutts you can offer a few yelps and clucks to send the message that all is calm on the ground.

When turkeys pitch out of the tree they often call on their way down, thus the name, fly-down cackle. Sometimes bubbly putts and brief purrs can be heard. In early spring, when birds are still in big flocks, it's common to have 100 birds or more flying down in unison, all making fly-down cackles. It's an amazing thing to witness, and is often all that needs to be heard in order to answer the question, "Are turkeys worth getting up early for?"

Fly-down cackles are associated with birds on the move, specifically, birds flying off the roost. When flying across some of the West's major draws and canyons, fly-down cackles can be long and drawn out. I've heard birds make cackles when flying into trees, out of trees, across creeks, over fences and when crossing from one ridge to another. I've also heard them throughout the day, but 95% of the time it's heard in the morning, when birds are leaving the roost.

In addition to being a good locator call early in the morning, a fly-down cackle is valuable for calling birds in, right off the roost. Avoid the urge to overuse this call. Once you perfect it, the fly-down cackle is one of those sounds you'll love hearing yourself make, but remember, it's purpose is to indicate a bird on the move, and toms don't often like chasing down hens, especially in the middle of the day.

To master the tempo of a fly-down cackle, watch birds actually doing it, themselves. What you'll notice is that with each downbeat of the wings, the bird lets out a call. This is because when the bird flaps its wings downward, its chest muscles contract while the bird simultaneously lets out air, thus producing a sound. This explains the tempo of this call, starting slower with slower wing beats, picking up as they launch into the air, then slowing again as the bird glides to the ground without pumping its wings.

The fly-down cackle sounds something like; tuck, *tuck...tut, tut, tut, tut, tut, tut, tut, tut.. tuck, yup.* How I choose to finish it depends on the mood of the day. On warm, promising mornings when the birds are vocal, I'll put more feeling into it, rounding it out with some clucks, yelps and even purrs. If things are quiet and cold, I won't string out the sounds.

When trying to get toms to fly your direction, right off the roost, the fly-down cackle is one of the best sounds you can offer.

Kee-Kee: Hunters who've spent time in the turkey woods know these birds are much more vocal in the fall than during the more popular spring hunting months. This is because the diversity and age class of turkey flocks are changing. In order to maintain the social structure within these growing fall flocks, communication is key. If you really want to learn about the wide-range of sounds turkeys make, spend October and November in the field, where you'll hear it all.

Of the fall chatter made by turkeys, the most commonly heard is the kee-kee, or kee-kee run. These are sounds made by young turkeys who've lost track of the flock and are looking to reassemble with adult birds. Variations of these sounds are also made by adult birds, mostly hens.

While the kee-kee is mostly used by hunters in the fall, it can also be effective in the spring, especially late in the season on years where early hatches occur. During springs where chicks may be born as early as late April, they grow fast, and by the end of many hunting seasons out West, are already becoming vocal. One of the first sounds you'll hear poults make is the peep, with the next progression being the kee-kee. If hunting late season toms in the spring, around areas with tall grass and growing vegetation, a kee-kee can be a good call to bring in hens, and hopefully a tom will follow.

While the sounds of very young birds are more of a peep than a kee, the notes will eventually progress into a kee as summer months advance. The kee-kee run is simply a kee-kee with a yelp added at the end.

The kee-kee is almost always made up of three fairly coarse and somewhat unevenly spaced *kee, kee, kee* sounds that, in total, last just over a second in length. The key to making this call work is sticking to the magic three note sequence, not extending it to five or six notes because it may sound good.

As birds mature, the kee kee sounds become slightly more raspy. Because fall turkey flocks are often made up of a wide range of poults–I've seen them born as early as late April and as late as early October in the Pacific Northwest–the kee-kee can vary greatly in tone, pitch, volume and roughness. When using this call in the fall, try to mimic what you're hearing in the woods on that day. Again, the key is hitting the right number of notes, not overdoing it.

The kee-kee run is also a call worth having in your fall calling repertoire. The kee-kee run is simply a string of three kee-kee's, usually followed by one to three yelps. The kee-kee run carries well, and is a bit more pleading; *kee, kee, kee, yup, yup, yup.* The notes are unevenly spaced, with each note lasting anywhere from 0.05 to 0.15 seconds long.

*Young birds commonly make kee-kee calls to reassemble
in the summer, fall and winter months.*

Again, the purpose of the kee-kee and kee-kee run is to reassemble broken flocks, and the sounds are largely made by young birds. This is a great call to use when breaking up a flock, or when you hear birds calling in this way.

One fall, right before Thanksgiving, I was bowhunting turkeys from a blind. I got set up on the edge of a predictable path of travel and not long after hitting the ground from the roost, the flock of over 40 birds started marching my way, feeding along the brush-line in which I sat. But as they got about half way across a meadow, the flock scattered. A golden eagle was dive-bombing them, trying to get a meal. After three failed swoops, the eagle gave up, and by that time all the turkeys were scattered into the surrounding brush and timber.

After about 10 minutes, the young started calling. When I heard this, I started hitting it hard with kee-kee's and kee-kee runs. I made the sounds with mouth and pot calls, to emulate multiple birds calling from my location. Within minutes birds started moving my direction, and before I knew it, more than 30 turkeys were standing within bow range. Picking out a jake, I let the BowTech do the rest of the work, and it put my Gold Tip arrow exactly where I wanted it. The bird dropped on the spot.

Gobble: There are few sounds in nature that capture the attention like a turkey's gobble echoing through a canyon. It's a distinct sound, one that's not mistaken, and one that, when you're in the woods in pursuit of them, gives a surge of adrenaline that makes you yearn for success. Sometimes getting a simple glimpse of a gobbling tom will suffice.

While the gobble is one of the main sounds made by male turkeys, it's not the only sound they make, nor is it only heard during the spring breeding season. In fact, I've heard turkeys gobble every month of the year, amid some very harsh conditions.

One day in mid-December, I was bowhunting deer in the northwest corner of South Dakota. It was below zero with a skiff of snow on the ground. While hunting through a creek bed I heard a kee-kee call. I slipped a diaphragm call into my mouth and emulated the sound. Soon I had much of the flock–hens and young of the year–talking to me. Then I heard a gobble.

In less than five minutes, not only did I have some 25 hens and young around me, but a bachelor flock of more than a dozen toms moved in, and they gobbled at every sound I made. Soon they broke into full strut and their heads turned from white and dull red, to the patriotic red, white and bright blue hues that make them so attractive in the spring.

Then many of the toms began fighting, with loud yelps, clucks and fighting purrs dominating the conversation. The flock of hens and young birds eventually moved off, but for more than 15 minutes the toms stuck around, gobbling at every sound I offered, and all within 10 yards of where I sat. Too bad there was no open season in that area that time of year, but it goes to show how aggressive and instinctual toms can be. Here it was, mid-winter, and basic calling got them fired-up as if it were peak breeding season.

Simply put, the purpose of a tom's gobble in the spring is to let hens know where he is. As hunters, we try defying the natural instincts of turkeys by calling toms to us, using hen sounds. In nature it's often the opposite, as toms pick a strutting ground and call from it, hoping to attract hens. However, toms will follow the sounds of hens in the wild, especially in areas where mature tom densities are high and the competition for breeding, intense.

Over the past decades of spending time in the turkey woods, I'm always surprised at the number of toms responding to calling hens, seeking them out rather than gobbling and waiting for the hens to find them. It could just be me, but it appears as populations move, shift and become established in a region, the competition to breed grows more intense, thus the explanation behind why more toms move toward calling hens than what people think.

Toms also express levels of dominance through gobbling. Gobbles send the message that there's a mature tom in the area and not only is he ready to breed, but to fight other toms for the right.

Remember, wild animals have two goals in life: to stay alive and reproduce, and the turkey is no exception. Once a hen is attracted to a male, or the tom finds a hen, his displays shift from vocal to visual. Now, instead of gobbling to get the hen's attention, it's puffed chest, fanned tail, head bright as the colors on the American flag, are on display in an effort to let his stunning coloration convince the hen(s) that he's the one most worthy of passing on his genes. As is the case with all wild animals, it's the strongest, healthiest males that largely do the breeding.

Over my years of hunting throughout the West, I feel there are certain factors that contribute to a tom's interest in gobbling. Photoperiodism, weather, flock dynamics, tom densities and hen activity are some factors impacting gobbling activity. We'll get into more of these details in our spring hunting chapter, but for now, it's good to know that there are outside factors that make a tom want to gobble.

Toms may gobble out of a reaction to sounds totally unrelated to anything that has to do with breeding rights or establishing dominance. This phenomenon is called shock gobbling, and while it can happen year-round, it happens most in the spring when testosterone levels are high.

Hormone-filled toms will shock gobble at just about any loud sounds. Over the years I've heard them gobble at chain saws, jake brakes, thunder, slamming car doors, yelling children, bugling elk, coyote howls, owl hoots, crows, geese, woodpeckers, honking horns, gun shots and many other sounds, both natural and unnatural.

Shock gobbling seems to be most intense during the peak of the breeding season, which means it's a great clue for hunters to pinpoint where toms are located. In many areas I've hunted, shock gobbling seems to peak during the first two weeks of April. Then again, if conditions delay breeding, toms may intensely shock gobble into early or mid-May.

Why a tom shock gobbles, I have no scientific explanation, other than the fact their bodies are producing increased hormones which, in-turn, heighten their aggressive tendencies. One way of establishing dominance is through gobbling, so shock gobbling at sounds not made by other turkeys could be a way of saying, "Hey, I'm here, unafraid, and willing to do what it takes to hold my ground and breed when the time comes."

Because there is always some level of male hormones in a tom's body, they can often be convinced to gobble anytime throughout the year. The biggest tom I've taken with my bow came in the fall. Jody Smith and I were out on a blue-sky day, on the heels of an intense week of rain. We decided to try some calling as birds often become vocal when such weather change happens.

We located three bachelor flocks in one valley, and proceeded to call in all three of them at the same time. Some 30 toms, most 1 1/2 year olds, came to us, gobbling, strutting and carrying on like it was April. The bird I arrowed that day was one of the mature toms in the mix, and carried a beard more than 11 inches in length and spurs that stretched the tape nearly 1 1/2 inches. I'm a firm believer that in the right situations hunters can make toms gobble any month of the year. Whether they respond by coming in is a different story.

More hunters are discovering the value of using gobbler sounds in the spring to bring in toms. I've had my best success offering gobbler calls early in the season and when breeding is delayed, usually due to bad weather, thus a setback in spring's arrival. I think gobbles work best in these situations because the toms are then breaking up from their winter bachelor flocks and when this happens, they also fight for dominance amidst one

Despite what many people believe, toms can be called in during the fall and winter months. I got this tom fired-up, then closed the deal with my Destroyer.

another. This fighting includes displaying and gobbling, which explains why hunters can find success through offering gobbling sounds.

Early in the season and in areas of high tom densities, using a gobbler call in conjunction with a mature, full-strut tom decoy can yield some exciting turkey hunting. If toms are aggressive and looking for a fight, once they hear your gobbles and get within sight of the full-strut decoy, they often come sprinting in. When hunting this way in the broken terrain of the West, be ready, as the action can happen fast.

Spit & Drum: I'll never forget the first time I heard a tom spit and drum. We'd called a tom off the roost, hoping he'd make his way through the forest and into the tiny, grassy opening in which we'd placed a decoy where my buddy could get a shot. The tom pitched out of the tree then went silent. I continued calling but only got the occasional gobble, just enough to confirm he hadn't left the area. Then he shut down for 10 minutes.

When movement to my extreme right caught my eye, I sat, statue-still. It was the tom and he was coming my way, chest puffed up and tail fully fanned. He came from a direction I'd not anticipated, catching me off-guard. I had to wait for the bird to cross in front of me, then proceed toward the decoy. As he strutted past me I could hear an almost clicking-like sound, followed by low rumbles. Instantly it reminded me of how a ruffed grouse drums, and how, though you may be right next to the sound being made, you can't pinpoint where it's actually coming from.

As the tom strutted by at three paces, I dared not move. Heart rapidly thumping in my throat, I was sure he'd bust me. Slowly the brilliantly colored bird slipped right passed me, spitting and drumming all the way. Once the tom reached the decoy, my buddy let him have it. That was many years ago, but it's a sound I'll never forget. Fortunately, I'm in the woods enough that I get to hear it every spring.

The purpose of spitting and drumming is to attract hens, and it's a difficult series of sounds for humans to hear. On calm days, the sound is said to be heard up to 100 yards away. Maybe it's due to my deteriorating hearing, but many toms I've heard spitting and drumming have been inside 30 yards, with most in the five to 10 yard range. Regardless, when I hear it and can't see a tom, I know he's likely within shooting range.

Spitting and drumming are heard when a tom is in full-strut.

Early in my turkey hunting days I thought the snapping of the tom's primary wing feathers into strutting position was what created the "spitting" sound, while the popping open of the fan created the "drumming." Then I heard a number of toms spitting and drumming while already in full strut. I also noticed that the spitting sounds seem to emanate from toms whose mouths are sometimes open. Whether that's coincidence or not, I don't know, but I do believe that both the spitting and drumming sounds are produced by the movement of air within one or more of the air sacks located in the chest and/or body cavity of the tom.

More specifically, I think the spitting and drumming sounds are likely caused by the movement of air flowing through the syrinx, the vocal organ situated at the base of a bird's trachea. Because the syrinx is situated lower in the body cavity than is the larynx in mammals, it receives several forced-air vibrations at once, meaning multiple sounds can be created.

Spitting proceeds drumming, and both sounds are unique and usually occur, together: *pffit, dooooommmmmm*. The drumming actually sounds more like how some grouse force air through their air sacks during the breeding season, rather than the actual "drumming" or the beating on the chest and trapping of air with wings, as ruffed grouse do when "drumming." Perhaps a better name for this call would be spitting and booming.

In the past there have been companies who've crafted spitting and drumming calls, but they didn't perform as intended, failing to get the guttural, reverberating sounds the birds naturally produce. The best spitting and drumming sounds I've made, and heard made, come from your mouth and chest, not a call. Try quickly forcing air through the front of a small opening in your teeth to get the pffit sound. For the drumming sound, try forcing air from your chest into your throat, while making a humming sound, *dooooommmmmm*. It's not a loud sound, rather a close-range call used to pull birds into shooting position, get a hen to move in with a stubborn tom on her tail, or bring in other toms in areas where tom to hen ratios are high.

Turkey Diet

When it comes to food, turkeys are very opportunistic and omnivorous. Upon field dressing every turkey I shoot–or can get my hands on that were tagged by other hunters–I make it a point to examine the crop. If you really want to learn what birds are feeding on during hunting season, examine their crop. This will not only tell you what they're eating, but likely where they are acquiring the food, thus, where to hunt if looking to fill another tag.

Of course, a bird's diet will vary depending on where they live and what the respective habitats are like. Diets can also change as food sources change, shift or simply go away.

Early in life, poults primarily eat insects. This high source of protein

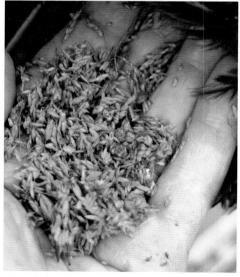

Examining the crop of a turkey will reveal what it's eating and where to concentrate future hunting efforts.

allows them to quickly grow and offers them the nutrition they need to survive. Grubs, worms, spiders and more, are sought in the spring, while grasshoppers constitute a large part of the diet in the summer and early fall months.

Adult birds also thrive on grasshoppers during the summer months, as well as various types of grass seeds. If the fall is mild, grasshoppers can survive well into October, even November, which makes patterning birds fairly easy as they concentrate on such food sources. As turkey flocks grow in size with the progression of fall, their daily movements become more routine. The more abundant and reliable the food source this time of year, the more predictable the bird's daily travel paths become.

For the fall turkey hunter, grasshoppers living in farmlands and along hillside meadows can offer very high percentage hunts. Keep an eye out for the grasshoppers during the summer month, then, as fall hunting season approaches, watch for turkeys to start making the rounds, quickly covering ground while plucking 'hoppers from blades of dry grass.

Another fall food source western turkeys love comes in the form of night crawlers. When the first warm rains of the season fall, make it a point to hit low-grass meadows and fields. The rain brings out the earth worms, and turkey's can literally flock to such areas in search of the high-protein morsels. If you're timing is off and you're not finding birds in a field that looks promising, take time to walk around, looking for droppings and scratch marks where turkeys have been hitting the field in search of worms in the morning or evening hours. From there, you'll at least have a starting point and confirmation that birds are using the area. If no sign is found, move on.

In addition to any insects they can round-up in the fall, turkeys also feast on a wide-range of berries this time of year. Huckleberries, snow berries, black berries and poison oak berries are just some of the fruits turkeys feed on in the fall. One fall I watched a flock of turkeys fighting over a lone, wild apple that had dropped from a tree. One bird would pick up the apple, then the others chased it, relentlessly, until it dropped it. Then they'd all peck at the apple until another bird picked it up and started running with it. This lasted more than 10 minutes, until the apple was gone; it looked like a kid's soccer game. Later in the fall, when the season opened, I returned to that area and took a nice tom.

Trail cameras reveal a lot about turkeys, including what they're feeding on.

During the fall and winter months, turkeys spend a great deal of time scratching for food. Once such sign is located, monitor it to determine when the birds are hitting the area, then devise a game plan.

Nuts also constitute an important part of the turkey's diet during the fall and early winter months. Acorns, pine nuts, myrtle nuts, filberts and a host of other nuts are all valuable protein sources turkeys thrive on in their respective habitats.

In the fall and winter, turkeys primarily scratch for food on the ground, trying to uncover anything that offers calories. Look for patches of fallen leaves that have been overturned by foraging flocks of turkeys. If birds find food in such areas, they'll be back.

During the winter months, turkeys simply try to stay alive by scrounging for anything they can get their beaks on. Any leftover mast crops are fair game, as are grass seeds, clover, sow bugs, worms, buttercups, rose hips and more. Winter is a very vulnerable time for turkeys, especially in wet climates like the Pacific Northwest, so their goal is to conserve and retain as many calories as they can in order to make it until spring, when the quality of forage greatly increases.

In the spring, grasses, grass seeds and clovers become a primary food source of turkeys, and these, along with other plant materials, account for up to 95% of the turkey's total diet. Not only will they eat the leaves, but the buds of clovers and flowers, as well. Dandelions, and a variety of other small, flowering plants are also target foods for spring turkeys, as are fern fronds. While the ground is still soft, turkeys can also be found clawing for roots and tubers during the spring months, then again in the fall when the ground moistens.

As grasses mature, turkeys will waste no time stripping the heads of their seeds. Some of my best turkey hunting memories were had in the closing weeks of the spring season, when pursuing toms in tall grass meadows. When the grass grows tall, it's not only a primary food source but offers sanctuary in the form of cover and relief in the form of shade. Birds may spend all day in such high grass fields, making them challenging but very effective places to concentrate hunting efforts.

When hunting on private ground where cattle or other livestock are run, make it a point to inspect their droppings to see if turkeys are digging through them. Often you'll find dried cow pies that have been fully turned over, or horse manure that's been picked through in search of insects, undigested grains and fresh sprouting grasses. Though you may not find birds actually digging through the droppings, the obvious sign will confirm that birds are in the area.

The most active times to catch turkeys feeding are during the first and last few hours of daylight. Hens that are sitting on a nest will get up to feed during the course of the day, often at random hours, which is why it's a good idea to hunt all day long if you're looking to fill a tag late in the season. The reason is, as hens get off their nest, toms will try finding them in hopes of getting a chance to breed. Toms usually know that hens are in the area, otherwise they wouldn't be there in the spring. So, if you can be the "lone hen" that's up and feeding throughout the day, late in the spring, you have a chance of calling in a tom. This is a great situation in which to use a lone hen decoy.

If overturned cow paddies are moist on the underside, it's likely the turkeys aren't far.

A wild turkey's digestive system is interesting, and understanding how it works can help us gain a more complete understanding of the bird's lifestyle. Turkeys have exceptionally long intestines compared to other birds, which means they get the most out of the food they eat thanks to complete digestion. But the gizzard also plays a large part in the digestive process.

As turkeys take in food, it's passed through the esophagus, into the crop, a sack-like appendage located at the base of the neck, at the top of the breast. From there it moves into the gizzard, which grinds it up into a pulpy liquid. Tiny rocks are often ingested by turkeys, which are moved into the gizzard to help grind the food which is driven by muscular contractions. This explains why turkeys–and other upland birds–are often seen along the edges of logging roads, creeks and rivers, gathering grit, usually in the morning and evening hours.

Because digestion is so complete, turkey droppings often come out in a liquid, pasty, green texture. This makes it tough to decipher exactly what they've been eating, though on occasion a hard to digest grass seed slips through. This is why examining crops of birds taken, and observing birds actually feeding, will help you better identify exactly what they have been eating.

The crop–where turkeys store freshly taken-in food–can be removed and its contents studied. What's inside the crop can be valuable information for future hunts.

Turkeys are commonly seen on logging roads, gathering grit.

48

Chapter 2:

GEARING UP FOR THE HUNT

Since the days when I first tromped into the turkey woods, it's been nothing short of amazing to see the progression in hunting gear that's made it's way into the marketplace. Gone are the days when a turkey hunter grabs his waterfowl gun, a handful of duck loads, slips into his green rubber boots and goes out turkey hunting. Not that this simple gear won't get the job done; it will, but there are advancements that make bagging a turkey a lot more comfortable and efficient than it used to be.

The first time I was invited on an outdoor writer hunt for turkeys in Idaho, I felt more out of place than a 6th grader transferring to a new school in the middle of the year. When I broke out my old, beaten-up duck hunting gun, leather boots and a few calls, you should have seen the looks I got from the boys who were on the hunt from back East.

Here they were, clad in more camo' than I even owned, camo' rubber boots, vests bulging at every pocket and short-barreled camo' shotguns topped with scopes. I'm sure the looks I gave them were equally as surprising as what I felt cutting through me. It was a high-elevation Merriam's hunt in Idaho, and while the rugged land was daunting to my eastern buddies, the gear they used to lure in tom after tom truly opened my eyes as to how behind the times I really was.

Though I did bag a bird on that Idaho hunt, what I really came away with was an education on how much I had to learn about turkey hunting. One thing I've realized is that hunting turkeys out West is quite a bit different than hunting them in the East. Eastern-based birds are more pressured, live on smaller parcels of land and are tougher to hunt, period. Because of this, the hunting industry has evolved to give hunters the added edge, hoping to increase success rates. Bottom line, we have turkey hunters from back East to largely thank for the advancement in turkey hunting gear across the nation.

That said, I'm not suggesting that every piece of gear highlighted in this chapter is something you should go out and buy in order to find success. Again, ultimate success comes down to knowing the birds in your area and how to most wisely hunt them. By knowing how you'll hunt, and where, then it's up to you to decide what gear will help you find more consistent success.

Because every year sees advancements made in hunting gear, I'm not going to focus on brand X or brand Y, for by the time you finish reading this book, they may be obsolete. The purpose of this chapter is to share what's out there, so you can make the choice of what best fits your hunting needs.

Shotguns

Had I written this book when I first started turkey hunting, in the mid1980s, this section would have been one paragraph: Pick a gun that fits you, feels comfortable and that you consistently shoot well. Cover the bluing and shiny wood stock with camo' tape, and you're set. But things have changed since then.

Nothing has impacted the turkey hunting industry more than the development of shotguns in recent years. Specialized guns and advanced loads have revolutionized turkey hunting and catapulted it to a level many people never thought possible.

As touched on earlier, I took my first turkey back in 1986, with my favorite duck and goose hunting gun. I'd shot the gun for years, before heading into the turkey woods, so knew how it handled and shot. With

Specialized shotguns for turkey hunting have reached new levels in design and popularity. Find one you're comfortable shooting and can handle with confidence.

the handloads I'd worked-up for it, the gun patterned wonderfully. The only extra work I invested was to cover the gun in camo' tape. Not only did my waterfowl gun account for my first turkey, but for my first several turkeys, in multiple states.

Honestly, I'd not hesitate using that gun turkey hunting, even today, because I had confidence in it and knew how it shot. When trying to pick a turkey gun that's right for you, simply find one you feel comfortable handling and shooting. Shot placement is the key to successful turkey hunting, not how cool your gun might look.

One spring season Jody Smith had clients miss 52 shots at birds, all with shotguns. That season they killed 51 birds. The year prior he had clients put 68 birds on the ground, with a total of 28 misses.

So what's to blame for these misses? It seems like a simple question, really, but when it comes down to it, it's more complex then one might think.

Twenty-five years ago I would have credited those misses to poor shooting. Back then, hunters were familiar with the guns and loads they shot because they were used to hunting everything from ducks to grouse, geese to doves, all with the same gun. In other words, things were simple, straight forward and hunters knew how their guns performed.

Then came high-tech shotguns, chokes and loads that performed in ways hunters weren't used to. Today's specialized turkey guns are made to shoot high-performance payloads long distances. Add after-market chokes to the equation and distance increases even more, while patterns tighten. This can be good and bad.

The good thing about added distance is that it gives a tighter pattern, which means more pellets hit the kill zone at sensible ranges. The bad thing is that it creates a false sense of being able to shoot farther, which is the case, but only if you pattern your gun and intimately know how it performs. I would not recommend taking shots much beyond 40 yards.

Over the years I've taken more than 100 turkeys, and have missed a half-dozen birds. One of those misses was at 35 yards, the rest, inside 20 yards, with two of those coming inside 10 yards. There were no excuses for the 20 and 30 yard misses, I simply pulled my head out of the gun too soon and shot over the birds. I missed a tom on the wing, too, smacking a tree as he flew behind it. Misses happen, and the more you hunt turkeys, the more misses will accrue. It's frustrating when it happens, but there are things to know that are different when comparing shooting a specialized turkey gun to a waterfowling scattergun.

On the close-range shots I've missed, both were with high tech'

guns, extra full chokes and hot loads. The next time you shoot your specialized turkey gun, pattern it at 10 yards and see what happens. The wad of pellets are tight, meaning there's no room for error. Because turkeys often bob their heads back and forth when moving, or nervously, randomly shift it from side to side, up and down, this can make connecting on a close-range shot, difficult. If the bird moves the instant you touch the trigger, it could result in a clean miss.

A 3-inch payload of sixes throws a tight group at 10 yards. Know how your gun performs at such close range.

When my oldest son, Braxton, was nine years old, we called in a turkey that he shot at four yards. I was pumped, excited and thrilled that Braxton was able to make such a shot. "Dad, it was right there, it was an easy shot," Braxton pointed out

Braxton Haugen with a fall bird shot at four yards. When this close there's no room for error–it's one of turkey hunting's toughest shots.

amid my hugs and high fives. What Braxton failed to realize was just how tricky that shot was. The bird was nervous and starting to move, head alert with eyes searching for something that wasn't right. At that moment Braxton pulled the trigger and literally took off the top of the bird's head with a load of 3-inch 6s fired from his 20 gauge. At that range, the pattern is small and is more like shooting a rifle than a shotgun.

After talking with Jody Smith about all the misses he encounters as a guide, he had this to say: "I think the biggest mistake people make is not patterning their shotguns, figuring out how they shoot with the loads they're hunting with. The next biggest thing is that people are afraid of the recoil on some of these new guns, which causes them to flinch or lift their head off the gun too soon. I'm seeing way more misses today, than I did 20 years ago, and with today's technology, it should be just the opposite. Hunters also need to be sure of the yardage before shooting at a bird, be it with bow of shotgun."

"Another thing that happens, when a turkey approaches from a long ways across open terrain, hunters get in their gun, early," Smith continues. "After several minutes of sitting in this position, the natural action is to eventually lift your head off gun to see what the turkey is doing. When it comes time for the shot, often times the shooter fails to properly get reset in the gun. If your cheek's not on the stock and the bird directly in your sights, don't shoot."

I was once contacted by a leading shooting magazine to test and write a review on what was being tabbed as the most advanced turkey hunting gun of its day. The 12 gauge pump action gun featured a 20-inch barrel with an overall length of 39-inches. It weighed 6.75 pounds and held 2 3/4", 3" and 3 1/2" shells, and came with an XXfull choke and red dot sight.

The gun patterned well, but after three shots my face was numb and it felt like my upper canines were cutting through my lip. The thing was beating me up. Knowing I had to come up with something positive, I removed the pitch plate, replaced the high profile sight with a lower profile Trijicon RMR, and added a butt pad with extra recoil absorbing properties. This allowed me to stay in the gun much better, and made all the difference in the world in how I shot the gun.

I ended up running nine different loads through that gun, and all shot surprisingly well. Once I got the gun dialed-in to fit me, it performed wonderfully, and I've taken a number of turkeys with it, since.

The point is, in today's age of specialized guns, don't expect to run out, buy one and have it shooting perfectly, right out of the box. Think of these shotguns more like a rifle, in that they'll need to be sighted in with various loads to figure out which ones pattern best.

Some guns shoot brand X loads perfectly, while they won't shoot brand Y loads worth a darn. The next gun might pattern brand Y perfectly, but not brand X.

"Several times I've had clients run out of shells," cringes Jody Smith. "When I gave them some of my shells to use, which were a different brand, they were all surprised when I asked them to pattern the loads. When they saw how differently they shot in their guns, they began to realize how different guns handle different loads."

When picking a turkey gun, choose one that feels comfortable, is something you can carry all day long and ultimately, shoot very well. Out West, the rugged terrain often encountered on turkey hunts can be demanding, and toting a shotgun all day is not easy. Find a gun that's fairly light, but that you can handle the recoil on, and carries well with a sling.

Search for a gun you can quickly and easily maneuver, so if you do have to move the gun for a shot, you can do so with ease, when the bird's head is behind his fanned tail or passing behind a tree. A short barreled gun is preferred by many western turkey hunters for the simple reason it's easier to walk with through woods and brush, not having to worry about the longer barrel getting tangled.

Ideally, look for a gun with a barrel length of 20 to 24-inches, weighing 6.5 to 8 pounds and that can chamber 3 1/2" shells. If not included, an after-market, XXfull choke is a good

idea. Chokes, themselves, have greatly advanced turkey hunting and the ability to shoot more accurately, but you need to know how they work.

All good turkey guns of today have good chokes. Labeled "turkey chokes," they have greater constriction than full chokes, but aren't so constricted that they hamper the pattern. Turkey chokes may be labeled as XXfull or Extra Full. The more open the constriction of a choke, the better it's suited for larger pellets, like 4 shot. Turkey chokes for 12 gauge guns range from 0.670-inches (long range) down to 0.640-inches, with the tighter constrictions in the 0.640-0.655 range being best suited for size 5 and 6 shot. A 0.500 or less choke will limit the effective range of your pattern, but could be used for closeup shots from a blind situated near a decoy.

Chokes come in various designs, each to perform specific functions. Find what works best in your gun, with your desired loads.

It is possible to use chokes with too much constriction. If you pair too tightly of a constricted choke with the pellets, the pattern simply disperses before reaching the target. An indication that the choke tube is too tight is that pellets may collide with one another in flight, yielding irregularly shaped holes in the target. If this happens, choose a choke with less constriction and see how it shoots.

54

Take the time to fit the choke and loads to the gun. If looking to optimize performance, it's a good idea to test multiple loads through different chokes, at different distances. From there, look at your results and choose the brand and shot size that shoots best from your chosen choke.

It doesn't matter if the gun is a pump, semi-auto or single shot. What matters most is that you can shoot it well and with confidence. There are some guns featuring a thumbhole stock, others with pistol grips and still others that more resemble tactical rifles than any shotgun you've likely seen. But all of these designs are for a purpose, usually to increase stability, decrease weight and expedite quick handling, and all in an effort to attain more accurate shooting.

Note that the more streamlined these guns, the harder they often kick with the heavy loads of today. Still, guns are being designed with the intent to reduce recoil, but when you cut weight through composite stocks and shortened barrels, the energy has to go somewhere. Semi-automatic shotguns feature the least amount of recoil as they utilize back-pressure to cycle the shells. Also, some of the heavier shot loads feature less velocity than some of the amped-up loads, but they offer reduced recoil.

If a 12 gauge packs too much punch, try a 20 gauge. The 20 gauge is also a great choice for youth and women hunters. Like the 12 gauges of today, the 20s are being specially made for turkey hunting, and do a great job. The effective range of a 20 gauge is 25-30 yards, while most 12 gauges are solid out to 40 yards, maybe a few yards beyond. My boys have confidently taken turkeys with their 20 gauges, out to 30 yards, the farthest coming at 42 yards. As is the case for the 12 gauges, loads and chokes for the 20s are very specialized, so pattern a selection of shells–both in brand and shot size–and see what works best.

As for shotgun shells and turkey hunting, the options keep growing each year. Loads, like the guns that shoot them, continue breaking new ground through technological advancements and precision design in not only the shot, itself, but the wads, too.

Today's 20 gauges are a great alternative if you're not a fan of heavy-kicking 12 gauge turkey guns.

Though the turkey is a big bird, it's kill zone is relatively small and having a high energy payload with a tight pattern increases the chances of delivering a lethal shot. To best do this, select a range of shotshell brands, in various size shot, to see what works best in your gun. I've seen some brands shoot perfectly in some guns, then perform terribly in others. The key is understanding that selecting a load to fit the gun is vital, and may take some time.

I had one specialized turkey gun that I ran five brands of shells through before finding one that fit. Other guns may require adjusting the sights to get the loads shooting perfectly. Though these shells aren't cheap, take the time to do it right and find a load that fits with your gun. Again, treat it like a rifle, not a shotgun.

Three different brands of magnum 6s, shot at 30 yards from the same gun. Note how the points of impact vary. This is why it's crucial to test loads before choosing one to hunt with.

As for shot size, anything from 4 to 6 shot works well. In an effort to decrease recoil, some shells are being made in 2 3/4-inch, carrying payloads of 7 shot. Personally, I like 5 shot as it offers mass and speed. But I've also taken many birds with 4 and 6 shot, and some with duplex loads (2 and 6 shot, combined). There are many options, you just have to find what works best in your gun.

Patterning your gun on a turkey target is the best way to learn what loads work best in your gun. To do this, shoot off a solid bench, ideally in a recoil-reducing device. I like shooting from a Caldwell Lead Sled as it's steady and takes away the recoil. Do not sight in your shotgun off-hand or from shooting sticks, as you'll not get accurate results.

Start shooting at 30 yards and make any necessary adjustments in windage or elevation. Once the pattern is dead-on at 30 yards, test it at 40, then 50 yards. Next, shoot it at 20 yards to see how tight the pattern is hitting. It's even a good idea to shoot the gun at 10 yards, even five, to see what to expect should a bird come in close. You'll be amazed at how tight the pattern actually is at 10 and 20 yards, confirming the fact there's little room for error. It's also a good idea to pattern it out to 60 and 70 yards, just to know what it will do should you need to make a follow-up shot at that range.

The rule of thumb for a good turkey load is that it should put 100 pellets inside a 10-inch circle at 40 yards. This pellet count equates to putting an ideal amount into the narrow, rather small kill zone of a turkey's head and neck. Ideally, at least 18 pellets should hit the kill zone of a turkey's head and neck at 40 yards. There are many loads capable of achieving and even exceeding this number. As a general rule, if you

When testing loads, it's a good idea to have a solid bench setup to reduce recoil and maximize accuracy. The Lead Sled is a favorite of many turkey hunters.

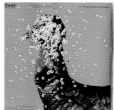

With a load chosen, pattern it at 20, 30, 40 and 50 yards,
so you know exactly what to expect on a hunt.

shoot at a 30-inch target and the percentage of shot inside that circle drops to below 65% of what's carried in the shell, you've exceeded the effective range of that gun, choke and load.

For reference, many turkey hunters try to achieve a goal of getting 70% of the shot to hit inside a 30-inch circle. This goes for whatever distance you're patterning the load at.

A two ounce load of 6 lead shot holds about 450 pellets, meaning about 22% of this payload would fit within a 10-inch circle at 40 yards. Two ounces of 5 shot holds about 340 pellets, so about 30% of those pellets will fit inside the circle. As for 4 shot, two ounces holds about 270 pellets, equating to 37% of it's delivery falling inside the magic 10-inch circle at 40 yards.

So how do you find the right choke for your gun, and is it really that big of a deal? Yes, it is that big of a deal, in fact, each year at the National Wild Turkey Federation national convention, there's a stationary paper target competition. The idea is to find the best load, choke and gun combination that will effectively take a turkey.

When picking a choke for your gun, understand that it's a three part process; the gun, load and choke are all interrelated. Start by picking a choke tube and shooting it. After the first shot, check to make sure the choke stayed tight. Next, pick at least three brands of loads, and shoot each at least three times into a four-square-foot shooting board so you can see where every pellet hits. Different loads put through the same gun have been known to change the point of impact by as much as 12 inches.

Test your gun and choke with both high speed and magnum loads. High speed loads have fewer ounces of lead but move fast, while magnum loads carry more shot at a lower velocity. Personally, I avoid the speed craze as it's not crucial on a 40 yard shot at a turkey. I'd rather have more pellets and know precisely where they hit. Finally, when picking a choke, make sure it's designed for the shot you'll be using. Some choke tubes are designed specifically for using with lead shot, and running steel through them may damage the choke and the barrel.

While on the topic of sighting in a specialized turkey shotgun, consider a device that can greatly increase your accuracy; a red-dot sight. If there's one trick that will help to connect on more shots with today's specialized guns and loads, it's the aid of a red dot sight. If this option interests you, make sure your gun is drilled and tapped to mount a railing system that will hold such a site. Most of today's turkey guns offer this feature. My favorite rail is a Picatinny style, as it securely holds sights and scopes in place and offers freedom when it comes to positioning the sight on the gun.

Before mounting a red dot sight, check current regulations in states where you wish to hunt to learn what restrictions may be in place. Some states may permit battery operated sights, some may not. Some may allow a red dot sight, some may not. If no batteries are allowed, the only battery-free red dot sight on the market at the time of this writing was Trijicon's RMR (Ruggedized Miniature Reflex). It also comes in battery operated models. I've taken a number of birds with both models of RMRs, and can't say enough about the accuracy they offer and the confidence they instill when shooting.

One feature I particularly like about the RMR is that it's low profile, meaning you don't have to raise your cheek off a gun with a steep pitched comb. This allows you to stay in the gun, maintaining proper form all the way to the follow through. It also means your face won't get pounded in the recoil, as often happens with sights that sit high on the railing system.

When sighting in red dot sight, make adjustments just as you would for a rifle. I like to position the red dot at the base of the turkey's neck–where skin meets feathers–so the pattern will cover the top of the head as well as the lower neck, which extends below the feathered region.

If a red dot sight is not an option, consider fiber optic sights. Most advanced turkey guns come with this feature, and it's best to get guns with both a front and rear sight. Look for the rear sight to be split, so the front sight can be centered between them. Not only will this increase accuracy, it will ensure proper adjustments can be made to properly sight in the gun.

Red dot sites, like this Trijicon RMR, are great for today's specialized turkey guns, loads and chokes. Be aware of state laws on such sites, and if battery operated models are legal.

If shooting an older model gun, or one without fiber optic sights, consider adding an aftermarket front sight. Trijicon makes a front sight that secures to the ventilated rib of 12 and 20 gauges, and comes in red or green fiber optic. The TrijiDot easily instals on the front of the gun and is held in place with small set screws. In low light situations or amid heavy shadows where a bead blends in and is hard to decipher, a fiber optic sight can make the difference between making the shot or missing it.

Fiber optic sights are another option when it comes to modifying your gun to increase the level of accuracy.

With the gun ready to roll, what else can be done to improve its performance in the field? If hunting from a blind, resting the gun on shooting sticks will greatly aid in your shooting accuracy. My favorite is a Bog Pod tripod shooting stick. Three legged shooting sticks offer more stability than two legged ones, and the sturdy nature of the Bog Pod is perfect. For youth hunters, this tripod is ideal in allowing them to stay in the gun for extended periods, where they'd otherwise not be able to support the gun. I've even had great success with youth using shooting sticks out of the blind, when sitting in front of a tree.

The important part in selecting a turkey gun comes with accepting the fact that it's a three-part process. First comes the gun, then comes the load and choke. While turkey hunting has never seen such upscaled, specialized guns and shotgun shells, they have to be tried and tested to know how they will perform. This can take some time, so be patient and thorough if you wish to get the most out of your setup.

Bows

I've been fortunate to take many turkeys over the years, with a bow. Braxton and Tiffany have also both taken turkeys with their bows, as have many friends along the way.

Bowhunting setups for turkey are much more straight forward than shotguns, but shot placement can be a different story. For the setup, it can be as easy as using your regular hunting bow. Personally, I use the same bow I hunt big game with throughout North America and much of the world, which is set at 72 pounds. Some people let off the poundage, and that's fine. Some hunters set up a special turkey bow at lower poundage, so they don't have to deal with increasing and decreasing weight, then re-sighting the bow each time.

Some archers set up a bow specifically for turkeys–
usually at lower poundage–while others use their big game setup.

Like many of you, I do enough hunting in big game seasons that I want to keep everything set the same, for not only does it allow me to gain valued, in-the-field practice, it offers more speed and kinetic energy than if I were to backdown on the poundage. Because turkeys can react fast once the string is released, I like a speedy bow for turkey hunting.

Personally, I'm not a big fan of expandable broadheads in the big game woods, but this may largely be due to my inexperience with using them since my home state of Oregon won't allow them. I have taken a handful of big game animals with them in other states and abroad over the years but am partial to my fixed blade broadheads.

While fixed blades work great on turkeys–especially on bows set at lower poundage–I prefer expandable broadheads when it comes to bowhunting turkeys. I like them because they fly with pinpoint accuracy and they leave big entry and exit wounds.

When hunting from a blind, be sure and have a rest for your bow so you can sit at the ready, arrow nocked. The biggest challenge when bowhunting turkeys is movement. Movement is required to pick up the bow, move it into shooting position then draw the bow. If not in a blind, turkeys will bust you more times than not.

One spring I was set on filling all three of my Oregon tags with a bow. I

hunted several days to do it, but pulled it off. I shot one bird from the ground, one from a treestand and the third from a ground blind. The one from the ground blind was easiest, for the obvious reason a blind hides your movement. We won't get in to the number of birds I spooked when hunting off the ground and from the treestand, but I didn't miss or cripple any; I simply waited for the right moment to take the shots.

When bowhunting turkeys, I like removing my quiver, as it allows smooth, easy movements to be made should a bird be moving. One thing I've done in recent years is to move my decoy closer to the blind, to raise the odds of successful shot placement. Usually I place my decoy five yards from the blind, 10 at the farthest. Due to a turkey's sense of sight, detailed in Chapter 1, they are not afraid of blinds. In fact, I've called in hundreds of turkeys to ground blinds and never had one spook from the blind or not come in due to the blind being there.

Of utmost importance when bowhunting turkeys, is shot placement. Honestly, I think the wild turkey is one of the West's toughest animals to kill with a bow, for two reasons: First, the wild turkey is nervous, by nature, so is alway moving, looking for danger. Second, turkeys have a surprisingly small kill zone, and precise accuracy is vital if you want to cleanly kill one of these birds.

A turkeys vitals are situated tight together, making the kill zone about the size of a human fist. At the same time, turkey vitals are set farther back and higher in the body cavity than on big game, which explains many of the misses by archers.

Be sure and devote plenty of time to practicing on 3D targets. It's worth the investment to get both a 3D target in full-strut and one that's standing upright. Devote time to shooting from all conceivable positions, especially if hunting from a ground blind. The biggest concern

I hear from bowhunters going after turkeys for the first time from a blind is that when they draw on the turkey, their sights aren't lit-up. This is because blinds don't let in enough light, so the fiber optics can't gather the light like they do when in the open. Placing a black pin on a black bird can be a shock, so practice and prepare for it. This is one of the reasons I place my decoy so close to the blind.

As for shot placement, where the arrow goes depends on what the bird is doing and what direction it's facing. Be aware that the vitals of turkeys are not only small, but are situated differently in the body cavity than big game animals you may be used to hunting. The lungs, for instance, sit against the back, tight to where the ribs attach to the spine. Conversely, the heart is situated in the center of the body, directly above the legs. These are the vitals of choice when it comes to lethal shot placement, but it's unnatural for many archers to aim so far back and so high on an animal when they're used to putting the pin behind the front shoulder of big game. In the past, some 3D targets haven't helped, as they indicated the vital organs being placed too far forward of where they actually are. My favorite 3D turkey targets are ones created by Cabela's and Rinehart, as they direct shot placement to where the vitals really are.

The best turkey target I've used in terms of physically showing where a bird's vitals are located is one made by Master Target. The photo quality image of the turkey, along with the anatomically correct vitals placement are a great learning tool. The image is printed on Durashot, a material designed to withstand hundreds of bow shots. They'll last many times longer than paper targets because the material is 100% waterproof, tear-resistant (the arrows do not tear the target apart) and UV protected.

I've arrowed birds in just about every position, from nearly every conceivable angle, and can say that there are shots to take and shots not to take. My favorite bow shot is when a bird is standing erect, feathers tucked in tight to the body, head extended and facing straight away. This exposes the entire spine, from head to tail. A spine shot will secure a turkey quicker than any other. I also like this position because it offers the best angle at the lungs. The lungs are situated in the middle of the body, between the wings. Place an arrow here and you'll get your bird every time.

My second favorite bow shot is when a tom is in full-strut, facing straight away. While I'm not a fan of the broadside shot when a tom is strutting, I like it when he's facing away because it elongates his body cavity, making it streamline for an arrow to slice through the entire section of vitals.

For the fully-fanned, facing away shot, simply put the arrow where all the tail feathers converge, right about at the anus. This will usually drive the arrow through the digestive tract, heart and lungs, and may strike the neck upon exiting the bird, depending on the angle of his head.

The anatomically accurate Master Target reveals how high the vitals are on a turkey, which can be deceiving when a tom's in full-strut.

One time I called in a trio of big toms and all were in full-strut around my decoys. I held my BowTech steady and when a bird showed me his fully-fanned backside I let loose. The Gold Tip arrow moved quickly through the bird but not before doing impressive internal damage. Upon impact about half of the fan collapsed, indicating I'd hit the spot where the tail feathers converged. The bird went six yards and tipped over. I've secured other birds with this shot that dropped on the spot.

When a tom is in full-strut, facing you, that's also a good angle as long as he's not moving quickly. For this, wait for the bird to be directly facing you then put the arrow where the featherless part of the neck meets the feathers. I've dropped birds on the spot by barley clipping the red skin at the base of the neck, breaking the neck and continuing to pass through the bird and exit near the anus, destroying key vital organs along the way. If sitting in a ground blind, near level with the bird, the arrow can also be placed about half-way between the base of the red neck and where the beard protrudes from the body. In other words, there's a little forgiveness with this shot angle as long is the arrow is kept in line.

Each of the birds below are in ideal bow shot position.
The green dot indicates optimal arrow placement.

If a bird is standing upright, facing you, feathers tucked in, then place the arrow where the beard comes out of the body. This will ensure an upper heart and lower lung shot, and if centered, will sever the spine. This can be a tricky shot if the bird is moving or seems nervous. This is one of those cases where it pays to know how the bird is behaving and anticipating what it's next move might be. If it appears nervous, this is not a good shot, for the bird can jump.

Another shot I like taking with a bow is when a bird is standing upright, facing broadside, feathers tucked in. This gives a true view of how its skeletal system will be situated, thus where the internal organs are located. A good shot here is to follow the legs straight up the body, placing the arrow in the center of the bird's body. This will ensure a heart shot, with the arrow traveling into an open triangle region that's created when the bird has its wings tucked in. This open triangle lies beneath the radius/ulna bones, to the side of the metacarpals and above the femur. A good thing about this shot, if you hit low, you'll bust the femur or sever tendons, meaning the bird can't jump to take flight. If you hit high, and are using enough poundage to break through the humerus and scapula, you'll hit the spine and lung region.

Another good shot, but one that can be tricky, is when a tom is in full-strut, standing broadside. The challenging part here is deciphering exactly how the skeletal system is situated, thus, where the internal organs are located. This is a deceiving angle as the bird's feathers are puffed up, his head retracted and his tail fully fanned. In this situation, most misses are made by shooting too high, hitting nothing but feathers. Avoid such a miss by drawing an imaginary line connecting the base of the neck (the red caruncles, or waddles) to the base of the tail. Next, come straight up from the legs. Where the legs bisect the horizontal line drawn between the neck and tail, right in the middle of the body, that's your sweet-spot. Shoot at the intersection of this "T" and you'll hit an open triangle leading to the heart. This triangle is larger than the one created when the bird is standing erect, but is tougher to pinpoint. This triangle window lies above the radius/ulna and below the humerus. Hit an inch high, above the humerus, and you're in the lungs and spine/scapula region. Remember, the lungs are situated horizontally along the back, meaning this is a small target to hit when the bird is standing broadside. Be careful not to hit the wing butt, or shoulder, as these can deflect arrows. I once watched a hunter bounce an arrow off a tom's shoulder, the same setup he'd used to kill elk. These hollow bones are very tough and can be impenetrable if hit wrong.

Some of the quartering-to and quartering-away shots can be tricky with a bow. Making these shots comes down to simply knowing the anatomy of the bird and where the skeletal system and internal organs are situated in relationship to the bird's body position. If in doubt, don't shoot. Instead, wait, the bird will likely move and offer a solid shot opportunity.

Another challenging shot can be the head shot. This should only be attempted by seasoned archers, or by exceptional shooters who have the knowledge to anticipate bird behavior and the patience to wait for the perfect shot angle. Unless the tom is in full-strut, a turkey's head is almost always in motion. It's already hard enough to connect on the small kill zone a turkey head offers, but when you throw in the fact it's moving, usually in a non-rhythmic fashion, then connecting on the shot can be near impossible. I've heard of many misses and crippled birds by people attempting head shots with bows. The oversized, 2- to 4-inch cutting diameter fixed blade broadheads that have become popular for the purpose of head-shooting toms, will likely fly best with larger fletching, so as to maintain consistent and accurate flight. Though it may sound cool, only you can determine if it's a good, ethical shot for you to take.

64

Though these toms aren't in perfect shooting position, if you know where the vitals are, they can all cleanly be taken. Put the arrow where the green dot is located and you'll fill a tag.

Turkey anatomy plays a big part in determining shot placement. While many turkey bones are hollow, they're strong. The humerus and its connective joints on both ends, is the number one spot I've seen send slam-dunk turkey shots with a bow, awry. This is a big bone to break and if hit wrong, the arrow may not penetrate. That's why it's important to hit below it, or in certain circumstances, above it, so the broadhead can do it's job.

While the keel, or sternum isn't hollow, it's big and thick where it attaches to the body. If taking quartering-to shots, know that you may have to contend with putting an arrow through this bone mass. Usually, however, most shots should enter the body above the sternum.

Knowing a turkey's overall anatomy is important when it comes to delivering an accurate bowhunting shot. Turkey anatomy diagrams are available from the National Bowhunter Education Foundation at www.nbef.org.

Within the hollowed bones of turkeys are a labyrinth of structures that act like trusses, to add strength and support. Though they may not be dense, the bones are remarkably strong, which is why I personally prefer shooting heavy poundage with a reliable arrow.

Of course, shot placement is key, but due to their small kill zones and the fact birds rarely hold still for very long, plus the fact the vitals are surrounded by bones and heavily quilled wing feathers, arrows don't always hit where intended. That's why I like fast shooting bows, dependable arrows and the right broadheads for the job.

My favorite setup includes a Diamond or BowTech bow set at about 70 pounds and Gold Tips Velocity arrows. I've taken dozens of birds with these setups, and they've performed well. I've been amazed how many good hits I've made on toms only 10 yards away and not had the arrow pass completely through them due to smacking hollowed bones and stiff wing feathers. This is the same setup I've experienced complete passthroughs with on elk, bison and even African lion and other big game. Bottom line, if not hit in the right spot, arrows may be stopped in the bird, that's how tough they can be.

If hit right, the arrow will slice through with ease, even when pulling 35 pounds.
Some folks like arrows to stop in the bird, so if it tries to fly or run, it's more difficult, thus keeping the bird on the ground where it can bleed-out. Others prefer a complete passthrough. I don't care if it passes completely through or not, all I want is two gaping holes on both sides, with the internal organs fatally damaged.

If choosing a lower poundage bow, in the 35-50 pound range, I'd suggest a fixed blade broadhead so kinetic energy isn't sacrificed. Upon impact, expandable broadheads cause the arrow to slow down and if they contact one of the large, hollow wing bones, first, they may not even reach the vitals if bows are set to a low poundage. Fixed blade broadheads will more efficiently transfer their energy upon impact, thus have a better chance of hitting the vitals when shot from lower poundage bows.

Turkeys are nervous by nature which means their lightning-quick response to a bow being shot–though it may only cause their position to shift an inch–can be enough to make a perfect shot turn out not so perfect. That's why I personally prefer shooting high poundage bows and getting birds as close as I can before sending my Velocity arrow on it's way. The faster the bow and the closer the bird, the less time they have to react, thus the shot usually hits the intended mark.

Find a setup that works for you, study turkey behavior and learn their anatomy. From there it's just a matter of practicing and gaining the confidence to make the shot when it counts. The more time you can spend in the

Braxton Haugen arrowed his first fall turkey at age six. Success came down to taking the right shot at the right time, and knowing where to place the arrow.

turkey woods, the more confident you'll become and the more knowledge you'll gain. There's no substitute for spending time afield, observing the animals we are so privileged to hunt.

Tiffany Haugen with a gorgeous gobbler. This is what spring bowhunting for turkeys is all about.

Optics

When my buddy from Kentucky traveled to Oregon to hunt turkeys with me for the first time, he understood the need for bringing binoculars. But when I suggested a spotting scope, he thought I was joking. Once he set foot in the vast, open, rolling hills and higher elevation, timbered ridges we'd be hunting, he understood.

Out West, binoculars and spotting scopes are important turkey hunting tools that can save valued time, helping cover ground with your eyes, not your legs. Binoculars have their place in turkey hunting arenas east of the Rocky Mountain states, when trying to locate toms in brushy terrain or size them up from a distance. But in the West, binoculars and spotting scopes are important, must-have necessities for many turkey hunters.

When hunting the rugged mountains throughout the American West, it's not uncommon to call from the point of a ridge, only to have multiple toms sound-off from various, distant places. Due to the nature of the topography–deep canyons, steep hills and big ridges–sounds travel far and birds can easily be a mile away, even more.

One spring, while hunting near the 5,000-foot elevation line atop Idaho's Joseph Plains, I hiked to the

end of a ridge and let loose with a sharp, aggressive cutt. Though my intentions were to light-up a bird I'd heard earlier, four different toms answered back, three of which were on distant ridges. The bird I was after hung-up with three other toms and a handful of hens, and wouldn't budge. But one of the distant toms was hot, double and triple gobbling at every sound I threw out.

Eventually the aggressive tom showed himself, proudly strutting into a small opening on an old logging road, well over a mile away. Breaking out the spotting scope I confirmed he was mature tom, all alone and was worth going after. Hopping on the logging road he was moving down, I got into position and kept calling. It took 45 minutes, but he eventually turned the corner on which I sat and strode within 15 yards of where I sat, gun at the ready. The bird gobbled at every sound I made, crossed through two big stands of timber, a big creek and came through 50 yards of brush to reach my location. One shot ended the hunt and soon I was packing out a 24 pound Merriam's sporting a 10 inch beard. Had I not confirmed through the spotting scope that the bird was a good tom, I wouldn't have invested the time in calling him.

Over the years I've located and confirmed mature toms on several hunts which not only saved me valuable leg time and guesswork but resulted in filled tags. There are various sized and powered spotting scopes on today's market, and at a range of prices. Find what fits your budget and figure out what size best fits your comfort level.

On extended, high country hunts, you might want a small, compact, lightweight spotting scope. These scopes are easy to pack and quick to set up on a small tripod for long-range viewing. Some of the lower powered models can even be held by hand, braced against a tree or rock for stability.

Then again, size may not be a concern, meaning a higher powered optic is the best option. For this you'll need a lightweight tripod, something to either carry in your bird pouch or over the shoulder. While there are many fine spotting scopes on today's market, my scope of choice is Swarovski's STM-65 (though this may change as newer, more compact models become available). This scope, combined with Swarovski's lightweight, carbon fiber tripod, makes for easy packing in rough country and saves hours of hiking time.

If toting a spotting scope, there's no need for bulky, high-powered binoculars. Instead, go with something in the 8 to 10 power range–something comfortable and lightweight. This makes a great combination with the spotting scope, allowing you to not only pick apart birds in brushy habitat, but also scope them out across big, open terrain.

If desiring high powered vision but don't want to carry both binoculars and a spotting scope, then consider a high powered binocular. It may be heavier than your 8x or 10x bino', but a strong, 15x binocular serves both the purpose of a bino' and spotting scope.

Should your western turkey hunting adventure lead you into big country, prepare for it as you would any big game hunt; this includes optics. Find what fits your personal needs and desires and go with it. Don't skimp on optics, not if you want to save valued walking time and increase your odds of filling a tag.

Calls

When I began acquiring turkey calls in the mid-1980s I thought everything that was possible to create had been invented. But with each passing year it never ceases to amaze me the number of new calls that are turned out. This is a big compliment to turkey hunters, nationwide, and proves just how popular this sport is, for it's the hunters who drive the market.

In this section it's not my intent to outline or highlight every call that's on today's market, for next year they may not be found. Besides, on any given year something new and innovative may come along. That's the beauty of a growing industry, you never know what the future holds in terms of tools and toys that make the adventure more enjoyable and productive. My intent is to raise awareness on what types of calls are out there, encouraging hunters to try any and all calls of interest.

One thing I've learned about turkey calls over the past 25 years is that turkeys can be picky, so the greater the variety of calls in the vest, the greater the chances of calling in a tom. To maximize the sounds a turkey hunter can deliver, many hunters utilize multiple calls; others stick with a type of call they can work with confidence. Take Splinters, for example.

Splinters was the nickname given to a guide I once met in northern Idaho, on a writer hunt I was invited on. He earned this title due to his aggressive calling approach which utilized strictly box calls. He called so aggressively with his wooden box calls that rumor had it, when he left a calling site, you could see where he'd been by the splinters of his box calls that were left behind.

The first morning I hunted with Splinters, he dug through his vest and showed me nearly a dozen box calls of all shapes and sizes. Box calls were the only calls he used, figuring he'd master each of them rather than worry about working slates and mouth calls. His approach made sense and it worked for him.

Splinters had two objectives: to create high volume with his range of box calls and to be able to offer different sounds with them. Just about every time he set up to call, Splinters would line up all his box calls in front of him, for quick, easy access. He'd usually set up 20 to 30 yards behind the hunter, out of sight, and was ready to offer different sounds if toms were reluctant to come in. His approach worked, both in producing various sounds and reaching high volume pitches that carried across canyons and heavily forested draws. All four of us tagged birds on that hunt, thanks to Splinters' impressive, aggressive calling approach.

Box Calls

The box call could well be the most popular turkey call available. Sounds are not only easy to produce but they sound very real. For young or new turkey hunters, box calls are the easiest to use. Then again, I know of many veterans who prefer box calls over all others.

Whatever box call you choose make sure they are freshly chalked, or treated, in order to produce the most authentic, realistic sound possible. Personally, I carry two box calls; one all-weather and one that's extra loud. I like using other calls–pot, mouth, push button and gobblers–so only have room in my turkey vest for two box calls. This means I'm very selective when it comes to picking those box calls.

Years ago, famed call maker, Larry D. Jones, created an all-weather box call. Larry lives in my hometown and I've known him since he got into the call making business. One thing I loved about Jones Calls is that Larry crafted these calls with the western hunter in mind. His turkey call was no exception.

Larry's all-weather box call was the first of it's kind in our area, but shortly after Larry created it, he sold his company. Not until the company changed hands again, five years later, did the call resurface. By that time many all-weather box calls hit the market but I still believe Larry's version was and still is, the best.

Jone's Calls changed to Point Blank Hunting Calls, and the all-weather box call, dubbed the Mother Load, has become not only my personal favorite box call, but a favorite of hunters throughout the Pacific Northwest. When Larry first developed this call I was able to grab a few, years before they hit the market. Jody Smith also got his hands on a few of these first box calls and between he and I, it's safe to say we've called in more toms with this call than just about anyone.

What makes the Mother Load so special is its unique waterproofing design, which incorporates rosin rather than chalk. Of all the waterproof box calls I've used, this one sounds and works the best. "If I had one call to take into the woods, it would be the Mother Load," comments Jody Smith. "I call in more big toms with this call than all others, combined."

I deliver numerous turkey seminars and one of the things I do prior to starting many of them, is place the Mother Load in a bucket of water prior to the crowd's arrival. I then place the bucket on a front table, for everyone to see. Then toward the end of the seminar, when I get to the part on the importance of all-weather calls when hunting in the rain, I reach into the bucket and pull out the Mother Load. You should see people's eyes light-up, not only when the crowd learns the box call had been sitting in water for 45 minutes, but when they hear the sound quality. Try different models and see what you like, or better yet, what the turkeys like.

Rain, dew, fog, snow, sleet and moisture in any form can shutdown a box call, fast, which is why, when hunting out West it's a must to have an all-weather call you can count on. I actually carry two all-weather box calls, one regularly designed call and a second that will cut through driving rains,

The best test for a waterproof box call is to get it wet...really wet, then see how it works.

heavy winds and carry across vast canyons and densely forested timber patches. For this I prefer a long-paddled box call that's different in design and volume than my Mother Load.

As for making sounds with a box call, they are one of the easiest calls to use. Many seasoned turkey hunters believe the best, most realistic sounds emanate from a box call. There are a wide range of sounds which can be made with a box call, including yelps, clucks, purrs, fighting purrs, putts, cackles and gobbles.

If you can get yelps, clucks and purrs to sound good on a box call, you'll routinely bring in birds. Before trying to make these sounds, play around with your box call. With the underside of the paddle chalked, pass it over both sides of the beveled edges, or the lip of the box, to see what type of sounds are produced. Usually one side will produce a different quality sound, and this has to do with the thickness of the edges and sometimes the angle at which they're cut. Normally, higher pitched sounds come from the thinner side of the call; lower pitch from the thicker side.

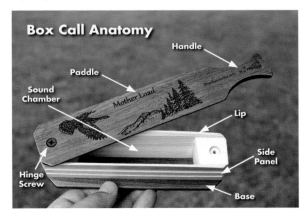

Many calls are intentionally made this way, to yield a wider range of sounds.

With the underside of your box call's paddle covered in chalk or rosin, you're ready to call. It's the curvature of the paddle's underside that creates tone and pitch differences, so don't ever sand this surface as it will change the call's ability to make good sounds.

Box calls are one type of friction call–slates, push-pull and scratch boxes also fall into this category. To produce a sound from a friction call, two surfaces come in contact with one another. It's the pressure, speed and intensity of these two surfaces rubbing together that produce sound.

To make simple yelps, hold the bottom of the box call between your thumb and fingers. Some people like cradling the call in the palm of their hand, but if you do this, be sure you're not muffling the sound of the call. With the other hand, pinch the handle between the thumb and index finger. With the center of the paddle about a 1/2-inch to the side of one lip, lightly drag or scrape the paddle across the lip of the box. Stop the dragging motion when the center of the paddle is about a 1/2-inch on the opposite side of the lip it was just moved across. This short, one inch stroke is a yelp. Apply three to five of these in succession at the rate of about one per second, and you have a series of yelps. Avoid putting too much pressure on the paddle, for it will produce unrealistic sounds.

To produce a purr—my second favorite sound to make on a box call—gently slide the paddle one to two inches across the lip. With some calls, the weight of the paddle is enough to generate a quality purr sound. Be sure not to apply too much pressure or the purr will sound unrealistic and may even transition into a fighting purr sound at an inopportune time.

Clucks are often used in conjunction with purrs and yelps, even as a stand alone call. Clucks are made by quickly plucking the paddle over the lip in an upward motion. With the cluck, the paddle only travels about 1/4-inch, even less, over the lip. Think of trying to create a popping-like sound, one that's quick and sharp, by quickly tweaking the paddle off the lip. Clucks are good to use at the end of a series of yelps and when made softly, pair well with purrs.

When locating toms, one of my favorite ploys is to try and get them to gobble with aggressive cuts, and these are simple to make with a box call. To make cutting sounds with a box call, apply pressure by pressing down on the paddle as it's dragged across the lip. Quickly and aggressively, scrape the paddle over the lip, covering an inch or so with each pass. Making a dozen or so loud cuts is a great way to get toms fired-up.

Cackles can also be made very easily with a box call. Start with a few yelps, then progress into five or six cackles by quickly striking the lip with the center portion of the paddle. End the sequence with a few yelps and you have a very realistic sounding yelping and cackling sequence both toms and hens will respond to.

As for gobbles, some hunters have a quick enough hand to rapidly pass the paddle over the edge, to where it sounds somewhat like a gobble. Usually, however, the best gobbles from a box call come by securing the handle to the body of the call with a rubber band. Find a rubber band of proper thickness and tension to match your call, whereby allowing the paddle to slightly move with a bit of a shake. To make a gobble, hold the bottom of the call with the handle pointing upward. Vigorously shake the body of the call from side to side, sending the paddle into motion. Make sure there's enough tension on the paddle that it aggressively scrapes the lip with each pass. With practice, you'll be able to generate a gobble, and though it might not sound great to your ears, it's the sequence you're after, for that's what can get a tom talking.

Box calls can be one of the most expensive tools a turkey hunter invests in and are worthy of diligent care and maintenance. If properly maintained, both in the field and at home, a box call will keep working for many years.

When in the field, it's important to keep that box call's surface clean, free of debris, dust and moisture. Some turkey vests come with built-in pouches designed specifically for carrying and protecting box calls. I've seen many hunters who've sewn in pouches to fit their favorite box calls. Some hunters elect to cary box calls in plastic bags, in the bird pouch.

If your call gets dirty, wipe it clean with a rag. The goal is to keep the edge of the box and the underside of the paddle, clean. If any debris or moisture finds its way on to these two calling surfaces, sound quality will be sacrificed, the call may also quit working, altogether.

If you do have to wipe the calling surfaces, it may be necessary to re-chalk the underside of the paddle. Only apply chalk to the underside of the paddle, not directly to the beveled edges of the box call as this could change the angle of those edges and hamper the call's sound. Avoid using abrasive paper to clean your box call as this will change the angle of the paddle and the striking surface, likely rendering the call useless. Be sure and use only chalks that are designed for turkey calls, ones that contain no oil or sugar base. Carpenters chalk and classroom chalk work, too.

When in the field, periodically blow or dump any debris out of the sound chamber. This is also a good way to clean out any chalk dust that may have settled in the chamber. When handling the box call, keep all fingers off the underside of the paddle and the beveled edges. Nothing will render a box call useless faster than oils from hands coming into contact with the calling surfaces.

When toting your box calls in the field, use a rubber band to firmly secure the paddle to the box. This will help keep the call quiet and prevent wear. You can also place a small cloth inside the sound chamber, or between the paddle and the call's edges, to protect it and prevent it from making sound when you walk. If placing a rag between the two calling surfaces, the paddle may need to be re-chalked prior to calling.

At season's end, simply store your box calls in a holster or plastic bag. Some hunters living in the Pacific Northwest, where moisture levels are high, store them inside plastic bags and place them in a cupboard to ensure they remain dry.

Mouth Calls

Due of the harsh weather routinely encountered throughout the West during much of the spring season, mouth calls are used by many hunters. Then again, a number of hunters are afraid of these calls, feeling they can't master them. If you can get yelps and purrs out of a diaphragm call, that's all you need to get started. Don't worry about fancy cackles, fly-downs, cutting, putting or fighting purrs. Simply get down the basics and go with it.

I'll carry anywhere from one to two dozen diaphragm calls at any given time. Within this selection is an array of single, double and triple reed calls, as well as ones with notched or split reeds. Also included are reeds with various cuts and designs that allow them to produce unique sounds. With mouth calls, as is the case with any call, the goal is to have models that produce different sounds, sounds the turkeys ultimately like.

As for diaphragm mouth calls, my best advice is to dive in and make them work. Once you get it, it's easy, and you'll be amazed at how quickly you can expand your calling repertoire. Don't be intimidated, as these calls are easy to work, offering the best hands-free calling there is. This can be vital when nervous toms approach, allowing you to generate realistic sounds with no movement. They also work in any weather conditions and the volume is easily regulated. Honestly, the diaphragm call is one my most important tools in my turkey vest, especially when bowhunting.

However, mastering diaphragm calls can be challenging. I know of some folks who've given up on trying to use them; others who got it the first time they placed a reed in their mouth.

Start with a single-reed call when trying diaphragms for the first time, as they are the easiest to blow. Your goal is to simply get a sound, not mimic a turkey right away. To generate a sound, it's all about properly positioning the diaphragm call in the roof of your mouth.

74

Using your tongue, position the call in the roof of your mouth about half-way between your front and back teeth, with the open edge facing forward. On multi-reed calls, place the short reed, down. Some people like the reed a bit more forward than others, some a bit farther back. Don't be afraid to trim the tape or slightly bend the frame to achieve a better fit. The more you experiment with call placement, the easier it will be to find a comfortable position. You'll know when you find it.

When preparing to call, place the top of your tongue against the tape, pinning it to the roof of your mouth. The idea is to create a seal so no air passes over the top of the tape (or foam) or around its edges. When blowing lightly, you want air

You don't have to be a championship caller to be effective in the woods, but you want to be the best you can be. Practice with diaphragm calls in order to get the most out of them.

moving over the top of your tongue, but beneath the diaphragm. Sound is generated by air passing beneath the latex reed(s), causing vibration.

Air should be forced from deep within your chest, or diaphragm. Think of fogging up a pair of glasses or binoculars to clean them; that's where the air should come from. Don't blow air out the mouth as you would blow out a candle. Here's a trick to get started. Before even placing a diaphragm in the mouth, force air from your chest while trying to create a static sound as heard on the radio. The sounds is made by bringing up air from the chest while pressing the tongue against the roof of the mouth, all the while forcing air through a small opening atop your tongue. Once you get this sound, you're ready to try it with a diaphragm call.

Keep in mind not everyone's mouth is the same shape or size. This means it may be necessary to slightly tweak the reed before you can generate any sounds with it. Personally, I slightly buckle the edges of my calls by pushing the two aluminum corners together at the front edge of the call. This takes the tension off the reed and allows me better control with my tongue. Right or wrong, that's what works for me. The more you call and work with diaphragms, the more familiar you'll become with them, finding what works for you.

The first and simplest sounds to make with a diaphragm are hen yelps. With the call in your mouth, slight pressure on the reed with your tongue, lightly blow while saying the word "yelp" or "chalk." Keep with it, repositioning the call as needed. At first it will likely tickle; that's okay and is normal. Keep working it until you get a soft yelp. Experiment with tongue pressure, air flow and reed position until you produce sounds without tickling the mouth, and which sound good. Once you get a single yelp, work on producing a series of yelps.

Once you get the yelp down, try for a purr. There are two ways to produce a purr: by blowing and fluttering the lips, or by blowing and fluttering the tongue. Either way, the goal is to get a soft, short, non-threatening sounds. Purrs–like yelps and any other sounds produced from a diaphragm call–can vary in volume based on how hard you blow, and in tone, based on how much tongue pressure is applied.

Clucks are next and can be made by expelling a short, sudden burst of air while saying the word "puck." Build-up the air pressure in your diaphragm (chest), then quickly release it while saying "puck." To end the call, quickly close the lips, cutting off the sound. It's a short, quick note that is used in combination with yelps and purrs, and is good to apply when a tom is hung-up just out of shooting range.

Putts can also be made on a diaphragm call, and, in fact, sound almost identical to clucks. In fact, I think they actually sound the same, thus are made the same way. Here's my rationale. Over the years I've heard hundreds of birds–both toms and hens–putt. They do this to alert other birds that possible danger may be near. I've also heard numerous birds cluck, but the cluck is usually followed by some purrs or a yelp, sending the message that the bird is content. To my ears, clucks and putts sound much the same, and at times can be impossible to differentiate. I think what sets them apart from one another is the situation in which they're heard.

When birds are nervous, they putt. When birds are content, they cluck, and usually team the sound with a yelp or purr. If a bird approaches and nervously starts putting, I'll answer right back with the same sound, but follow it up with purrs or yelps. This sends the message to the bird that, I hear your danger calls, but things are okay where I am. Hopefully this relaxes the nervous bird and gets it to come in the rest of the way.

Some callers make the cluck or putt sound by blowing a burst of air while simultaneously popping the lips open. This requires a lot of air pressure and can be accentuated by

When toms pull their feathers in, retract their snood and crane their neck high, you know they're nervous.

pushing the tongue tighter to the reed, narrowing the channel through which air must travel. The condensed air flow will help create a short, crisp sound.

Cutt and cackle sounds can also effectively be made with a diaphragm call. The cutt is nothing more than a hyped-up version of the cluck. To make cutting sounds you can loosen up a bit, as the sounds are simply a drawn-out series of clucks made in succession. Rather than saying the word "puck" when you call, think of saying the word "pick" or "peck" when cutting.

When cutting, the airflow is more strung-out than when clucking, and sounds are usually made in rhythmic groups of ones, twos, threes and fours. Think of it like this: *Pick-PickPickPick-PickPickPickPick-PickPick*. When making this call, be excited and loud. This can be one of the most fun and rewarding sounds to make with a diaphragm call but it will take some practice to master.

If you can make simple yelps with a diaphragm call, that will likely account for 80% of your calling repertoire. The remaining 20% will consist of clucks, purrs and cutts. There are other sounds to make, but these four are the most widely used and most applicable in the spring turkey woods. Kee-kees are easy to make on a diaphragm call and work well in the fall season. To make this sound, apply tongue pressure toward the front of the reed, narrow the air passage in the tongue and semi-aggressively blow, whereby creating a high-pitch sound while mouthing the words, *kee-kee* or *tee-tee*.

Spend time in the woods listening to real birds, then trying to copy them with your mouth call. You can also do the same by listening to recorded turkey sounds on the internet. There are some great resources out there if you're not able to get afield as often as you'd like, or if birds are scattered in your hunting areas.

When afield, I carry a diaphragm–often two–in my mouth all day long. When not using it, I'll slide it to the side of my mouth, against my cheek. This keeps it moist and easily accessible. It also allows me to play with the call throughout the day, getting comfortable with its position in my mouth and even practicing calls from time to time. This is a great call to practice with when driving, as it's hands-free and allows lots of repetition.

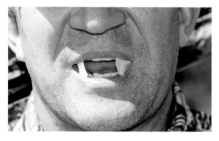
One of the biggest challenges faced by avid users of diaphragm calls is properly taking care of them so they last. I'm as guilty as the next person. Often I get in a rush, traveling from one spot to the next and take out my mouth call, setting it in the dash of the truck. I usually forget to grab it, but return hours later to find it glaring in the midday sun, being cooked through the windshield.

It's critical to keep all your diaphragm calls in working order, not only from day to day, but from season to season. If not cleaned and stored properly they can dry out, split and become useless.

When getting a new diaphragm call, I give it a quick rinse with warm water to remove any powdery, latex residues. When carrying diaphragms afield, I like doing so in leather or synthetic pouches that allow air to circulate around the calls. Often I'm using more than a dozen diaphragms a day and putting them back into plastic, enclosed cases doesn't allow them to properly vent. The result is
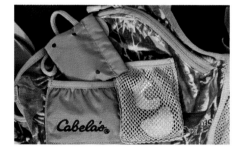
quicker rotting of the reed and sometimes the glue on the tape will separate.

Once home at the end of the day, I like rinsing every diaphragm I used in mouthwash to rid them of bacteria. I'll often run a toothpick between stacked reeds at this time to clean them and keep them from sticking together. Then I'll lay them out on a towel to air dry, overnight. Come morning I'll place them back in my pouch and I'm ready to go.

During the season, if I'm not hunting for a week or so, I'll place all of my diaphragm calls inside a sealable baggy and put them in the refrigerator. Storing them in a cool, dark place not only protects them but keeps the latex tight, producing the best sounds.

In the off season be sure to thoroughly clean each diaphragm call, even if it wasn't used. Inspect used calls for tears in the corner, or warping of the latex. If in doubt, throw away and replace the following season. It's not a bad idea to place toothpick pieces between stacked reeds to keep them from sticking together. Store them in a cool, dark place, keeping in mind that heat and direct sunlight breakdown latex, ruining the call.

Before the start of the season test each and every diaphragm call. Make sure each produces crisp, clear sounds, not any muffled sounds with uncontrolled vibrations. If the sound quality is poor, toss it and get a new one. That's one thing about diaphragm calls, each spring new, innovative designs are introduced and most of them work very well. Try as many as you can afford, that's my motto.

Pot (Slate) Calls

Pot calls–often called pot-and-peg or simply, slate calls–are another friction call option, and are a must-have for all turkey hunters. These are some of my favorite calls, producing what my ears perceive as the most realistic turkey sounds I'm capable of generating. Their volume is easy to control, allowing soft sounds as well as blaring sounds to be produced. This allows you to talk to birds when they are close–as long as they can't see you move–and locate them several hundred yards away.

A pot call consists of three parts: a pot, a calling surface and a striker. The pot serves the purpose of supporting the calling surface and acts as a sound chamber. The calling surface is what the striker is skipped across to produce sound.

Calling surfaces range from slate (Pennsylvania slate being the best), to glass, aluminum, plexiglass and more. Each surface yields a different sound, and each type of striker produces a different sound.

The pot, or sound chamber, has holes drilled in the bottom for sound to escape. Be careful not to block these holes when holding the call and generating sounds. Some pots are very tediously designed to optimize sounds. Some even feature metallic plates or specially coated internal parts with the intent to produce loud, sharp, realistic sounds.

Pot calls can be made to be all-weather, with the right striker. There are dozens and dozens of striker options, each producing their own unique sound, some of which can be all-weather. Humans have terrible hearing compared to turkeys, so what might sound

78

the same to us, may sound totally different to a turkey. That's why many slate lovers carry multiple strikers.

Personally, I carry about 12-15 strikers in my vest. My buddy, Jody Smith, carries 20 to 30 on all of the hunts he guides. "Even though we may not hear the difference between an oak or maple striker, the birds can," Smith shares. "I don't know how many times each season I start with one striker, and before I know it I have 20 of them laying on the ground beside me. A lot of times a tom won't even respond to the first 10 or 12 strikers, then one will light him up! If he loses interest in that striker, I might have to move to something else. You never know how these birds will respond, which is why I'm always prepared to throw a lot of different sounds at them."

One spring while hunting with Smith in western Oregon, we were after a specific tom. A couple days prior I'd received a call from Jody, telling me about a weird looking red and white tom. I immediately knew what it was, a rare erythristic color phased bird.

Note how the strikers used on this setup–where a tom was called in and taken from–have their tips pointing into the air to keep them dry.

Early the following morning we were near where Smith had spotted the tom, in place well before first light. With a stuffed hen decoy situated 10 yards in front of us, we both called, and called and called. We heard toms gobbling and eventually three started our way, but they weren't the big red bird we'd hoped for.

We were on a small parcel of private land, with no option to move, so we kept calling. Two hours later we heard a faint gobble in the wooded draw below us. That's when Jody went crazy with the strikers. "He's liking the high pitch sounds," Smith whispered. I agreed.

I kept working a mouth call while Jody rifled through his strikers and slates. Three pots and 17 strikers later, he found what the tom liked. I'll never forget the image of the red and white tom strutting through the thick grove of madrones, moving uphill, right at us. He was even more brilliant than I'd envisioned, and the fact we were capturing all the action on film for one of our TV shows made it even more special.

As the bird got closer, Jody kept his interest piqued by continuing to offer toned-down versions of the high pitched sounds. The tom loved it, kept gobbling, and kept moving our way.

Looking at that big red bird through my Trijicon RMR sight, I'd never felt so nervous about closing the deal on a tom. My intent was to shoot him sooner, but he was so gorgeous, I was enthralled with simply watching him. I knew this special moment would never repeat itself. After more than two minutes of his strutting around the decoy, I lowered the boom, dropping Big Red on the spot.

That bird was memorable for obvious reasons, not the least of which was Jody offering up over 30 different sounds–and me tossing in nearly a dozen sounds through various diaphragms–before getting the tom to physically move our way. The odds of getting a wild, erythristic color phase tom, about 1 in 300,000. This bird was a prime example of just how finicky toms can be, and how vital it is to have multiple calls and be able to use them.

Strikers for pot calls are specialized, in and of themselves. In fact, there are call companies that do nothing but manufacture strikers for turkey hunters. Dozens of types of woods are utilized to create strikers, as are laminates, synthetics and various metals. The prices of a single, specialized striker may exceed the total cost of all the calls in a hunter's vest, that's how serious pot calling is to some turkey hunters.

The shapes and designs of strikers are another art, some would say a science. In an effort to produce just the right sounds, strikers are strategically fashioned with various tip designs, stick thicknesses and handle shapes and tapers. While some may say it makes little difference, seasoned callers agree that design has a lot to do with delivering desired sounds.

Detailing each type of striker, either in design or composition, could take up most of this book, and that's not my intent. However, I will say that if I had to head afield with five strikers–hopefully that will never happen–it would be a purple heart, oak, maple, laminate and an all-weather, respectively. What you'll discover is that each striker produces a unique sound on every pot. If you really want to diversify your call offerings, doing it with multiple strikers and pots is the best way.

Take my vest, for instance. I carry at least three pots: slate, glass and aluminum. I also carry a minimum of 12 strikers. This combination gives me 36 different sounds I can produce, and all the components are stored in a single pocket. The key here is understanding that picking the striker to fit the pot is not necessarily dictated by the hunter, rather the turkeys.

80

Throughout the hundreds of turkey hunts I've been on, I've kept careful track of what strikers have worked best, that is, got the birds moving my direction. Some of the sounds seem great to my ears, some don't, but if they result in birds either verbally or physically responding, then I make note of it. Often, what sounds best to me isn't what the birds like. That's what I like about pot calls, you can easily switch out the pots and the strikers to get different sounds.

As mentioned, my buddy Jody often carries multiple pots and at least two dozen strikers in his vest. On some setups he'll carefully position each pot and striker on the ground in front of him so they're easy to reach. He takes care to keep the surfaces of the pots and the tips of the strikers dry. Sometimes he might go through every pot and multiple strikers until he finds what turns on a tom. Once he gets a tom

My turkey vest contains a variety of strikers and pots to offer different sounds to finicky toms.

moving, that's the sound he sticks with. If the tom loses interest in that sound and quits coming then Jody will switch to a different sound. This approach has worked very well for Jody over the years.

As far as producing sounds from a slate call, I believe they're one of the easiest calls to work and they deliver very realistic sounds. Some folks struggle with a slate call and this is where practice and persistence come in. You don't have to be a world-class caller to work a slate call, just being able to produce basic sounds is all that's needed to be successful in the field.

Whether the pot's surface is slate, glass, crystal, aluminum, coper, plastic or some other material, and no matter what type of striker you're using, the motions are the same when it comes to producing specific sounds on different pots. It's the wide range of designs and types of materials used to create both pots and strikers that make them the most wide-ranging turkey call there is when it comes to producing a variety of sounds.

Prior to making any sounds on your slate call, rough up the surface with abrasive paper (more on this later). Drag the tip of your striker across the abrasive paper, too, making sure it's clean. Hold the striker about one-inch up from the bottom, like you would a pencil. Tip the top of the striker away from you, so the peg is at about a 45° angle when contacting the pot's surface. This angle should remain constant throughout the calling process, no matter which sounds you're making.

Note that some strikers will be tilted at slightly different angles than others when in use. Play with each striker to determine what angle creates the best sounds. You'll also want to find the sweet-spot on each pot. Most pots sound best when the strikers are "scratched" across the surface about one-third of the way in from the outer edge of the pot. Some

When holding a pot call, be careful not to cover the sound chambers.

have sweet spots a little closer to center. Devote time to roughing up–or "dressing" or "conditioning"–your pot's surface and dialing in to its sweet spots.

With the sweet spots of your pots determined and with the angle of the striker consistent, you're ready to make turkey sounds. As with other calls, yelps are the most commonly used to call in turkeys, and are fairly easy to mimic on a slate call. Begin by holding the pot in one hand. Grip it around the outer edges with and extended thumb and index finger or middle finger. Be sure not to cover the sound chambers in the bottom of the pot, whereby muffling the sounds. Some slates have beveled outer edges which are great for gripping the pot.

When making a yelp on a slate call, the striker remains in constant contact with the calling surface, even when traveling away from the pot's center. Place the tip of the striker on the pot and draw an oval shape. The oval shape should fit on the surface of a dime, that's how small of a radius you're dealing with. The "yelping" sound is made when the striker is pushed downwards, toward the center of the call, skipping across the pot's surface. When returning the striker to the starting position, no sound will emanate as the angle of the striker traveling across the pot's surface is opposite what it should be to "skip" over the grooves in the pot. Each time the striker moves downward, it creates a yelp. Repeat, making the oval three to five times, in sequence and you've created a yelp.

By applying more or less pressure on the striker, you'll get higher or lower pitched sounds. What tones you get depends on the pot and strikers being used. Experiment to see what you get. The higher pitch notes simulate young hens, while raspy hen yelps and tom yelps can also easily be produced in the same way.

Bigger ovals create a pleading yelp, or lost yelp. For this, think of drawing the oval so it fits on the surface of a quarter. This drawn-out yelp is great for calling in hens, hoping toms follow, and I've even used it to pull toms off uninterested hens. It's a great sounding call to make with a pot-and-peg and has many applications. If you're an aggressive style hunter, you'll like this call.

The following sounds can all be created by moving the striker across the slate's surface in a straight line. Of the five sounds remaining, purrs are my favorite to make on a slate call. Personally, I can come closest to mimicking the sounds of real turkey purrs

82

with the use of a slate call more than any other. To do this, grip the peg about a half-inch higher from where you gripped it to make yelps. This will expose more of the peg, allowing perfect tones to be reached. With a slight bit of pressure, draw the tip of the striker toward you, from the outer edge of the slate to the middle. As you draw the striker toward you, it will lightly skip across the slate's surface in a straight line, producing purrs. Practice with this and it will be one of the easiest sounds to make on a slate call.

To create fighting purrs, simply pick up the pace of the purrs, using the same motion. Gripping the peg a bit lower down and applying more pressure will create a louder, sharper tone. Increase the frequency and urgency of this call and you'll create flock excitement often encountered during a real fight.

Clucks can also be made on a slate call. To do this, grab the striker about a half-inch from the bottom and firmly press down on it when pulling it toward you on the slate. The peg should make a quick, sharp jump, creating a one-note sound. To get the cluck tone you want, simply move the striker around on the

On a slate call, yelps (A) are made by dragging the tip of the striker toward you while pushing down, then returning it to the starting position. When making this oval-shape motion, the striker never leaves the slate. Purrs (B) are created by gently applying pressure on the striker while skipping it over the slate's surface. Clucks (C) are made by firmly pushing the striker into the slate while quickly moving it toward you, producing a sharp, one-note sound.

slate's surface to find the sweet-spot for this sound. Of course, this should be done prior to heading afield.

Cutts can also be emulated on a slate call. To do this, make the same stroke as you would for a cluck, except slightly extend the length of pull on the striker and quickly follow it up with five or six more of the same sounds. Start each pull at the same point, quickly returning the striker to the starting position so the sounds can be delivered in a fast sequence.

Add some yelps and clucks to the front end of a cutt and don't apply quite as much pressure during the cutting action, then you'll produce a fly-down cackle. This is a great early morning call when working birds off a roost.

Try a variety of pots and strikers to determine what works best for you. Get to know the pots and where the sweet-spots are. I've seen many hunters dismiss a call as unusable due to its poor sound quality. In reality, all that was needed to make the call perform was proper conditioning and finding the sweet spot. Patience and persistence, that's how you'll find a good slate call and get quality sounds from it. Personally, I like slate calls that give off high pitch sounds, but that's just me; I call in more birds with these higher frequency sounds, no question.

As for maintaining your pot-and-peg calls, there are certain steps that will ensure they make the best quality sounds as well as prolonging their lifespan. Whether your pot call is made of slate, glass, aluminum, polymer or other material, keeping it in good working condition is important.

Be sure to never touch the surface of your slate call with bare fingers or hands. The oils that transfer from your hands to the call's surface will render it useless, meaning it has to be reconditioned with abrasive paper to get it back up and working. Some pots come with a plastic lid that snaps over the top, and is a great way for protecting the calling surface. If there is no hard plastic cover, put the pot in a plastic bag or storage pouch to ensure it won't rub against the inside of a vest pocket or pouch, whereby wearing the surface flat. Also, keep any oils, rain or dust from coming in contact with the call's surface, all of which will impede its sound-making ability.

When conditioning your pot's surface, that is sanding it to create grooves for the striker to skip across, do so by moving the abrasive surface in one direction across the slate. Avoid sanding back and forth or in a crossing motion, as coming back across the surface you just sanded will knock down the ridges you just created. Remember, the purpose of conditioning or sanding a slate is to create grooves that cause the striker to skip when it's dragged across the surface. If the ridges of the grooves are sanded away, the call won't sound as good as it should. Sanding your slate in one direction or in a circular motion will ensure a consistent sweet spot, thus producing more realistic sounds, no matter what call you want to replicate.

When sanding real slate, use a lighter abrasive paper than you would on glass or aluminum. Real slate is softer, thus doesn't require the rigorous sanding that metals, glass and plastics do. For those harder surfaces, use a larger grained abrasive paper, something in the 80 or even 40 grit class. Conditioning stones also work great on hard-surfaced pot calls. For real slate, I like 220 grit abrasive paper, so as not to wear down the surface too quickly.

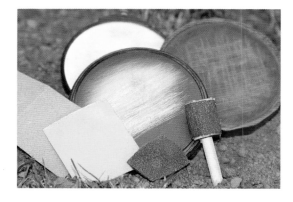

That same 220 grit can be used to sand the tips of your strikers. This is something I can't stress the importance of, enough. Often a poor sounding slate–no matter what the surface may be–is the result of the tip of the striker becoming clogged with sediments from the slate's surface. Once done sanding the surface of a slate, blow it clean or wipe it with a dry cloth. Though this will remove most of the dust, it won't get it all, and dragging the striker over it will result in the dust being imbedded in the pitted end of the striker. To clean the striker's tip, drag it in one direction across the abrasive paper. I keep a small square of abrasive paper secured to the outside of a vest pocket, in an alligator clip, making sure it's easy to access. This ensures I'll clean the striker as needed, which is surprisingly often. The more you use a slate call, the more familiar you'll become with knowing when the striker needs to be cleaned and the pot's surface, reconditioned. When afield, be sure to keep your striker tips dry and clean.

When storing pot calls and strikers, keep them in a cool, dry environment. This will prevent warpage and weathering due to exposure to the elements, and will keep the call functioning well for years.

Miscellaneous Calls

Tube calls and push-pull calls are also popular among some hunters, and are good alternatives to offering different sounds. I'm not a fan of tube calls, probably due to my lack in ability to get them to sound good. Flute-style calls are also popular among hen-focused callers. I do like the ease and sound quality of some push-pull calls.

The tension is already set in push-pull calls, so all you have to do is move the button one direction. As the sliding portion of the call moves across the stationary, chalked portion of the call, it emits sound. These are great calls for beginners as they can quickly make great sounding yelps and purrs. Clucks can also be made, as can cackles and sometimes cutts.

The biggest drawback of a push-pull call is their inability to produce loud sounds which may be needed in rugged, timbered terrain or amid rainy, windy conditions often encountered out West. However, on calm days, or if birds are close, push-pull calls are great.

Many models can even be attached to a gun and operated by pulling a string, a setup that allows hunters to shoulder the gun and simultaneously call. This is great for hunters who can't work a diaphragm call and is especially of value when working birds in field settings where you have visual contact with them for extended distances, where movement must be kept to a minimum.

Other calling devices include a gobble call and a wing, yes wing, not wingbone call. We'll look at how to make a wingbone call in an upcoming section.

As for gobbler sounds, there have been many attempts to create the perfect gobbler call, but most have not hit the mark. It's a very difficult sound to produce, given the rapid rhythm and volume a real gobble reaches. The best gobbler calls I've heard coming from humans are produced from their mouth, not a man-made device. But few of us have the ability to do that, so we're stuck with man-made contraptions. I've tried tubes, box calls, handheld calls and shakers, and for me the shaker calls produce the best sound.

Shaker calls can be shaken to produce a series of gobbles or they can be manually manipulated to produce the sounds. Experiment with the call and find what works best for you.

Why would a hunter want to use a gobble call? There are many cases where a gobbler call has helped me seal the deal on toms over the years. In areas where tom-to-hen ratios are high, the competition can be tough and toms often respond to the calls of other toms as a challenge. For this reason, I've had good luck getting toms to gobble on the roost, and ultimately getting those toms to physically come in to my calls. I think they get the message that says, "Hey, you're in your tree with your hens, but there are other hens over hear and I'm roosting with them." Once I get a tom to answer every gobble I throw his way, I'll follow it up with some fly-down cackles, yelps, clucks and more gobbles. Aggressive toms often come into this approach, sometimes gobbling, sometimes silent.

I also like gobbling early in the season, when heavy rains and cold temperatures have delayed the breeding process. In these times, toms often remain in bachelor flocks longer than usual, which means they are still establishing a social dominance amongst themselves. If they hear another tom in their area they'll often seek him out, looking for a fight.

If I can get between two toms, or groups of toms that are henned-up but not moving to my hen sounds, I'll start gobbling. The purpose of this is to get the toms gobbling back and forth, hoping one of them will make a move on the other.

One year I did this while hunting high in the mountains of Idaho. I had four toms hung up with a few hens to my left, two toms with hens across the ridge to my right. All the toms gobbled at just about every hen sound I made, but wouldn't leave the hens. Then I started gobbling. Though the toms still answered, they didn't budge. Then an old, raspy sounding hen began loudly yelping. Every time I gobbled, she yelped. Every time she yelped, I yelped right back at her with a raspy diaphragm call. That hen yelped nearly two dozen times, and reached my calling site, fast. Right on her heels was a mature tom. I'm confident I wouldn't have got that tom in were it not for gobbling up the hen.

No matter what calls you choose to carry into the turkey woods, know how to use them and use them with confidence. If you can't use a call with confidence, then don't carry it in your vest. The more time you spend in the woods, hunting, calling and observing turkeys, the more versed you'll become in learning what sounds to make, when.

A dried turkey wing is another calling device that can work, though isn't utilized very much by hunters. This tool is easy to make and can be used to simulate the fly-down sounds made when turkeys leave the roost. Take the wing of a tom you've killed, separating the 10 primary feathers from the rest of the wing at the wrist joint, or where the ulnare and metacarpus bones attach to the radius and ulna bones. From the underside of the wing, carefully remove the muscle tissue from the ulnare and metacarpus bones, making

sure the 10 primary feathers stay attached to the bone. Next, spread out the wingtip, nail it to a board, cover with borax and let dry. After a week or so the wing will be dried in an open position with the primaries spread out.

Now you have a wing that can rapidly be moved through the air, simulating a flying turkey. The 10 primary feathers create much more noise as there's less resistance than using a whole wing. It's about impossible to generate enough volume by flapping it in the air, so hold it in one hand and flap the tips of the primaries against your other hand. It works to calm and entice birds early in the morning and works when simulating fighting toms. When toms fight they often flutter around, flapping their wings. The action is loud and the sound carries.

Fly-down wingbeats and fighting sounds can be simulated with a dried turkey wing. Rapidly slapping it against a hand will add even more realism.

I've also used the flapping wing call with effectiveness in the fall, when simulating birds competing for food. Often times turkeys get in a rush when they locate a food source and birds from the back end of a

Drying the 10 primary feathers makes a great wing call, versus using a whole wing which creates too much drag and not enough noise.

large flock will fly their way to the front end of the flock so as not to miss out on the newly discovered food source. Combine the beating wing sound with aggressive scratches amid dry, fallen leaves and you have two realistic sounds often heard in the woods that time of year. Throw in some yelps, purrs and kee-kees, and you've just simulated a feeding flock, something that can bring birds in on the run.

When it comes to turkey calls, if you want to really hone your turkey calling skills, go into the woods once you're tagged out for the spring and try calling in as many toms as you can. You'll be amazed at what can be learned when hunting without a gun. When hunting with a gun, or bow, the intent is to quickly kill. When you have no weapon it can be amazing to actually see how long a tom will hang around a decoy, or how making different sounds will keep a tom interested and holding within shooting range.

Wingbone Calls

As mentioned earlier, turkey hunting has a rich history in the eastern part of the country, and as is the case in any sport, with historical significance comes nostalgia. The wingbone is one of the most historically rich, nostalgic pieces of equipment when it comes to turkey hunting. Dating back thousands of years when Native Americans subsisted off turkeys, wingbone calls have been made. I've read some reports that say wingbone calls were made as early as 6,500 B.C.

Whenever and wherever the first wingbone calls were crafted, there's no denying that, today, this call is fun to make and emits excellent yelps. I've made wingbone calls out of hen, jake and tom wing bones. Personally, I like the sounds that come from hen wing bones, from birds taken in the fall. Incidentally, the skin from the same hen can be used to make a decoy and the meat can be eaten. Talk about making the most from all parts of your bird.

A wingbone call can be made of two parts (radius and ulna) or three parts (radius, ulna and humerus). Simply remove these bones from the bird's wing, at the joints, making sure no breaks have occurred. Strip the bones of any meat then saw off the ends of each bone, exposing the pith. With a wire and tap water, force the marrow out of all bones.

It's best to remove the marrow before boiling the bones, and avoid flushing it with too hot of water as the fat will begin to cook and stick to the inside of the bone.

Wingbone calls can be built from three bones (left), radius, ulna & humerus, or from two parts, the radius and ulna.

With the marrow removed, boil the bones for 15 minutes in a 50/50 solution of water and hydrogen peroxide, adding about five drops of dishwashing liquid to the mixture. Add enough of the solution to cover the bones by at least an inch. Once the water reaches a high boil, turn it down to a slow boil.

Remove the bones and rid them of any excess flesh or marrow. If desiring a pure white set of bones, boil again for 15 minutes in only water.

Bones can be further whitened by placing them in a solution consisting of 50% water, 50% peroxide. Let stand 30 minutes to two hours, depending on how white you want the bones. The bones may not appear to be whitening when in the solution, but once removed and left to dry, will transition to white. Avoid letting stand too long in peroxide or bleach, for you don't want the chemicals breaking down the bones.

Take the bones, lay them out from smallest to largest, and start dry-fitting them together. With a fine-toothed saw, gradually remove the ends of bones so they snuggly fit inside one another. This is the longest, most tedious step, but is what eventually ends up being the most important if looking to get authentic sounds. If desiring a perfect fit, you can sand the ends of the bones. If using the humerus to make a three-bone call, it may be necessary to file down the interior bone structures at the wider, bell-shaped end of that bone with a small file or dremel tool.

At this point, whether making a two- or three-boned call, the bones can be pieced together by inserting them about 1/2-inch inside one another. Next, small bits of cotton can be shoved into the joints with a toothpick. A two-part epoxy will then be added, filling the gaps. If you want to skip the cotton insertion, simply apply epoxy, making sure none collects in the hollow center of the bones which will impede calling. You can also use Plastic Wood to fill the gaps and join the bones together.

Let the epoxy dry, trim away excess glue and you're set. If wanting to polish-up your wingbone call, do so with 200 to 500 grit abrasive paper. Size 0000 steel wool can also be used to buff the call and get it shining.

If desiring a lanyard, that can be made and attached to the call in a number of ways. Just avoid drilling any holes in the bones, as you want the sound chamber clear of obstructions.

To make yelps with your wingbone call, place the tip of the small end just off center between your lips, flattened side facing down. Put the call into your mouth just enough to create a suction, ensuring air can't enter around the sides. Next, suck in, just as you would suck a thick milkshake through a straw. With practice you'll be able to generate excellent sounding yelps and clucks. For you fall hunters, kee-kees can also be made with the wingbone call.

In the mid' 1900s, the wingbone may have been turkey hunting's most widely used call. Today, the art of using–and making–these calls has waned, but it's not gone. As your turkey hunting experiences grow, you owe it to yourself to craft your own wingbone call. When you call in and take your first tom with a call you created, you'll understand the culture behind this special call, and you'll appreciate the historical ties this grand bird has impressed upon many peoples throughout the Americas for centuries upon centuries.

Locator Calls

There are other calls that are important for turkey hunters to know about. These calls have nothing to do with calling in turkeys, but everything to do with finding them. They're referred to as locator calls and are meant to do just that: locate turkeys. A locator call is a call that's meant for hunters to find turkeys, without sounding like a turkey.

If locating turkeys with hen calls you may put toms on the move before you're ready to set up. It may also make them nervous and alter their behavior, or alert them that there's another turkey in the woods that they didn't know about. But if you can get a tom to gobble to a sound other than a turkey, then you know where he is and have a valuable point from which to start your hunt.

Locator calls are meant to get a reactionary gobble from a tom, usually early in the morning while he's still on the roost. It can also work during the day but as a rule of thumb, the hotter the day and the further into the season it is, the less likely you are to get a gobbler to respond. But locator calls work especially well early in the morning and late in the evening, all season long, and are most effective when toms are roosted.

Though locator calls are largely used in the spring, I've found success with them in the fall in many parts of the West. This is because the purpose of the locator call is to elicit a reactionary gobble. It's sort of like sneaking up on

Find a roosted bird by using locator calls and your chances of filling a tag will rise.

someone and scaring them; when this happens they usually jump, gasp and often holler out loud. They don't think about doing that, they simply react to the startling moment that caught them off-guard. Getting a tom to gobble at a locator call is the same thing, with the intent to get him to gobble out of a sense of being shocked. This is what's often referred to as "shock gobbling."

Ask any hunter whose spent time in the woods and they'll tell you they've heard toms shock gobble at many sounds. This is why it's a good idea to carry a selection of locator calls in your vest, because birds won't always respond to the same sounds.

Owl hooter calls are likely the most popular locator call in the eastern turkey woods, and work well out West, too, in the right situation. The thing with owl calls is they're not very loud, so are most effective when used on calm mornings when hunting open, flat country, or amid timbered country where turkeys aren't far.

Personally, I prefer locator calls that have the capability of hitting high volumes that will reach out and touch toms on the roost. Crow calls are a favorite, as is a coyote howler.

I know some hunters who don't like coyote calls, reasoning they scare birds and keep them on the roost longer. If hunting low elevation lands where coyote numbers are high, this may not be a call you want to use. Then again, there are few things as loud as a coyote howler, and given the fact you're trying to elicit a reactionary gobble, really it shouldn't make much difference as the birds don't think about responding to a call; they just do it.

There are many types of locator calls. A coyote howler, hawk, owl and crow call are among the best.

In the morning I like crow, owl and other bird sounds. Often the birds are so fired-up they'll gobble on their own, so there's no use throwing out locator calls. This is a fun time to sit back and watch nature awaken. It also allows you to mark the precise position of toms as they gobble.

In the evening I like louder, more aggressive locator calls. This is when coyote calls have worked best for me. I also like loud locator calls on rainy, windy days, in thick habitat and when calling across canyons because I want the sound to carry as far as possible.

In addition to owl, crow and coyote calls, elk and peacock calls work well. Yes, there's a company or two who make peacock calls for the sole purpose of locating turkeys; that's how effective the shrill sound is at getting a tom to gobble, never mind the fact the turkey has likely never seen or heard it's colorful cousin before.

Woodpecker and hawk calls are also great shock gobbling calls. Many hunters feel the raspy sound of a box call imitating a cackle, or cutting, is a top locator call, and it is, but keep in mind it's also sending the message you're a turkey, which has now alerted the tom that there's another bird in the woods.

When delivering locator calls, do so in quick, short, loud bursts. Don't drag out the calls. The goal is to introduce loud, crisp sounds that make a gobbler react. If a hunting partner is along with you, have them stand 20 or 30 feet to the side, so they can better hear a shock gobble.

If hunting alone, it can be challenging to hear a tom answer back, especially if he

does so early in your calling sequence. To lower the chance of this happening, keep your locater calls brief and loud, then be ready to listen. Once you've delivered a locator call, don't move a muscle. Stand still and don't shuffle things around in your vest, for missing a faint, distant gobble may mean the difference between filling a tag or being left empty handed.

One thing locator calls can offer hunters is a chance to move in on a stubborn gobbler that's talking but won't budge. Instead of trying to pull that tom your way with hen calls, keep him gobbling with a locator call and you go to him. As long as he's talking, you know where he is. The final yards might find you covering ground on your belly, Rambo style, but it's a very effective approach to tagging a tom that you know won't come to your hen calls.

Though it may feel awkward, opening your mouth and cupping both ears to form mini-satellite dishes, will dramatically increase you ability to hear distant gobbles.

Locator calls are one of the most important tools in the turkey woods and can save valued time and help locate birds you otherwise would have never known were there. I can't begin to count the number of birds I've seen called in over the years due to getting them to shock gobble, thus divulging their whereabouts. After all, once you know a tom is out there, and know precisely where he is, then you can devise a solid game plan.

Decoys

I'll never forget the first tom that came into my decoy. I'd placed a foldable, lone hen decoy some 25 yards in front of me, then sat against the base of a big oak tree. I called, a tom gobbled, and soon he was sprinting to the decoy. The moment he reached the decoy, I shot him. It happened so fast, it was one of those times where you find yourself asking, "Did that just happen?"

The next season I took another tom over the same hen decoy. This time I wasn't so quick to pull the trigger. Two toms approached and I just watched. Once they reached the decoy, they strutted, pecked at her, pirouetted and even fought amongst themselves, totally neglecting the decoy. Eventually one tom tried breeding the hen impostor. The whole performance only lasted a couple minutes, and concluded with my tagging the biggest of the two toms. What the incident confirmed was just how effective decoys can be when hunting turkeys, and how long toms will actually stick around them.

Had I written a book on turkey hunting 25 years ago, I'd have suggested getting a foam, collapsible hen decoy, placing it 20 yards in front of you, then calling. Today, an entire book could be dedicated to the types of turkey decoys on the market and how to use them.

Each season more and more turkey decoys hit the market and the creativity and precision with which they're designed is nothing short of amazing. Some decoys look even better than the real birds.

What will likely most influence what decoy or decoys you get, will come down to how much money you want to invest. A simple, two-dimensional decoy can be purchased for as little as $20.00, or you can actually have a bird mounted to use as a decoy, and that could run upwards of $500. Some hand-made, hand-painted synthetic models will run $400-$500, even more. Or you can mount your own bird for about $70, plus labor.

Hen decoys come in a variety of body postures, color-ranges and some are even moveable. Jakes come in a range of body positions with heads painted various colors and with tails at full or half-fan, all in an effort to exude specific moods and behaviors. Some jake decoys even spin, raise and lower a partially fanned tail.

Tom decoys are also available in a wide selection, with an array of different colored heads. They can be found in full-strut, half-strut, feeding positions, aggressive postures, submissive stances and more. The key is knowing which decoy sends the message you want to convey at the time of your hunt.

Then, add to the decoy options, breeding pairs, even entire flocks of decoys, and it's not only overwhelming, but it starts taking up a lot of space. There are even tom decoys where one appears to have two heads, when in actuality, the 2nd head is set off to the side to create the illusion that another tom is standing behind the full-body one. Flocks of multiple hens, jakes and mature toms can also be purchased.

With most turkey decoys you can get simple, two-dimensional cardboard, plastic or fabric models. These are great for packing as they are lightweight but if a wary tom sees them from any angle other than broadside, he could get nervous and flee. Plastic, molded bodies are available, as are inflatable decoys. Some are big and bulky, making them somewhat challenging to carry a long distance, while some, like foam, plastic decoys, roll up and fit nicely into the game pouch on the back of a vest.

Whatever decoy or decoys you decide to get, make sure you're getting them for a reason. In other words, make sure you know what message each decoy is sending. Based on turkey populations and patterns, decipher what objectives you want your decoy set to convey.

A word of warning. Prior to heading afield, make sure the state in which you're hunting allows the use of decoys. Also, if looking to use moveable decoys–mechanically, battery or manually operated–be sure it's legal in the state you're hunting. One more warning, when

Decoy options are many when it comes to turkey hunting.
This flock arrangement, with one tom and four hens is a good way to lure in a mature tom.

hunting pressured public grounds, be sure to hide the head of a mature tom decoy in your pack; you don't want it sticking out when walking through brush, for fear of being shot. At the same time, when calling, be watchful of fellow hunters who might approach your decoy, looking for a shot.

Fortunately, much of the American West is expansive, meaning turkey hunters have a lot of room to spread out. In fact, in all my years of turkey hunting throughout the West, I've never encountered another hunter while physically in the woods. This is largely due to the fact I avoid pressured areas and try securing private lands to hunt on. I've seen a lot of hunters when driving logging roads and passing through small towns, but never have I seen a turkey hunter working the same areas I'm hunting. That's not an invitation to be careless, just a simple fact that our turkey hunting population is not as densely packed as places in the eastern part of the country.

Decoys detract the attention of approaching birds. On this setup the author and Jody Smith nailed a big tom with the decoy placed nine yards in front of them.

So, you're looking to get a decoy. What should you buy? If you've never hunted turkeys before, I'd start with a lone hen, that's it. A lone hen decoy has accounted for more than 75% of the toms I've taken over a decoy or decoy spread. In other words, a hen decoy has worked for years, and it will continue working.

The purpose of a hen decoy is to capture the attention of a tom who is looking to breed. If he sees her, he'll likely come to inspect. It's that simple.

If you're looking to acquire multiple decoys, your next best purchase might be a jake. A jake decoy situated near a hen decoy sends the message to adult toms that there's a hen nearby, and she must be ready to breed, for the jake is courting her. This will often draw a mature tom in, fast.

When a mature tom approaches a lone hen decoy, he'll usually break into full-strut to get the hen's attention. Often he'll strut and walk around the hen, sometimes gobbling, spitting and drumming and pirouetting. When walking behind the hen decoy, a tom might try to approach and mount her. I've had numerous hen decoys knocked over by toms trying to breed them. This is why, when using a lone hen decoy, you want her facing away from or to the side of you, to keep the tom from staring your direction.

94

When setting up a hen decoy for bowhunting from a blind, I'll usually stick her five yards from the blind, no more than 10 yards. If hunting with a shotgun, 25 yards is good, for this will give the pattern time to spread out. This is where patterning your shotgun is important so you know exactly how they'll perform at what range.

Turkeys are tough to kill with a bow and the closer you can get them for a shot the higher the percentages for connecting on a quick, clean kill. The first turkey my oldest son, Braxton, killed with a bow, walked within 10-inches of the blind. I've had numerous turkeys within a foot of the blind, some toms even touching it in strut mode.

When bowhunting turkeys, I like placing the hen decoy slightly to the side of the blind, opposite from the direction which I think a tom will approach, and facing away. This is so when the tom does see her, he'll have to cross in front of the blind to get in front of the decoy so he can start displaying.

If using a jake decoy in conjunction with a hen, positioning is important, especially for bowhunters. When using a jake decoy–or any tom decoy for that matter–it's a good idea to set them so they're either facing you or standing broadside to where you're sitting. This is because when a tom approaches, he usually goes in front of the intruding male decoy in an effort to visually impress and intimidate him. For a bowhunter, getting the live tom to stand between you and a jake decoy will offer the best shot.

As for mature tom decoys, there are many thoughts to using them, in fact, they are so new to the world of turkey hunting, the verdict is still out on just what these decoys can and cannot do. Personally, I'm amazed at how their application continues to expand and just how effective they can be throughout the season.

The key to choosing and using a tom decoy comes down to intimately knowing what's behaviorally going on with the birds in your hunting area. One season I phoned a buddy in Oregon, suggesting he give a lifesize, full-strut decoy a try. I'd just finished hunting three Rocky Mountain states where friends and I absolutely hammered the big toms, and all with the strutting tom decoys. It was the most amazing thing I'd ever witnessed when using decoys as it brought toms in on a dead sprint the moment they laid eyes on the tom decoy.

When my buddy back in Oregon tried it, he thought it was the worst invention ever introduced to turkey hunting. While various friends and I filled more than a dozen tags on big toms charging in to the lifesize decoy, it didn't work so well for my Oregon friend. In fact, the first three times he used it, approaching toms saw the decoy and quickly turned, running away.

The more we thought about it, the more we reasoned why the strutting tom decoy likely failed to work in one place, but did so well in others. Where my friends and I used the decoy in Montana, Wyoming and Idaho, tom densities were high. Where my Oregon buddy used it, tom densities were low that year. Interestingly, about six years later, tom densities rose in my Oregon buddy's hunting area and he hammered the big toms with the aggressive, full-strut tom decoy.

Over my next eight years of using a strutting tom decoy, I'm a firm believer that where tom densities are low, the decoy is not as effective as using a hen or jake and hen decoy. This is because the birds simply don't want to fight. They've likely already been pounded during the winter bachelor flock break-up and fights were likely incurred early in the breeding season when multiple toms battled over a few hens.

In regions with high tom densities, I've observed fights amongst mature birds throughout much of the season, and it's especially high during the first half of the season. During wet, cold, delayed springs, I've seen toms remain in bachelor flocks two to three weeks longer than normal, meaning these are also great situations to use a full-strut tom decoy in. I also like them later in the season when hens have gone to nest.

I also like using full-body, strutting tom decoys in agricultural area. Here, toms are used to seeing hens, and know what gobblers are in the area. But introduce an aggressive tom decoy and the live bird will often come barreling in to see who the new bird in the field is.

Some hunters like using tom decoys that are in half-strut or a walking position, as this sends the message that they are interested in the hen (decoy), but not overly confident. This semi-submissive decoy position can be an open invitation for a live tom to come in, strutting his stuff as he approaches with the attitude that he's going to establish dominance, then breed.

Then there are tom decoys with red, white and blue heads, and ones with nearly all white heads. Brightly colored heads send the message, "Hey, look at me, I'm good looking, I'm brave and I'm worthy of breeding." A white headed tom is one looking for a fight, and if he's strutting at the same time, he's saying, "Hey, hen, look at me, I'm big, tough and mad, and for you other toms, come fight me, I dare ya!"

I've had the best success using white headed tom decoys in conjunction with hen decoys in a submissive, breeding position. I think this combination is so effective because it sends the message that a hen is ready to breed, and that an aggressive tom is ready to mount her, but also willing to take on any challenges. Where tom ratios are high, or many hens have gone to sitting on their nests, this can be a great decoy combination to get toms fired-up and moving in.

I've also had good luck using a brightly colored, full-strutting tom decoy over both a submissive hen decoy as well as one in a feeding position. I don't think these tom decoys issue such a sign of urgency. Placing three or so hen decoys around a strutting tom decoy can be very effective. When a live tom sees one tom with a group of hens, he knows his chances of pulling away a hot hen is good, so he'll approach.

Some of today's decoys feature great detail. When selecting an aggressive tom decoy, be aware of the message it's sending.

I'm always trying different things, experimenting around to find what works and what doesn't. After a few years of having solid success with a strutting tom and multiple hen decoy arrangement, I thought, "Why not toss in some more toms, just to see what happens?" My intent was to create a testosterone-induced scene that, once an approaching tom saw it, would make him want to come in and be a part of it.

The first trio of big toms I called in to this setup turned and ran the moment they saw it. The next time I tried it, three single toms came in over a 45 minute period, all from different directions. Every tom gobbled his way to the setup, through brush and patches of broken oaks. But when each tom laid eyes on the decoy flock, they shut up, froze and quit coming. All three of their heads changed colors, from red, white and blue, to white. They all pulled their feathers in and totally shut down. All three held up out of bow range. That was the last time I tried using four hens, a jake and three mature tom decoys.

For years, hunters thought that tom decoys would scare off turkeys, and in many cases that's right. But once you know when to use them, they work unlike any decoy

I've seen. They create some of the most eye-popping memories you'll ever witness in the turkey woods, and leave you wanting more.

One thing I do with all my strutting tom decoys is replace the factory supplied synthetic tail with a real fan I've made. When heading to Merriam's country, I'll use a Merriam's tail fan, and in Rio country, a Rio fan. I like the real tail fan because it doesn't reflect light and the feathers move in the slightest breeze.

I also use a real tail fan in other decoy situations, which I'll elaborate more on. But first, let's look at how to make a tail fan.

When you kill a tom, one you're not going to mount, you can save the tail. With the bird on its stomach, gently grab the fan, fold all feathers together in one hand and push it forward, toward the head. This will expose the base of the tail and you'll easily see the white skin where each of the quills of the tail enter in.

Beneath the bulbous juncture where the tail feathers meet, and above the anus, take a sharp knife and start cutting. Push the fan forward as you continue cutting, which will make it easy to see what you're doing. Cut around the rounded edges of the base of the tail and through the spine. Continue cutting down the back a few inches to ensure the lower tail

Dried tail fans, ready to use.

coverts and some back feathers remain attached to the tail section. Not only do these feathers add color to your natural tail, they add movement.

With the tail removed, work from the backside to remove the meat and expose the base of the quills. Once most of the meat and fat have been removed, pin the tail down to a piece of thick cardboard and cover the exposed tissue with borax. Let set until dry, usually a few days to a week, depending on conditions.

Incidentally, this is the same way to preserve a turkey tail fan for display in your home. The only difference is, if being removed for display, be sure to remove as much fat and meat as possible from between and around the quills to prevent spoiling.

Once dry, you're left with a tail fan that can be used alone or placed in a full-strut or half-strut decoy. Tail fans can also be used to hide behind and make a stalk on a tom, or used to lure toms to you.

To use the turkey fan as a decoy, simply place the dried fan in a piece of stiff wire or a wooden stake that's about a foot long, and you're set. Bend a piece of wire in an S-shape at the top, then slide the turkey fan into the curve. This will securely hold it.

Throughout the West many hunters are addicted to stalking their turkeys for the sole purpose of improving stalking skills on big game. Those who've dedicated themselves to this technique know turkeys can be every bit as hard, if not more challenging, than stalking big game. This is largely due to the bird's nervous nature and superior ability to detect movement.

Stalking turkeys is also more applicable out West than in other parts of the country for the simple reasons there are vast tracts of land to hunt and fewer hunters. If hunting in an area where other hunters will be, avoid stalking toms. Keep this approach for hunting private land, or public lands where you're certain no other hunters will be.

A tail fan is effective for stalking turkeys, but make certain it's on private land, no other hunters are around and know your target.

There are two ways to hunt with a tom turkey fan. First is to spot a tom, then hold the fan in front of your face as you crawl towards the bird. If trying to call a tom in, but he won't move, try stalking your way to him with a fanned tail as your portable blind. I cut a notch in my tail feathers so I can peek through them rather than having to lift my head to look over or around the fan. Many times you can simply stealth your way to within shooting distance of a tom by staying hidden behind the fan. Sometimes a tom might even see you and come running. When this happens, be ready for a potentially close-range shot.

Second, the fan, alone, makes a good decoy. Get the fan in a position where a distant tom can see it. Usually, if he sees it, he'll either commit right away or he'll stay put. If he commits, stake the tail into the ground and get ready to shoot, for a sprinting tom can quickly close the distance. If he hangs-up, then use the fan to stalk in on him.

A tail fan makes a good decoy, alone or when placed near a hen decoy.

The same tail fan can also be placed in a 1/4-sized tom decoy. This decoy adds the realism of a bird's body as well as a tom's colorful head. DO NOT use this decoy on public land or any place where other hunters even have a remote chance of being. This is one to use only on private land where you're positive no other hunters will be. This is because the realism of this decoy–a detailed painted head and real turkey tail– create a very realistic looking decoy, one a novice, amped-up hunter might pull the trigger on. This decoy would be used the same way as the fan.

On one early season hunt in the higher elevations of Idaho, toms were very active and just splitting up from their winter bachelor flocks. Some toms were strutting and aggressive, others were content on feeding. I'd just called in two big toms but they approached from behind and I couldn't get a shot, as we were filming it for a TV show and the camera man couldn't get turned around. Though those two toms came to within six yards, I never got a shot. But moments later I spotted a lone tom feeding on the ridge below me.

I tried calling that tom with a range of sounds, and calls, but he never once lifted his head. Taking the 1/4-lifesize decoy with a real fan shoved into place, I began stalking toward the tom, slowly covering ground on hands and knees. The ground was rocky and slow going, so I reached into my vest and pulled out a pair of knee pads. That allowed me to make better time.

Note the eye-hole cut into the feathers of the tail fan, allowing you to keep track of the target. Only use this approach on private land, or where certain no other hunters are around.

As the tom moved toward a brushy, timbered thicket, I had to pick up the pace. I was amazed how quickly I cut the distance from 90 to 70 yards, then to 50. At 27 yards I had to take the shot, for the tom was moving out of sight. Though he could clearly see me on the open, rocky, shortgrass hillside, he was never for a moment nervous. I think I could have walked right up to that tom. The crazy thing, my camera man was behind me, with a large camera on his shoulder. That tom carried a 10-inch beard and weighed 26 pounds, a whopper of a Merriam's.

Real tail fans can also be placed in lifesize tom decoys, adding realism to them. Jake tail fans are also valuable when looking to use them alone or in a decoy. A jake tail fan sends a message of submission, allowing you to sneak up on a tom without him feeling threatened, or to encourage a tom to come to you, making him feel confident that he can displace the insubordinate jake.

In coming years, turkey hunters will learn more about decoy use and applications. Where it will be decades down the road is anyone's guess, but that's what's so great about turkey hunting–the learning never stops.

Blinds & Stands

As with other tools in turkey hunting, the expansion and advancement of ground blinds and treestands is never ending. Every year new, innovative designs hit the market and surprisingly blinds and stands keep getting better and better.

Here, the intent is not to dissect individual blinds and stand designs, for they are perpetually changing. The purpose is to share the effectiveness of these tools and suggest the best conditions in which to use them.

The first time I ever hunted turkeys from a treestand, I thought I'd never fill a tag. Turkeys always seem to be looking up due to the large number or avian predators they have. Not until I hung treestands where they needed to be, not where I wanted them to be, did I start filling tags.

At first I hung stands in open, exposed oak trees. With this setup, birds could see me from a great distance and if I had to move to get a shot they'd bust me. This made getting a shot tough, even with a shotgun, but with a bow, it was near impossible.

Then I started placing stands in thicker habitat and just inside the edges of bigger timber stands. I hung them in places where birds had to be called into light cover. Birds out West don't mind entering brushy habitat, since they live in it each day. If a tom is fired-up enough, he'll venture into just about any type of cover.

Placing a decoy or pair of decoys near the base of the tree helps focus the attention of approaching birds on them, taking it off the hunter in the stand. If desiring to take a tom with your bow from a treestand, place the decoys as if they're moving away from you, and have the stand situated on the backside of the tree opposite the decoys, not in front of the tree. The purpose here is to bring a tom by you, then when he passes, his back will be at you, allowing you to reach full-draw without being seen. Keep in mind that 300° field of view a turkey has. The hard part here is that if the tom approaches from a different angle, he might be able to see you for a long time. This is where you'll need to calm the nerves and sit still until he passes by. It's best if you can reach full-draw when the tom is strutting with his head behind his fanned tail.

Treestands can be effective, but keep movement to a minimum as turkey's often look up.

No matter where a treestand is hung, keep movement to a minimum. This elevated situation is one of the most vulnerable positions there is for a turkey hunter, as any movement is almost sure to catch a wary tom's eyes. A buddy who has taken a lot of turkeys over the years, including dozens with his bow, believes taking a turkey from a treestand is the toughest hunt there is in the spring woods. I would almost agree, ranking it a close second behind arrowing one from flat ground with no blind or cover.

I think more success can be had from a treestand in the fall, when hung along a trail turkeys routinely use. Pattern the birds to see where they're moving, when, and along which specific trail. Then hang your stand on the backside of the tree. This will allow the birds to walk past you and be facing away when it comes time to shoot, be it with shotgun or bow.

When I first started turkey hunting, I'd never heard of a pop up ground blind–I don't even know if they existed in the mid-1980s. So, like many hunters, I created my own ground blinds from brush, logs, tree boughs and grasses. Though they worked, consistent success was marginal. This is because, unless the blind is created to look like a solid curtain of vegetation, holes of daylight will exist and any bird will likely bust you at the slightest movement.

Natural blinds work when properly constructed, but doing so can be time consuming, and if the birds aren't around, that blind can't be picked up and moved. Enter man-made ground blinds.

There are many options for man-made ground blinds. The most basic is taking a sheet of camo' fabric, spreading it across sticks or trees, and sitting behind it. The problem here is you have to rise above the fabric to get a shot, and birds often bust you. If using this kind of blind, cut a small hole in the fabric that you can shoot your gun through. The benefits of this style blind is that it's easy to transport. The drawbacks are the lack of 360° concealment and how tough it can be to get a shot, especially if bowhunting.

One-person blinds are nice, in that they are small and portable. But they do limit your range of motion which means if a bird approaches and hangs-up anywhere but directly in front of you, you may not get a shot.

The 360° popup ground blinds that totally cover you are the best blinds there are for turkey hunters. This is because they completely conceal you, allowing you to move about. Not only can this freedom of movement be critical in getting a shot, but also in changing calls to convince that finicky tom to come in the rest of the way. They also allow you to use box and slate calls, which obviously require movement of both hands to operate.

Total concealment ground blinds are also great when hunting with a buddy, especially youngsters. One of the biggest challenges faced by youth turkey hunters is sitting still, which can be tough to expect from them, even under the most ideal situations. Take the pressure off by using a ground blind which conceals them.

I'll never forget the first tom my youngest son, Kazden, took where it was hung-up out of shooting range. We'd called a pair of toms off the roost and they were headed right toward our blind until three hens fed across the grassy meadow between our hen decoy and the approaching toms. A jake eventually passed by the decoy, but I encouraged Kazden to hold out for one of the big toms, something I wasn't sure would even happen.

Fortunately, we were in a ground blind, covered on all sides. Had we been caught in the open I doubt the hunt would have ended in success. Two hours is a long time for anyone to sit, let alone a nine year old. I tried different calls, and Kazden scratched on his box call. Though the toms often replied with courtesy gobbles, they wouldn't commit to us. So we sat, quietly, hoping the hens might come our way. Even my pleading, raspy hen helps didn't get their attention, and when three more hens joined the flock, I questioned denying Kazden the opportunity to take that jake.

Then, ever so slowly, after two hours, the hens started feeding into the brush. That's when the biggest of the two toms decided to come check out the hen decoy. He was nervous, I think more due to my overcalling in a desperate effort to coax him in sooner rather than later, but he was at least making a move.

Kazden sat, 20 gauge resting securely in the tripod, patiently awaiting the tom to waltz within range. Finally, after what seemed like an eternity,

Kazden's first spring tom, taken with good friend and noted guide, Jody Smith, of Elkton, Oregon.

the tom finally hit the mark. "Take him when you're ready," I whispered to Kazden. "There's no hurry, he's not..." Boom! Before I could get the words out, the tom had taken a payload of three-inch magnum 6 shot.

Kazden was excited and relieved. Had we not been set up in a blind I doubt he'd have killed that bird, for at one time we had nine turkeys within 50 yards of us, and that's simply too many eyeballs to contend with. Kazden's tom was big and heavy, sporting 1 1/4-inch spurs, a 10 1/4-inch beard and weighing in at a whopping 24 pounds. The mounted tail fan, beard and spurs hang on a wall in our home, a daily reminder of one of the most memorable turkey hunts of my life. It was all possible, thanks to a ground blind.

I've never seen a turkey shy away from a ground blind that's been secured in place, that's how effective they are. Be sure there are no window flaps that may move in the wind, and make certain the model you choose allows the fabric to be stretched all the way across the frame when erected. A buddy had a blind that he threw away because the material was too loose across the mid-section when it was set up; every bird that saw that blind spooked when the slightest breeze blew.

Most of the blinds I set up for turkeys are done moments before the hunt, not days or weeks as commonly associated with big game hunts. Again, their monocular vision isn't keen enough to detect the outline of a blind, which explains why they will routinely approach so closely.

For bowhunters a ground blind is the most valuable turkey hunting tool there is, period. No other approach allows you to knock an arrow, reach full-draw, swing on a tom and release without being busted. I've taken over two dozen turkeys with a bow and have never spooked a bird when hunting from a pop up blind. We won't talk about all the birds I've alerted from natural blinds, treestands and hiding behind what I thought were big enough trees to conceal me. Sure, birds can be killed from these latter mentioned blinds, but the odds of success greatly decrease compared to being in a blind that offers total concealment.

When getting a pop up blind, look for one with a carrying case that comes with shoulder straps so it can be more easily moved afield. Be sure and put in practice time prior to hunting from your ground blind, especially if bowhunting. Practice shooting from every conceivable position so there are no surprises come time for the shot on a tom. Make certain you know the parameters of your bow inside the blind, so you can move with the confidence of knowing

104

your bow won't contact any part of the blind.

Ground blinds may cover you well, but they aren't sound proof. Be sure to keep unnatural sounds to a minimum so as not to spook any approaching birds. Don't let metal parts come in contact with one another and be sure the bulky turkey vest is set aside, out of the way. Make certain the chair you sit in allows for easy, silent movement. My favorite "chair" to sit on in any ground blind is a plastic-framed milk crate with a padded cushion on top. These crates are low-profile, dead-quiet and allow you to easily achieve any shooting position necessary, especially with a bow. Of course, if having to pack in any great distance, the crates are cumbersome to carry, so I might opt for a little stool.

If using a shotgun in a ground blind, implementing shooting sticks may be a good choice, especially for youth and aging hunters. Tripod sticks are best, for they more solidly anchor a gun and are less likely to fall and create noise like an unbalanced monopod or bipod might. They are great for helping smaller framed hunters keep the gun barrel up and in shooting position, rather than deferring to resting the barrel on the edge of an open window which can not only scare a bird, but doesn't offer proper support.

When selecting a blind or treestand, ask yourself where you'll use it and how you'll be hunting. From there, make the decision on what best fits your individual hunting scenario. I'd venture to say total concealment pop up blinds will allow you to hunt in 95% of any turkey terrain out West, with natural blinds and treestand rounding out the remaining 5%. Then again, if you're up for the challenge, honing your hunting skills by employing a variety of blinds may be what you're looking for.

That's the beauty of turkey hunting, there's always flexibility in how to go about filling a tag. The challenge comes in knowing when you're making headway or just educating already wise toms you may never close the deal on.

Miscellaneous Gear

Up to now this chapter has been devoted to what I call important, must-have pieces of gear. After all, you can't kill a turkey without a weapon, and using calls, blinds, optics and decoys greatly increase the odds of success. But there are other pieces of gear that can help improve success and keep you more comfortable.

Every serious turkey hunter I know is excited when it comes to gear and gadgets. That's because they know how finicky wily toms can be, and that any little gizmo that might remotely help close the deal on a tom is likely worth trying. The best turkey hunters I've spent time in the woods with are the ones who are aggressive, open to trying new things, confident and regularly apply woodsmanship skills. Of course, woodsmanship, or a working knowledge of the outdoors, comes only with spending time in the woods.

The advent of new gear often allows hunters to expand their tactical repertoire which ultimately makes them better hunters. There are pieces of gear on the market now that didn't exist a decade ago, allowing hunters to fill more tags in ways never thought possible. I'm sure, in years to come, even more gear will make its way into hunters' hands, and though we have no idea what that gear might be, we'll look back and ask, "Duh, why didn't I think of that?"

One of the best ways to learn about turkey hunting is to look into the vest of proven hunters and see what they're carrying. More importantly is an understanding of why they have the gear they do, and when and where they use it.

With that in mind, here's what you'll regularly find in my vest. Don't feel like you have to invest in every piece of gear mentioned, but know that it's available as what could be a valued addition should you desire.

Listed in no particular order, each item can directly impact your ability to effectively hunt, or allow you to be more productive and comfortable when in the field. Some apply to wherever turkeys are hunted out West, others may be confined to specific geographic locations or situations.

As for bonus gear, the most important tool that has not only increased my comfort level, but has allowed me to hunt longer and in situations I'd otherwise not be able to withstand, is the ThermaCELL mosquito repellent. If there was one mosquito in the woods it would find me. I've used a ThermaCELL in the most mosquito-laden lands and swamps throughout Alaska, Canada and the Pacific

106

Northwest, where no repellents have ever worked 100% of the time. But the ThermaCELL unit has, and continues working wherever I take it.

The ThermaCELL mosquito repellent unit is powered by a butane cartridge that screws into the bottom of the unit. With the push of a button the butane starts burning, heating a metal grill that holds a small mat saturated with a non-toxic repellent. As the mat heats up, it releases a vaporized repellent which rises into the air. The repellent, allethrin, is a synthetic version of a repellent that occurs naturally in chrysanthemums. It's said to repel up to 98% of mosquitos, black flies and no-see-ums, and is not harmful to humans. I'll attach the ThermaCELL unit to my turkey vest, the inside of a blind, or set it on the ground in front of me where I set up to call. Nothing has increased my hunting time in the mosquito infested woods like this device. I use it on many hunts in the spring and fall, and the family also uses it around the home and on camping trips.

While on the subject of Therma-CELL, they have also developed a wireless heated insole. The ThermaCELL Heated Insoles can be trimmed to any size and will fit in most adult-sized boots of any style. The wireless remote control lets you adjust heat levels, with maximum temperatures reaching about 112°. The insoles, themselves, recharge like a cell phone and can be charged up to 500 times. They keep the feet warm unlike any heating device I've used and are invaluable on those early season, cold hunts.

Another tool that helps add comfort is a set of knee pads. The first time I saw these hanging in the turkey section of a sporting goods store, I laughed. "Ah, another gimmick for turkey hunters," I thought to myself. Then I crawled through a soaking wet, rock-riddled pasture and wished I'd had them. The next day, I did. Since then I've used the military, tactical-style knee pads on numerous turkey stalks. They take up some space in the back pouch of my turkey vest, but weigh virtually nothing. They've allowed me to execute more stalks, in comfort, than I ever thought possible.

Knee pads are worth having when stalking through rough, rocky country.

A tool that's great for turkey hunters out West is a small pad to rest your gun on. The padded rest straps to your knee and when in a seated position, keeps the shotgun comfortably at rest in a ready position. When sitting in an awkward position on a sidehill or uneven terrain, the padded gun rest not only allows a gun to be kept ready, it frees the hands for using a call.

Having a pad to rest the gun on your knee not only allows you to work calls with both hands, but ensures the gun is ready.

Speaking of small tools, a lens cloth and some wet-wipes also come in handy. The lens cloth is great for cleaning optics and more. There always seems to be a need for wet-wipes, be it cleaning your hands, wiping blood from birds for photos, or much more.

In cold regions where you'll be out all day, matches and fire starter are also worth having. We once spent the day at nearly 5,000 elevation, chasing Merriam's. That afternoon a snow squall came through and the temperature dropped fast. It was nice having an instant fire as the storm passed.

While talking of sitting in an awkward position, one of the most important bonus devices is a stool or padded seat. When hunting without a blind where you're on the move and sitting against trees to break-up your body's outline, a comfortable stool or pad is a must. One of the vests I use has a thick, built-in cushion that flips down and stays attached to the vest. This usually provides ample comfort, but on steep hillsides I slide off the pad. A Cabela's vest I use has a built-in kickstand and thick pad, where an external frame extends, securing the pad in place and giving a great backrest.

If the built-in pads or stools aren't enough, there are many styles of chairs out there. A favorite of many hunters are ones that offer back support as well as ample padding on the bottom. Some have aluminum frames that sit low to the ground, like a mini lawn chair, keeping your backside completely off the ground while simultaneously offering a backrest. Some roll up and collapse, taking up little space while giving much needed back support. Some are shorter than others, some wide, some narrow, some designed at different angles. The best advice is to find what size and style fits your personal needs and choose accordingly. If you're like me, you'll

108

agree there are different seats that fit certain situations, which can mean you might find yourself investing in more than one stool.

A piece of gear that has a direct impact on turkey hunting success is a facemask. If you wear a facemask, be sure to pack an extra along, for they often get lost. Personally, I like the caps with a headnet sewn into them, for they never get lost and fit nicely to the face. They also make for quick, easy transitions when you have to set up fast. Bottom line, your face must be covered to cut down on the glare that turkeys will surely detect and the easier and more comfortably this can be achieved, the better off you'll be.

If you're a bowhunter, face paint may be the way to go so you don't have to worry about the string getting caught in your facemask. A buddy and I bowhunted for turkeys all day one spring, eager to score by way of spot-and-stalk. Finally, in the closing minutes of the hunt, my buddy had a shot at the first tom of the day. The distance was not a problem, but when he released his arrow, the string knock caught in his facemask. His shot wasn't even close, and a full day of hunting found us going home empty.

Whether hunting with a bow or shotgun, a rangefinder is a must. A lot of turkeys are missed due to misjudging distances. Looking at a turkey head through a little hole from a dark blind, or under the bill of a cap through a tiny hole in a facemask, appears far different than judging that same animal at that same distance while standing in the open. When you get set to call, range various landmarks so you'll know exactly what distance an approaching bird is at prior to taking any shot.

On those cold days, hand warmers are nice, especially if kids are along. Warm gloves are also a good idea, as are thin, camo' gloves to slip on as the day heats up to cover the glare on your hands. If hunting in already warm conditions, bring an extra pair of thin, camo' gloves, as one is often lost. Whatever gloves you wear, be sure you're comfortable shooting in them with bow or shotgun.

Bringing along a camo' stocking cap or beanie to keep warm is also a good idea.

There are even heated clothes that have a place in the cold, early season turkey woods. I've fallen in love with my Cabela's heated vest. What I would have given to have it when hunting turkeys at 3,500-feet elevation, in snow with temperatures dipping into the 'teens and winds blasting through the mountains of southeastern Washington.

Rubber boots are worth having, especially on those mornings when grasses are wet. They also keep the feet dry when wading creeks, trudging through snow and hunting in the rain. I always make sure to have a pair of hiking boots and rubber knee boots in the truck, wherever I hunt turkeys, along with extra socks.

If toting a shotgun, be sure to install a sling before hitting the woods as it allows the gun to be carried in comfort when hiking for extended periods in rugged conditions. If bowhunting, attach a bowhook on to your turkey vest to make it easier to glass and use locator calls with both hands. If bowhunting from a blind, have a bow stand to hold your bow in an upright position, arrow nocked–this will allow you to grab the bow with minimal movement and remain quiet while achieving shooting position.

Turkey vests come in many styles. Take time to find one that meets your hunting needs.

Speaking of turkey vests, pick one that fits you. Turkey vests could well be the most oversized pieces of hunting clothing on the market, and the last thing you want is a loose fitting vest that flops around making a racket. If possible, try several vests on and see what fits your frame; it will be worth it the moment you take to the woods.

It's also worth packing about 20-feet of lightweight rope, mole skin, a variety of band aids and a roll of athletic tape. Turkey season means allergy season, so bring any allergy medication you may need, along with aspirin and ibuprofen. Be sure and take plenty of water, either in a hydration system, water bottle of water purification bottle. I like the filtered purification bottles for they allow you to keep refilling throughout the day, without the added weight of toting a hydration pack. Staying hydrated in the western turkey woods is a must; you can't have too much water, especially on those hot days. It's also nice to have water when field dressing your bird so you can rinse out the body cavity and prevent spoilage.

Other bonus tools include a GPS, compass, topographical maps, fire starter, ribbon and reflective tape. The reflective tape is good when finding your way to a hunting spot in early morning darkness. Hang the tape the night prior, when staking out a spot to set up and hunt. In the morning, use a dim light to find your way into the hunting locale, picking up the pieces of tape as you go.

Navigational tools are great for not only hunting amid the big, rugged country throughout the West, but for also finding your way out of any storms or heavy fog that may roll in. Some models allow you to communicate with and track fellow hunters, too.

A knife always comes in handy, but I especially like having one so I can immediately tag and field dress a

tom. Quickly field dressing a tom will release body heat and keep the thin, internal organs from leaching through the body cavity and tainting the meat. I like Kershaw's folding fillet knife for cleaning and breaking down birds. Rubber gloves are nice for cleaning birds living in habitat laden with poison oak. Pruning shears are great for cutting shooting lanes or trimming vines that are in the way.

Toss in some snacks, toilet paper, a camera and maybe a cell phone and you're about set. There are other items you may find yourself in need of–like extra rubber bands to secure box call paddles–but that comes down to your own personal needs and preferences. Having an extra pair of socks is also a must, especially if hiking rugged country for Merriam's or Rio's, where feet might sweat. Sunscreen and lip-balm are handy when in the woods all day.

If covering ground on a quad, one tool worth having is a LoopRope. Constructed of durable, doubled-up, 1/4-inch heavy duty shock cord, this multifaceted securing system doesn't stretch or wear like a bungee. The multiple, duo-lock clips allow securing the LoopRope easy, making it great for transporting blinds, cased guns, vests, stools, decoys and downed birds. The LoopRope is one of those diverse tools that has a wide range of applications, and anyone who spends time in the woods or on the water will find them to be a valuable piece of equipment.

The more time you spend in turkey country, developing your woodsmanship skills, the better you'll be able to accurately evaluate the worth of your gear. Only by spending time afield, where gear can be put to the test, will you be able to draw your own conclusions as to what works and what doesn't. Chances are you'll over-invest on some items but you won't know how good any piece of gear is unless you try it. It's better to buy it and try it than wonder if a piece of gear might work, and never give it a chance.

The LoopRope is great for securing many things, be it on the hunt, in the truck or back at camp.

Chapter 3:

SPRING HUNTING SEASON

There's no greater time to be in the turkey woods than in the spring. Warming temperatures, budding foliage and an array of mesmerizing wildlife are all part of the spring turkey hunting experience. Throw in gobbling toms with some of the most stunning plumage in the bird world and the stage is set for one of North America's most coveted hunting seasons.

Spring hunts can happen fast or take days, depending on how the birds are behaving. In the West, variables are continually changing, whereby altering how toms act toward one another and interact with jakes and hens. Being cognizant of bird behavior, and why it's happening, will help hunters find consistent success. Knowing what methods to apply, when and where, is also crucial.

Behavioral Progressions

Turkey behavior in the spring is different than any other time of year. For a couple months in the spring the number one thing on a tom's mind is breeding. Hen's are also intent on breeding, but once that's done a hen will retreat to brushy nesting habitat where her goal in life is to raise a brood of chicks and stay alive; to do this she becomes reclusive.

While the urge to reproduce is what makes spring turkey hunting so special and so productive this time of year, don't forget that turkeys must eat, drink, take dust baths and roost. I think one of the biggest mistakes hunters make is focusing too much on the breeding cycle of turkeys, neglecting a turkey's other needs in life.

In many western states, both Merriam's and Rio Grande populations of birds will undergo a seasonal migration where they move to higher elevations as spring approaches. True, many turkeys are year-round residents at low elevations, especially amid valley floors, around ranches and private properties where food is easy to get and they are safer from predators. But in their more wild, higher elevation settings, turkeys naturally move to higher ground come breeding season.

Why the move to higher ground? Hen's often move to higher elevations to nest in seclusion. This is also their way of spreading out the population, for often times the brood will remain in the area they were born, then drop into a different drainage come late fall or winter. Sometimes, however, the hen takes her brood right back to her traditional wintering grounds.

Turkeys also move to higher elevations to seek new food sources. Melting snow means lots of water entering the ground, and with water and sunshine comes new plant and grass growth.

One thing that's for sure in the early half of spring, wherever a hen goes, toms are sure to follow. Adult hens are very mindful of what their needs are to be successful mothers. They know when to feed, eat and take cover in the shade. Wherever they go, whatever they do, toms won't be far. The only time a tom won't be with a hen this time of year is if she's sitting on her nest, or got up for a quick bite to eat.

Once the egg laying process has begun, hens won't stray too far from their nest. The experienced hens know they'll be dropping about one egg per day, and don't want to miss depositing it in the nest. Young, first-year mothers, however, often get caught off-guard, unaware that their biological clock is telling them it's time to lay an egg. These are the hens that may wander further from their nest, and the ones toms will likely stick to.

As mentioned earlier the peak of the breeding season for turkeys in most western states usually starts about one month prior to any hunting seasons opening. This is to ensure successful breeding takes place. However, peak breeding seasons can see delays, which can be good and bad for hunters.

The more hens hunters have to contend with in spring, the harder the hunting can be. It's tough trying to lure a tom away from a real live hen that may become receptive to breeding at any moment. This is why many turkey hunters prefer the last couple weeks of the season when it comes to calling in toms, their reason being that most hens have been bred, yet the toms are still looking for breeding opportunities.

Early in the spring season can be tough pulling toms away from hens that aren't yet nesting.

Typically, on an average year throughout the West, peak breeding is in full-swing when turkey season opens. This means hens are not yet tending nests and that toms, hens and jakes are all living very near one another. As hens get bred and go off to nest, some toms may follow them while other toms stay behind. In many areas, toms live in the same place year after year, meaning when hens get bred and seek nesting ground elsewhere, the toms stay put. These are fun toms to hunt for they're still interested in breeding, they just don't want to leave their comfort zone. This is where hunters can move in and have some great results using decoys and alluring hen calls.

As the spring progresses, usually in the latter weeks of the hunting season, toms will start roosting and feeding in small bachelor flocks. They're not as cozy with one another as they will be in the fall and winter months, but with no hens to compete with, they're more tolerant of one another. Slowly their focus in life shifts from breeding to survival.

Exactly how a turkey behaves and when behavioral changes take place can vary from year to year, even drainage to drainage. I used to think their behavior was dictated by photoperiodism, or shifts in daylight hours. But the more time I spend in the turkey woods, I'm not sure this is the case like it is with most big game animals.

114

Based on personal observations, the number one innate response to lengthening daylight hours that I've seen turkeys display is on their movement to higher nesting grounds. In some of the higher elevation areas–3,500 to 5,200 feet–I hunt in Washington and Idaho, birds seem to start moving high in late March and early April, no matter how nasty the conditions or how much snow is on the ground. Though the actual breeding may not take place for a few weeks, the birds begin their move early in these areas.

Turkeys can be found surprisingly high early in the spring.

I believe much of a spring turkey's behavior is dependent upon weather conditions, and I feel stronger about this the more time I spend in the woods. Many years I've seen the peak of the breeding season delayed when conditions were cold and wet. One morning on opening weekend I set up and called to a pair of toms I got to shock-gobble on the roost. I could hear a few yelping hens but didn't think much of it, as that's normal early in the season. But as daylight broke, the trees came alive with turkeys. Soon I had two toms, one jake and 17 hens in front of me. I saw those same 17 hens almost two weeks later, in the exact same place. The conditions that spring were extremely wet and very cold, and no doubt the breeding process was delayed because of this.

To say a turkey behaves in a specific way, day in and day out, year after year, is not something I care to do. While this may be the case for turkey hunters back East, I think the big, rugged country, wide range of habitats and exposure to severely cold, harsh, late winters and delayed springs, affects turkeys differently in their western habitats. When you talk about hunting birds near sea level, amid jungle-like rainforests, on up to 7,000-feet in elevation in the Rocky Mountains, it's only logical that behaviors can and will shift on any given year.

This is where the western turkey hunter must pay close attention to what transpires from year to year within their hunting area. I'm hunting some of the same areas I hunted 25 years ago; some places I'm no longer hunting because there are simply no birds there. Something caused those turkeys to move, be it a change in food sources, increase in predators, habitat shifts or a die-off. The key to successful spring turkey hunting out West is knowing how the birds live in and react to environmental conditions in the areas you hunt. All the while, it's important to note changes in bird behavior, not only during the hunting season, but throughout the year. Keep careful notes and you'll be surprised at how much there is to learn.

Reading Signs

Though we've already detailed how to decipher the tracks and droppings of a tom and hen turkey, there are other signs to look for during the spring season. Some of the most important signs are feathers, tracks and wing drag marks in the same area, all of which indicate a strutting ground. By nature, toms visit the same strutting area day after day, calling in an effort to bring a hen to them. In such areas I've found there to be high hen densities. These are great places to hunt, for you know a tom is there.

Early in the morning when dew is still on the ground, get high and glass down on grassy ridges, open meadows and pasture land. This is when it's easiest to see trails made by turkeys, where the dew has been knocked off the grass. Such trails often reveal roosting sites and feeding areas, as that's what turkeys are moving from and to, respectively.

When looking for tracks, if you come across a hen and tom track together, look closely. If there are no drag marks from the tom's primaries, or tracks that indicate he's pirouetting for the hen, then try to stay on them. If they're traveling in a fairly straight line with little sign of pausing, likely what you've found is a hen on the move, temporarily away from her nest in search of food. Once that hen goes back to her nest there will be a lone tom eager for some hen companionship.

Using a spotting scope from elevated vantage points also allows you to find toms trailing hens from a safe distance. Watch where they go and when the hen retreats into thick brush, make your move. We've especially had success doing this in the latter half of the season, once hens start nesting. They'll get up to feed in the morning hours, then again in the evening and sometimes in between, so keep a watchful eye for toms sticking with a lone hen.

As evening approaches, watch where birds go to roost. In some of the big valleys and timbered ridges I've hunted over the years, the roosting sites change as spring progresses. One area I hunted at 4,700 feet in elevation found all the birds roosting on the same bench early in the season. A week later, when I returned to hunt them, the birds were still using the same strutting ground atop that bench, but they'd split-up and were roosting on two different ridges, both across gaping valleys that required flights of a half-mile or more.

Another area my wife and I hunted one spring also saw a change in turkey roosting sites, but this one was due to weather. A week prior to the season the weather was warm and it felt like spring was here to stay. The toms were roosting in a stand of 40-year old Douglas firs. Then the monsoons hit. We were hunting Oregon's Willamette Valley, about 500 feet above sea level. For days the rains continued, and despite a torrential downpour, Tiffany and I decided to still give it a try on opening day. Making our way up an old farm road, we moved toward an abandoned hay barn to escape the rain.

As we approached the dilapidated structure, the back of a turkey caught our eye. Quickly we got set up and I gave a few yelps on the diaphragm call. Even at 60 yards, the tom couldn't hear me over the hard-hitting rain. So I turned it up a notch. Not only did he gobble, but so did a couple other toms. Seconds later, along came four toms, sprinting to the call as fast as their legs would carry them, right through the driving rain. With each stride their wet feathers moved from side to side across their bodies, resembling suits of armor. When they got nine yards from us, they stopped, then started gobbling and strutting. Tiffany made a perfect shot and had her tag filled less than 10 minutes into the season.

The author's wife, Tiffany, tagged this bird in a driving rain.

Grabbing her bird, we moved into the barn to tag it. What we found caught us off-guard. The old barn was littered with turkey feather and fresh droppings. A closer look at some of the poles revealed toenail marks, and below that, a line of droppings. What had happened was once the heavy rains hit, the toms started using the hay barn as a roost site. A couple days later I returned to the area, and though the rains had stopped and the birds were no longer using the barn as a roost, we did manage to get my dad a nice tom.

Fresh sign reveals turkeys roosting in an old, abandoned barn. You might be surprised where these birds roost.

One of the biggest clues that have helped us fill multiple tags over the years is what's in a turkey's crop. Remember, the rut is only one portion of what goes on in a turkey's life during a spring day–they have to eat and sleep. Once you tag a tom, open it's crop to see what it's been eating.

Early in the spring you'll often find grasses and clovers. Later in the spring the diet largely shifts to grass seeds. But there are other food sources, and it's up to you to learn what they may be in your respective hunting area(s).

I once took a nice Merriam's in Idaho, and with a second tag to fill, I was curious to see what the first bird had been eating. When I tore open the crop, I found bits of grass, as expected, but what I didn't anticipate seeing was a big collection of rose hip berries. They were obviously hold-over berries from winter, but where did they come from? Covering ground I found an entire hillside covered in wild rose hip bushes, a place I'd not seen before. I later filled my second tag, and it's crop also had scads of rose hip berries.

As spring progresses, signs will change. Get to know the land you're hunting and interpret the signs accordingly. By learning what signs there are, and deciphering their meaning, you'll develop the hunting skills needed to consistently get on birds.

Private Lands

In many areas where turkeys live throughout the West, they've congregated on private lands. When transplanting birds throughout many western states, it was not the intent of game officials to get turkey flocks established on private land; in fact, quite the contrary. Officials know that more animals on public land means increased hunting opportunities. Nonetheless, birds gravitate to private lands to escape predators, find food and roost in safety. It's no one's fault, it just happens. Well, sort of.

The number one factor that attracts turkeys to private land is food. Often birds are seen feeding amid cattle and sheep feed lots, picking grain fields, raiding grain bins, scouring crops and even getting seed from song bird feeders in backyards. In some suburban areas, turkey's have become a major nuisance.

Getting permission to hunt these private lands is wherein the challenge, and frustration, lies. Though turkeys may congregate on private land, landowners may not want you hunting them. I've tried reasoning with landowners, some will listen, some are reluctant. Some have gracefully granted permission to hunt, some have not. Even when I made it clear that the turkeys were planted in their region thanks to tax dollars given

by hunters, and that the turkeys wouldn't be there were it not for hunters, I was still turned down. When getting turned down, I ask if they would stop feeding the turkeys so they would return to public land, a service myself and thousands of other hunters helped fund.

There are ways to gain access to private land hunting. First, start early in the year. Don't wait until hunting season starts, or even a day or two before it starts, until you begin knocking on doors. Much of the private land access I've gained over the years has been found in the fall and winter months, when turkeys overrun private lands in their large winter flocks. At this time birds can be a nuisance and farmers and ranchers can be eager to thin their numbers.

Some landowners are willing to allow youth an opportunity to hunt, but you never know who they are unless you ask.

I've also offered the landowners something special. Taking them a smoked salmon or fresh steelhead fillets is often a good gesture. Not only will I do this when hunting, but during the off-season, too.

A buddy has gained access to some great land by simply pitching-in to help the rancher with chores a few days out of the summer. Another friend keeps his private land access by getting the landowner's wife a $250 gift card to her favorite store each year.

If looking to get youth on a turkey hunt, landowners are often more receptive to the idea of allowing families to hunt, versus an adult or groups of adults. When approaching such landowners I've had the best success doing it well before the season. Dress nice, represent hunters well and be polite if there's a "no."

There was one ranch Dad and I tried getting on for years, but the widowed landowner wouldn't let us, or anyone, hunt. Still, each summer we'd stop in and visit, and give her a fresh-caught steelhead. She was a sweet lady, she just liked her turkeys. One day in July we pulled up to her house and she quickly met us at the door. "I was wondering if you two were going to show up," she piped. "You can shoot all the turkeys you want...go get them now if you want!"

She'd recently had three big toms sail off the bald hill in front of her house, crashing through the plate glass window of her living room while flying at full speed. Two birds were killed on impact but the other ran rampant throughout the house, making shambles of the place. The 83 year-old lady had to replace all her furniture, carpet, curtains and more. We had some great turkey hunting on that property for a few years.

Above all else, be polite and courteous and know that you're representing all hunters when talking to landowners. If they say "no" that's okay, they don't owe us anything.

One year, early in the season, I knocked on the door or a rancher. I'd seen some nice toms on his place so stopped to ask for hunting permission. He met me at the door, took one look at my camo' clothing and partially closed the door without saying a word. He opened the door again but this time he was holding three arrows, all different colors. "I know what you're going to ask, and the answer is no!" he exclaimed, waving the arrows in my face. "These are what I got from my field over the last two days, from hunters trying to shoot turkeys from off the (paved) road," he ranted. I couldn't blame him, and found myself feeling sickened that anyone would stoop to such a selfish, illegal act.

Of course, not all hunting is on private land. For example, in western Oregon, nearly all the birds have moved to private land, but in eastern Oregon, large numbers of turkeys are found on public land. Pockets or regions like this can be found in just about every western state. There's no question that overall the hunting is better on private land as the birds are less pressured. Then again, how you go about hunting any turkey depends on many factors, be it on public or private land.

Following is a look at proven ways to go about consistently filling a spring turkey tag. Fall tactics are different and will be covered in the following chapter. Within many of the approaches, anecdotes will be shared on what has worked, and maybe hasn't worked, for me over the years.

Pattern Birds

No matter how you plan on hunting western turkeys, it's a major benefit to first try and figure out their daily patterns. Find where they're roosting, where they fly down to, where they spend the day and how they re-enter the roost. Observe the flock dynamics and see who is running the show. Is it aggressive toms warding off one another, calling to attract hens? Or is it hens going about their daily routine, being pestered by puffed-up toms with only one thing on their minds?

Some flocks travel more than others during the course of the day, and knowing where they go, when and why, is a big bonus. Note their food sources as well as where they might get water, or retreat to when it gets hot. One thing I've noticed over the years is how often turkeys go to water despite how much moisture is on the grass. Even on rainy days I've watched turkeys walk through drenched grass to drink from a creek. In other words, knowing where a turkey drinks, be it in a river, creek, spring or puddle, is valuable information.

When patterning birds, do so from as far away as possible with binoculars and a spotting scope, so as not to get busted. Disturbing a flock can throw them off their daily routine for a few days and by that time a hen's breeding status may change which could result in the birds leaving your area, altogether. I once got too aggressive on a flock that I'd patterned. I pushed it, trying to scoot across an opening and the flock busted me. They sprinted, then took wing to the neighboring property. Those birds never returned to where they'd been roaming for the previous six weeks, but the neighbor tagged a nice tom, thanks to my bonehead mistake.

Trail cameras are another valuable tool when patterning turkeys. Not only will trail cameras reveal where birds are, but they'll show how many birds there are, what they're doing (feeding or strutting) and what time of day they're around. Trail cameras have allowed us to pattern and take many birds over the years. The best part, trail cameras work all the time, even when you're not in the woods. Talk about an efficient way to scout.

Pattern birds from a distance so you can observe their natural behaviors, undisturbed.

Some folks like positioning trail camera's two feet off the ground. I like hanging them at least three, closer to four feet off the ground so they can cover a wider area. Increasing the field of view is what it's about when using trail cameras for turkeys, so you don't miss something. Situate cameras along known trails, on the edges of meadows and near where birds travel to enter and leave the roost. Watering holes and strutting grounds are also great places to hang trail cameras. Anywhere you see turkey sign–droppings, feathers, tracks–is fair game for a trail camera setup. You can even make mock dust sites as well as mock scrapings in the leaves of feeding areas, and place cameras there. You'll be surprised at some of the brushy habitat these birds live in throughout the West, especially amid the Coast Range and the west-facing slopes of the Cascades.

One spring we were catching a big, lone tom on trail camera that was using a Roosevelt elk trail in Oregon's Coast Range. He wouldn't come to any calls and where he lived was very difficult to hunt due to dense timber, brush and sharp breaks in the terrain which offered no place to set up. The only thing we could think of was to hang a treestand on the trail. Two days later will killed that tom, not two paces from where we'd caught him on trail camera.

Often times when turkeys start making their way to the roost, they'll split up and go to roost in different areas. I've seen this more in mountainous country throughout the West than in flat river bottom habitats. This can be a good time to close the deal on smaller flocks as they cover ground, heading toward the roost, for there are fewer eyeballs to contend with. Knowing where these separated flocks reconvene in the morning is also important, as it allows you to figure out exactly where to set up.

Keep in mind that as flock dynamics change, so too does turkey behavior, thus the bird's daily routine. How a flock moves and acts on opening day could be far different from how they move and act a month later, and again, at the end of the season.

Thanks to a trail camera, this wily tom was caught strutting on a game trail.
Soon afterwards, on a rainy day, he was taken from a treestand while using the same trail.

Open the eyes, observe and interpret turkey movement. Don't wait too many days before making a move as you don't want their patterns to change and catch you off-guard with no backup plan. Once a pattern is recognized, figure out a game plan and get after 'em.

Calling Spring Turkeys

It goes without question that calling in a hot, spring gobbler is the adrenaline-rushing thrill that epitomizes this great sport. For those who've experienced such excitement, they're left wanting more. For those who have yet to live it, the desire only runs deeper with each passing hunt.

As with calling any game birds–or animals for that matter–it's never a slam-dunk proposition. You might not get a single bird to come in on your first several attempts, then again, you might incur a stampede of toms the very first time you try calling.

Since we detailed in Chapter 2 the types of calls hunters can use, what sounds they make, how to make those sounds and what turkey vocalizations mean, in this section the intent is to share information on calling options, or philosophies. Throughout the rest of this chapter and Chapter 4, we'll take detailed looks at calling situations based on seasonal conditions and specific hunting situations.

There are many schools of thought when it comes calling turkeys. Some hunters are very shy in their calling, making sure not to overcall or spook any birds. Some hunters are very aggressive, calling much more frequently than others. Some hunters like getting close to a roost early in the morning, then calling, while others like setting up where birds will feed to, and call an hour or more after they've left the trees. Keep in mind that calling approaches vary with each hunter, and that while some methods may be better than others, some may all make sense at one time or another.

When I first began hunting turkeys I had no one to teach me how to call; remember, it was new to our region and my dad and granddads never had the opportunity to hunt them. I read all I could get my hands on and watched what few TV shows were on in those days. Largely, my progression into the world of calling turkeys was learned through personal trial and error. I've never had anyone actually sit down and show me how to use a call, or share with me what sounds to make in what situations. Though this slowed my learning curve, I feel it made me a better hunter.

The first hunt I went on I called sparingly, afraid of making mistakes. Then a big tom came thundering in, chest puffed, tail fully fanned. I shot him and instantly my calling confidence skyrocketed.

As seasons came and went, I found myself utilizing more kinds of calls and diversifying my calling approach. Some of it worked, some didn't. Then I stepped into the world of outdoor writing. Now the pressure was on to not only perform consistently, but to be able to thoroughly explain the details of what went on in the woods–and in my head–when calling turkeys the way I did.

I'll never forget the first four-state turkey hunting adventure I embarked upon. The quest began in Oregon, where I tagged a bird on opening day. Soon I was in California, Idaho then Montana. Each hunt was a success, but due to the short timeline of each hunt, I found myself being more aggressive than in the past. The best part, the aggressive approach worked.

A few years later, I unexpectedly entered the world of outdoor television. Now, not only did I have to consistently fill tags, but my timeline was even shorter, given our brief windows of hunting seasons. To top it off, I now had a cameraman–sometimes two cameramen–following me into the woods. As if trying to kill a turkey isn't hard enough, alone. But we made it work.

For three years I hosted two TV shows, which meant I had to turn in 52 episodes a year to producers. This meant the days spent on each hunt were limited. If we weren't turning a turkey show every two to three days in the spring, we got behind. To do this, I turned extra aggressive.

Not only did my calling sequences and setups grow more aggressive, but so did the way I covered ground. I found myself locating birds then quickly moving in much closer than I had in years past. I also called louder and more aggressively than in past seasons. The results amazed me. Sure there were blown chances, but surprisingly few. In fact, my success rates soared over the next 12 years and I found myself getting even more aggressive as seasons passed.

I was simply amazed at what I could get away with; not dumb stuff or being careless, but making moves I was afraid of applying in prior years. The first time I placed a decoy four paces from the blind, I was skeptical. But when a tom approached from behind, whisking the sides of my blind with his fanned tail before jumping on top the decoy, my optimism levels rose.

As I began imitating more pleading yelps of hens, dragging the sounds out long and hard, I was more than impressed with not only the number of toms that came in, but with how many adult hens responded. One of the biggest progressions I made was in experimenting with different calls. I soon found myself listening more intently to what the birds were telling me. Their responses told me which sounds they liked best, so that's what I used with growing frequency. The result was my using calls that wouldn't likely place in any calling contest, but who cares as long as the birds responded to them.

One of the best turkey callers I've been afield with, Cory Peterson, is aggressive, but hunts smart.

I think one of the biggest mistakes hunters make is trying to sound too much like a competition caller, and being afraid to call if they're not of this caliber. Believe me, some of the most awful calls I've heard have come from wild turkeys, both toms and hens. I've hunted with some competition callers, guys who are far better callers than I'll ever dream of being. Some had great hunting skills, but a few had no clue about how to interpret turkey behavior and adjust their calling, accordingly. They called because they liked the sound of it, or because they wanted to hear a tom gobble. These are the two worst reasons in the world to work a turkey call.

Calling turkeys is a vocalized process of communication. Each sound you create should be made for a reason, to send a specific message.

Don't get frustrated if a tom doesn't come in. It's nothing personal, it's that he's likely stuck with hens or is on a set schedule and feels he needs to get somewhere, so keeps doing what he's doing. This is often the case when trailing a tom or trying to call him from behind. If a tom that's moving away from you won't respond to your calls, circle ahead of him and try calling. This aggressive move often pays dividends.

I was once giving a seminar on hunting throughout the West. At the end a man presented the best question I've ever been asked. "So, if TV went away, would you still keep hunting aggressively, or would you go back to hunting the way you used to, more conservatively?"

Without hesitation or thought, I responded, "Aggressively!" I went on to explain the increased encounters I'd experienced since hunting more aggressively, but also made clear that many of the decisions I make are based on what's unfolding in the woods, not on what my preconceived notions might have been.

One of the best moves I made was switching to higher frequency slate and box calls. This is a prime example of where technological advancements in the call making industry has had a direct result in more hunters finding success by calling.

Glass, slate and crystal surfaces have been standard for many years, but when aluminum and ceramic surfaces came out, things changed. Of course, the type of striker you use on any particular surface can directly impact frequency. Personally, purple heart is my favorite striker when talking high frequency. Hickory, another tight-grained wood, and some laminated strikers are also great. I like some of the bell-shaped strikers, ones with a flared tip on the end, when it comes to reaching high frequency sounds. Try different combinations of slate surfaces and strikers and find what matches up best for you.

The creation of box calls from different wood types and varied designs are also capable of reaching high frequency sounds. Cherry is the best wood I know of for achieving high frequencies on box calls.

Initially I'll begin by offering soft clucks and see if a tom responds. Avoid starting off too aggressively, as you don't want to spook a tom that may be holding close by. If no gobbles follow, I'll get a bit louder. If nothing, then I'll toss out some cuts and pleading yelps. If I hear a bird I'll mark his location and move in closer if I have to, and keep hammering him. Once he's turned on, I don't want to lose him, so keep him fired-up by calling a lot. If I hear nothing after three to five minutes, usually I'll keep moving, unless I'm hunting with a stiff wind at my back (more on this later).

While turkeys don't call with such high frequency, these calls unquestionably receive more gobbles from toms. They also allow me to hunt more effectively on windy, rainy days and amid thicker timber commonly encountered throughout the West. Not only that, the high frequency sounds carry much further across gaping canyons and vast, open country, and ultimately result in my finding and calling in more toms.

In the mornings I usually call a bit more aggressively than most hunters. But I'll progress to this level, not start out with fast, frequent, intense sounds. I'll typically start with some soft tree yelps, followed by more seductive yelps. Clucks and louder yelps usually follow. If approaching hens start calling as they move your direction, mimic every sound they make, as this often entices a tom to follow.

If a loan hen starts hammering back with pleading yelps, and is obviously closing the distance, I'll not only mimic her calls but will also include some gobbles on my shaker call. This is because the hen is coming for a reason, and that's usually to breed. If she knows a hen is already on the tom's strutting ground, she'll likely keep coming. Many times a tom will follow her in.

If a tom is hung up with some feeding hens early in the morning, I'll often stay put, hoping to pull him my way when the hens return to their nest. This is a very good mid to late season approach. If he seems interested but won't quite commit, have your hunting partner sit tight while you move away from the bird, calling as you go. Often times, if a tom hears a calling hen moving away, he'll rush to check her out as he doesn't want to miss a breeding opportunity.

Early in the season when hens are still roosting with toms, I'll call a bit more aggressively right off the bat. This is because there's more competition happening within any given flock. If there are five toms and a dozen hens in a flock the chances are good for pulling one or more of those toms your direction right off the roost. I'll start with light yelps but quickly progress to pleading yelps with more clucks and purrs thrown into the mix. Below, we'll take a closer look at mid-day hunting tactics.

In the evening, it can be tough calling in toms but it can be done. Before hunting in the evening hours, be sure to check state regulations to ensure it's legal, as some states don't allow hunting after certain hours.

When calling toms late in the afternoon and evening, I've had the best success in setting up near where I know they'll be passing when going to roost. Because toms might work their way along timbered or wooded edges, or along the fringes of brushy creek draws and even meadows, this is where I set up. I like using a lone hen decoy for this, usually in an alert of feeding pose. I also call more subtly, with more feeling and less aggressiveness. When the air is calm, I'll even scratch the ground to mimic feeding activity and offer contented purrs from time to time.

When setting up for these evening hunts I might stay in one place for a couple hours, especially if I've patterned birds and feel confident they'll be passing my direction. I won't change much of my tempo or intensity, for the objective is to imitate a content, feeding hen.

Should you encounter what's called a satellite tom, it may be necessary to get your loudest calls and move in close. Satellite toms are two year old birds that are capable of breeding, and want to, but hang on the fringes of a mature tom's strutting ground, hoping to pick up a hen as she moves by. When a satellite tom is located, move in as tight as possible, get him gobbling and keep him gobbling. These birds are reluctant to leave the flock, so you've got to be persistent. Placing a hen decoy where an approaching satellite tom can see it can yield good results.

As the spring season progresses and hens go to nesting, mature and satellite toms will start hanging together. When this happens they often fight with one another. Find these toms and move in as close as possible before issuing any sounds. When you do start calling, offer soft yelps and purrs. While the act of physically moving in is aggressive, the calls are subtle. The purpose is to get those competitive toms racing toward you, and the closer you can get to them before calling, the greater the chances of them quickly responding.

The more time you spend calling in the turkey woods, the more proficient you'll become. I learned most all my calling approaches and the sounds I make from listening to wild turkeys. To do this, a great deal of time must be spent in the field, as there's no substitute for learning from the best callers out there...the birds, themselves.

Hunt The Rain

If many hunters out West waited for good weather to go hunting, they might not set foot in the spring turkey woods. I don't know how many turkeys we've taken over the years in the rain, but I can say it's 100% more than we've gotten while staying home.

While rain isn't the most comfortable of conditions to hunt in, and certainly takes some of the fun out of being in the spring woods, it presents some great hunting conditions. Think of big game and how we often yearn for rain. Rain quiets the forest floor, helps mask movement and knocks down our scent (thank goodness that doesn't apply to turkeys).

Early in my turkey hunting career I used to believe turkeys hated the rain and ran for cover anytime a raindrop fell. But the country I started hunting in was big timber interspersed with oaks. In some of the Rocky Mountain states I hunted, I also spent most of my time in areas with big trees and low growing Russian olive and willow groves. In other words, the habitat limited the visibility which made it difficult to interpret what was really going on.

As I began hunting turkeys in other, more open habitats, I found that when rains fell, the birds simply hunkered down in the open. A turkey's waterproofing system is surprisingly efficient for an upland bird its size. They like the open as they can more easily keep an eye out for approaching danger. If huddled in the brush, falling rain causes foliage to move and impedes their vision, making it tough to decipher predators. Today, I'm a firm believer that turkeys like to remain in the open during rain storms.

One day an area I hunted received just over two inches of rain. In traveling to and from different hunting areas that day, several times I passed by a flock of about 15 hens and a few toms on a piece of private property. They didn't move from that grassy meadow all day long. Since that time, I've seen this same scenario played out in many places across the West.

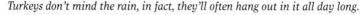

Turkeys don't mind the rain, in fact, they'll often hang out in it all day long.

Only on a few occasions have I taken birds holding under heavy cover on rainy days. It's tough pulling birds out of cover in this situation, so what's worked for me is walking the outside fringes, calling loudly as I go. This is where a diaphragm or waterproof box call comes in handy. The toms will often respond, and though they may not sprint into the open, they may approach the fringe, offering a shot. When a tom does bust out of heavy cover, feathers wet yet puffed and gobbling, you know he means business. We've had that happen a few times over the years, and it's just plain exciting.

My favorite condition to hunt in on rainy days is when there are sporadic breaks in the weather and the sun briefly pops out. During these quick breaks, turkeys often ignite in aggressive behavior, complete with fighting, gobbling and breeding. These are great situations to call in. As the blue sky closes and the birds start to shut down with another approaching rainstorm, move in fast and offer up some hen chatter. Often the toms will remain interested, even when the rain starts to fall. During a hunt in eastern Montana, I pulled a nice tom to the edge of a field he and the hens had been holding in during passing rainstorms. It took a while, but the tom approached to within shooting range.

When temperatures drop and it's raining, that's when the birds really shut down. My best success in these situations has come by way of spot-and-stalk (more on this approach later). These don't have to be early morning hunts, as the birds usually leave the roost later than usual when such conditions prevail. When it's raining hard, I've seen birds stay in the roost up to two hours longer than normal, though that's more the exception than the rule.

Should snow begin to fall, as long as it's a dry snow not driven by high winds, I'll hunt all day. I've found birds to be more active when it's snowing than when it's raining. If the snow turns wet and the winds kick-up, birds will often seek cover, likely because the don't like their feathers getting blown and snow getting under them.

While on the topic of snow, spend time looking for birds around the fringes of melting snow. If sunny days prevail, this means snow will quickly be melting in mountain meadows, adding moisture to the ground. The snow will also melt quickly around brush and timbered edges, both of which usually hold prime food. Also, when fresh snow hits the ground, search for sign to learn where the turkeys are.

If a rainstorm subsides prior to darkness, I think turkeys will stay up feeding a bit longer than usual before going to roost. One rainy day Jody Smith and I were trying to call in some toms. We had no luck as winds were high and temperatures cold. In fact, no birds were moving that day. What we did see were multiple flocks holding in the same wide-open spots, all day long.

Calling it a day, we decided to head for home. About then the rain stopped and we figured the morning might be a good time to fill a tag, seeing as how the birds were inactive all day long. When we passed by one of the fields where a flock of turkeys had been

Four-inches of fresh snow didn't keep Ron Janzen from scoring on this spring tom in western Oregon.

holding tight all day, we were surprised to see them up and feeding. "Usually they're in the roost by now," Jody noted.

Jody dropped me off and I worked down a line of fir trees, waiting for the birds to get closer. Eventually a big tom fed into range and I dropped him with a muzzleloader shotgun. That tom carried an 11-inch beard. He had little food in his crop and was trying to collect what he could prior to going to roost rather later that evening. That's a prime example of how waiting out the rain can pay-off, along with intercepting birds on the move.

Jody Smith and I have tag-teamed toms on many rainy days over the years. Don't let bad weather keep you out of the turkey woods.

If there's thunder in the hills, this can be one of the best times to locate birds, as toms often shock gobble with each boom. As with big game, when the barometer is falling, turkey movement slows; they'll often find a place and not move far. But when that barometer levels out or begins to rise, get out there.

When it rains, don't be afraid to hit the woods. What you'll learn about turkeys and how tough the really are, might impress you. Besides, you can't fill a tag sitting at home.

Hunt The Wind

Hunting in the wind is one of western turkey hunting's greatest challenges. The birds can be up and active, but having them hear your calls, or worse yet, you not being able to hear them answer you, can be frustrating. When the wind is howling up and down big canyons, or sweeping across prairie flats, don't give up. There are steps that can be taken on days when the wind is blowing.

The first place I head to on high-wind days are the leeward side of hills, knobs and ridges. Normally I'd walk atop the ridge lines calling from above, awaiting a tom's reply from below. But this won't work on windy days as the birds likely won't hear me, nor me, them.

The protected sides of hills are where birds often retreat to in high winds. Before committing to a hunt, check the wind direction. It's best to move with the wind, as it allows your calls to carry further. If you have to hunt into the wind, stick close to cover and keep your eyes open as birds can be close. On windy days turkeys don't move as much as on calm days, but when they do it's closer to cover and out of the wind. Stay alert and scan the ground ahead of you.

When calling with the wind, allow time for the birds to respond. Though your sounds may be easy for them to hear, you may not hear them. If you feel birds are in an area, find a good place to set up, call and wait. Give birds up to 10 minutes to respond, being aware that they may come in silently.

While hunting eastern Montana one spring, an intense windstorm picked up early in the morning. Moving my blind from the edge of an open meadow to the north side of a knoll, I sought any relief I could find.

After nearly 15 minutes I heard a faint gobble. Nocking an arrow, the instant I looked out the blind, the glowing hues of a red, white and blue head materialized. The tom gobbled again, but I could barely hear him. In fact, had I not actually seen the bird gobble, I wouldn't have believed he was so near. I let my BowTech fly, anchoring the tom on the spot. The distance was seven yards. At seven yards that big tom let out a gobble, yet I could barely hear it, that's how intense the wind was blowing. Fortunately we caught it all on film for our TV show.

Search the backside of protected hillsides on windy days, as turkeys often hold tight in them.

When hunting in windy country–places you know where the wind blows day in and day out–there's no better edge to gain than knowing where birds hang out. I've run up against this in many Rocky Mountain states, as well as in the Dakotas, Nebraska and Texas. Bottom line, turkeys have favorite places to hang out on windy days, and if you can get into those places the chances of success are good.

One thing I've noticed–and that's confirmed by writer friends, guides and buddies who live in and hunt windy terrain every spring–is that toms respond quicker on such days. Though you may not

My buddy, Bret Stuart, and I scored on these three big Merriam's on a very windy hunt in Montana.

hear them gobble, often times they approach on a dead run for they don't want the sweet sounding hen (you) to get away. For this reason, when calling on windy days, set up and be ready for immediate action. Set up in the same place you would if the wind wasn't blowing, but be ready for a quick response. On a calm day you might call, move, and call some more. On windy days, set up, then call, giving toms 10 to 15 minutes to respond. If nothing happens, push forward, for maybe the birds couldn't hear you.

A big bonus hunting in the wind offers is that it keeps the brush and trees moving and covers your movement. Don't mistake this for an invitation to be careless and move around, but if you have to make slight adjustments as birds approach, as long as it's done subtly, you can likely pull it off without getting busted. This is why I like setting up in front of trees with limbs growing to the ground, as their movement helps conceal me.

While nestled beneath the limbs of a juniper tree one spring, a lone tom approached from my extreme right, not from in front as anticipated. When that bird got to 10 yards, I had to slowly move to make the shot. The tom didn't even see me, thanks to the harsh wind whipping the tree limbs. Unfortunately, I rushed the shot and threw an air-ball right over his head.

Work tree lines, both inside and out, on windy days. Often toms will hold in the trees, but pop out to see what hens might be in their strutting area.

131

One piece of advice when hunting on windy days: avoid wearing loose clothing. Turkey vests, face masks and jackets can all run large in size, and if too loose fitting will flop uncontrollably in the wind. Secure these garments or wear tighter fitting clothes so unwanted movement doesn't alert a tom at an inopportune time.

As for using decoys on windy days, I've personally killed more turkeys without them. This is because the wind offers so much movement of brush, trees and grasses, and sound is so hard to pinpoint, it keeps toms searching and on the move for the sounds that brought them there. This also explains why so many shots come at very close range on windy days.

But decoys do have a place on windy days. Don't do like I did early in my turkey hunting career and use a flimsy, foam decoy in the wind. Though a little movement is okay, an unnatural spinning decoy will only spook birds. I had two big toms almost within range, then my decoy started spinning on the stake. The toms couldn't get out of there fast enough.

On windy days, use hard-shelled decoys that won't collapse in the wind. Place it facing the way you want, then put sticks on both sides of the decoy, firmly securing them into the ground. This will keep the decoy from spinning around in the wind.

I like using a real turkey tail on windy days, and all days, for that matter, as any movement is more realistic. If you've ever seen a strutting tom get hammered by hard wind, his tail often whacking him in the face, you know what I mean about tail movement.

On calm days you might hunt a field with a decoy placed 30 yards from the edge, in the open. On windy days, move back into the trees and situate the decoy on the very edge of the field, even just inside the tree line. Though toms may not be strutting in the open, they will often cruise by these strutting grounds, checking to see if any hens are near. If your decoy is in the right place it can offer great results, as I learned one windy day.

I'd placed a hard-shelled decoy on the inside edge of a field, then sat against a cottonwood tree, 35 yards deeper into the forest. I called, but heard nothing respond. Then, 200 yards away, two toms worked across the edge of the field. They were too far off to hear my calls in the heavy wind, but the instant they saw my decoys they came on a sprint. It was spectacular to see, and a testimony that decoys can work wonders on windy days, even without calling.

Because toms strut aggressively on windy days, using the wind to move their fanned tails, this is not an action that spooks them. In fact, just the contrary, moving tail fans of other toms gets their attention. Using a homemade tail fan and nothing more, you can often sneak to the edge of a field, clearing or gully, gently moving it in an effort to capture the attention of toms. Often, when a tom sees this movement he'll come on the run. Be ready and hold tight, for toms will often approach the decoy looking to challenge it. In such cases, shots may come only a couple feet from your gun barrel. If this is an approach you're going to use, try taking a lightweight 20 gauge with light loads and no sling, so you don't get tangled in the chaos.

When calling on windy days, get the loudest, highest pitched calls you have. Boxes and slate calls are favorites of windy day turkey hunters. As detailed earlier, I'm partial to high-pitch sounds pretty much all the time in the turkey

On windy days, use calls that create loud sounds. Here, good friend and colleague, Chad Schearer, tries reaching out with his slate call.

woods, but am particularly fond of them on windy days. On windy days, the goal is to get sounds out there, hoping the birds hear any part of it. You don't have to be a championship caller on windy days to find success.

It seems like turkey hunters are always faced with some sort of challenging conditions. Either it's too windy, too rainy, too calm, too hot or too cold. If you have time to hunt, then get out there. The birds have to eat to live, you just have to find them. Learn what the birds are doing when conditions are tough and figure out what has to be done to put a turkey in the pot. After all, overcoming challenges will only make you a more complete hunter.

Hunt Tall Grass

One of my favorite times to hunt turkeys is late in the season, when grasses grow tall and have come to a head. When grass stands three feet tall in meadows or fields, it offers turkeys just about everything they need to stay alive. It gives them food in the form of grass seed, shade when they hunker low and an open place to keep a watchful eye for predators. The only thing it doesn't always offer is water.

These can be tough habitats to hunt, but there are ways to consistently secure birds that have started carrying out their daily routines in tall grass settings. The first is to intercept them as they approach the field from the roost. Often times the tall grass fields are so tall, bird's don't like flying directly into them. Instead, they may pitch off the roost, landing on the edge of the long grass, then walk their way in to the feeding area.

In this situation, get into the field well before any hint of daylight. Take a low profile chair or cushion, something that allows you to sit in comfort, but keeps your head below the grass line. If the field the birds are using borders a fence line, erecting a pop up blind along the fence will work.

As daylight approaches and you hear birds on the roost, toss out a few subtle hen helps. If a tom replies, keep quiet. This is one of those situations where it's not necessary to overcall. The birds will eventually be heading your direction, and if they know you (the hen) are there, they'll often come by to inspect. More times than not I go without a decoy when hunting the long grass because I want the toms to come in searching for a hen, something that may take them a while to find.

When you pattern birds in tall grass, watch their movements throughout the day. One day, while watching a flock of birds in a grassy field from daylight to dark, I actually drew their daily pattern on a piece of paper. The crude map looked like the scribblings of a toddler, but my plan worked. That night, when the birds went to roost and well after dark, I moved in and set up a ground blind. By 3:30 the next morning I was back in the blind, where I was prepared to wait all day. At mid-day, just like they'd done the day before, the turkeys fed right in front of my blind and I filled my tag. Given where the birds were roosting, the private land on one side of the field, a well used road on the other and a river

flowing behind the field, it was the only way I could think of to access those birds. They had no clue I was there. Incidentally, I opened the crop of that tom and it was stuffed full of grass seeds, nothing else.

If you don't have the time to devote to sitting in a blind in a grassy field, waiting for birds to move your direction, then try calling. But do so sparingly. The birds are in the field, not going anywhere. You want to sound like a hen that's come in from a different direction, one that's contentedly feeding. Wait to make such calls, after the birds have been in the tall grass for an hour or so and feel relaxed. Though toms may not gobble because they may not be as

134

"rutty" this late in the year, chances are good they'll still come check you out. Be patient and let the tom's behavior dictate how loud and how often you should call.

If you're on private property, or on public land with no one else in sight, toms in tall grass can also be stalked. You can go about it the old fashioned way, on hands and knees or with the aid of a tail fan as a decoy. If you commence stalking with no decoy, wear knee pads, maybe even elbow pads, and remove the sling from your gun. If using a tail fan as a decoy, attach a long enough wire to the tail so it can be seen through the grass.

While toms may not come running through the tall grass to the tail fan decoy, they might hold steady long enough to allow you to move within range. One day I used this approach and slithered to within 30 yards of three big toms. Two days later my buddy did the same thing and a big tom ran right up to him; he shot it at four yards.

Tall grass fields can also be hunted in the evening when birds start moving toward the roost. Scout the field to make sure you know exactly what time the birds are leaving and precisely what part of the field they're exiting. From there, formulate your plan and wait for the birds to come to you. This usually comes together in the last few minutes of shooting light, so be patient and hold tight.

One of the biggest advantages hunting turkeys in long grass fields has to offer is that you can see the birds, so you know they're there. The biggest challenge is getting to them. If the grass is too short and spot-and-stalk is the only option, you might have to return a week or two later when the grass has grown tall enough to hide you.

If you're up to the challenge, hunting tall grass can be one of turkey hunting's greatest rewards. Patterning birds, then figuring out a plan, then executing it, will remind you of deer and elk hunting, and will serve as a reminder that hunting turkeys out West can be quite different than hunting them in other parts of the country.

Hunt Hot Days

Of the many guides and fanatical turkey hunters I've talked with over the years, on average they claim upwards of 65% of their birds taken come between 10:00 and 3:00. Remember, many of these are guides who are taking multiple clients into the field each day. Though they may get a bird early in the morning, they often have another tag or two to fill by nightfall. To do that, they keep at it all day.

While it may be mentally taxing, hunting during the heat of the day can and will pay off. The key is knowing where birds are when it's hot. Figure out where they find relief, where food and water sources may be located, then start hunting.

For hunters who aren't in to stalking, or who physically can't, don't be afraid to sit in a blind for most of the day. These two hunters, ages 84 and 86, doubled on a pair of mid-day toms.

JODY SMITH PHOTO

Some of my most productive calling encounters have come in the heat of the day. This is when hens tend their nests and toms go to feeding, preening and take dust baths. It's also a time for them to hit the shade in order to stay cool. There's definitely some traveling going on at times.

Earlier in this chapter I touched on high frequency calls. I've got more toms to respond by gobbling, and physically coming to the calls, with high frequencies more than any other during these mid-day hunts.

Once I've dialed in to where toms are spending the middle of the day, I'll move in as close as I can before setting up to call. While they may respond by covering a lot of ground in an effort to reach the decoys or the calls, keep in mind they are often conserving energy at mid-day. This means the closer you can close the gap, the better the chances of a tom moving your direction.

Be careful not to infringe too tightly on a tom's place of rest during the heat of the day. I've done this way too many times, and rarely are there are any second chances. Instead, work the fringes of holding habitat, call and see how the birds respond. If they're reluctant to move, either step-up the intensity or pitch of your calling or move closer. This is one of those situations where, if I don't dare move any closer, I'll go through every call in my vest until I find one a tom likes. At the end of such a calling session, it's not uncommon to have two box calls, three slates, a dozen strikers, ten or more diaphragm calls, and maybe a push-pull call scattered around me. Variety can be the key to closing the deal on these birds. Then again, the best callers in the turkey woods might not be able to budge those

birds. You never know what will happen unless you try.

Out West, with the many deep, wooded ravines turkeys have access to, they may not necessarily hang out in the creek bottoms. Often times the shade offered from towering fir trees, pines and dense brush are all a tom needs for relief. This means they may not stray far from their roosting site or primary feeding area. I've taken and seen many birds taken over the years, from just inside the brush line of a meadow. That's where the birds moved to when it got hot and that's where they spent much of the day. In areas like this, the tiniest of puddles may hold enough water for turkeys.

If scouting for places to hunt during the middle of the day, check out small water holes, creeks, the edges of ponds and even river banks with brushy paths leading to them. If fresh tracks are in the area, you can bet turkeys will return to them.

I've found spotting and stalking turkeys to be tough when they're shading for the day. This is because they're in rest-mode, as opposed to feeding or strutting to impress hens. When resting, every bird is on alert, looking for approaching danger. With so many keen-eyed birds scouring the woods, spot-and-stalk can be near impossible unless the situation is absolutely perfect.

If birds aren't approachable, try setting up a decoy or two across from where they entered the woods. Often times throughout the day, toms will enter the edges of fields to see if any hens are present. If they see your decoys, that's often all it takes to get them moving your direction.

While hen decoys work great during the middle of the day, don't overlook full body strutting tom decoys. When toms have their territory established during breeding season, if they see an intruder in their domain they'll often come looking for a fight. This is especially true in areas with high tom-to-hen ratios, as well as where hens have gone to nesting.

The middle of the day is also a time when turkeys often take dust baths. While this is done to delouse their bodies, it's also done to cool them off. Often they'll retreat to heavily shaded areas where soft dirt and rotten logs or stumps exist. This allows them to dig in the soft soil, accessing the cooler dirt below.

Setting up a blind on a dusting area can pay-off, though the wait can be long with little action. I've tried calling over dusting areas but with very little success. I think this is because mid-day dusting sites are destinations birds gravitate to by choice when their bodies tell them they need it. It's not a reactionary response like you get from calling birds.

If you want to take a tom in a wooded, secluded dusting area, do your homework. Make sure there are multiple dusting holes, depressions in the ground that are being used day after day. Look for body feathers and droppings. Remember, the breast feather of a tom is lined in black while the outer edges of a hen's body feathers are light colored. Also, tom droppings are J-shaped, while hen droppings are coiled. These signs will tell you if toms and/or hens are using the dusting sites.

Of course, the best way to tell what birds are using the dusting area is to set up a trail camera. This will reveal what birds are there, what time they're coming and how long they're spending there. If you don't want to set up and wait near a dusting area, you might be able to intercept the birds as they're coming or going, if you know what time visits are being made.

Just because it's hot doesn't mean it's time to give up. Stop and think about where the birds in your area should be, or will be, then figure out how to best hunt them. Because toms are pumped with testosterone, calling can work like magic any time in the middle of the day, as can decoys.

Be creative, have fun and learn as you go. No doubt, you'll make mistakes, but that's how we improve.

I'm often accused of being too aggressive of a turkey hunter, but that's the way I like to hunt. Sure, I blow my fair share of opportunities, but I also feel I create more due to this hunting style. After all, turkey hunting isn't about perfection, it's about learning from mistakes and continually pushing forward...just like in life.

Spot-&-Stalk

If there was one hunting style to describe western hunters it would be spot-and-stalk. I'll never forget the response I got when asking the question, "How many of you hunt deer from treestands?" I was giving a seminar on blacktail deer hunting, and of the 111 people in attendance, four raised their hands. It drove home the point that deer hunting blacktails on the ground was how it's done in these parts, not by methods that are mainly used in other areas of the country.

For many turkey hunters out West, they never call or use decoys. They go 100% spot-and-stalk, on the ground, just them against the turkey. Try that with your bow and you'll see why many hunters consider turkeys one of the West's greatest challenges.

Fellow outdoor writer and one of the men I most respect for his hard work, dedication and ability to find continual success, Patrick Meitin, has arrowed more than 60 turkeys with his bow,

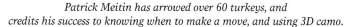

Patrick Meitin has arrowed over 60 turkeys, and
credits his success to knowing when to make a move, and using 3D camo.

and many of them via spot-and-stalk. His approach is simple; move smart, be patient and dedicate yourself 100% to using a bow. He also uses 3D camo to help break-up his body's outline.

In the late 1990s I queried several magazines on writing a turkey hunting story with the focus being on spotting-and-stalking, western style. Not only did every editor turn down the idea, they scorned me for even thinking about advocating such a dangerous, unethical approach. When I tried convincing them that's how most folks were hunting out West at the time, they still refused to look at it, claiming that's not how turkeys were hunted back East. In recent years, I've seen spot-and-stalk turkey hunting stories run in every magazine I'd originally bounced the idea off.

Spot-and-stalk hunting is frowned upon in many parts of the country, but out West where endless miles of open range exist, and where turkey hunters may not see another human in the woods all season long, it's a way of life. I know of many hunters who would not hunt turkeys if they couldn't do so via spot-and-stalk, for they feel it's the best practice there is for fall big game hunts.

Keep in mind, spot-and-stalk hunting for turkeys should only be done on private ground or on tracts of public land where you're positive no other hunters are around. Be certain of your target before making a move. There are some excellent callers in todays turkey woods, and some even more impressive tom decoys. Don't be fooled.

The greatest danger of spot-and-stalk hunting occurs where a hunter stalks in to a decoy, shooting beyond it and hitting a hunter who is sitting behind where the decoy was situated. Again, make absolutely sure of you're target. There's no excuse whatsoever for mistaking a decoy for a real turkey, even if it's a mount.

When spotting-and-stalking turkeys in wooded settings, use trees, shadows and broken terrain to hide your approach.

With that said, proceed with caution when stalking a turkey. Always be on the lookout for fellow hunters, even if you're confident they're not around. If you do happen to see another hunter simultaneously stalking the same turkey you are, pull away. It's just a bird and not worth any risk or hassle.

When stalking a turkey, do so as you would when stalking any big game, but with even more caution. Their nervous nature and exceptional eyesight make them some of North America's toughest animals to get close to.

However, get a bird in the right place and like anything, it can seem simple. I once made a stalk on three Dall sheep in Alaska's Brooks Range. When I popped over a rocky ledge, there they stood, three full-curl rams, barely 20 yards away. The shot was easy, and though the stalk was rigorous, the animals were in the perfect spot to pull it off.

If new to stalking turkeys, make sure the birds are in a place where you can approach them, unseen and unheard. This is where windy, rainy days play into the hunter's favor.

Glass the birds from a distance, try to predict where they're heading, then get in front of them. Intercepting birds as they move is the most effective way to get them and it's also the best way to keep from getting busted.

Should you find yourself trying to catch up with a flock of birds, be patient and move when they have their heads down, feeding away from you. If they're stuck in strut mode, see if there's a brush line you can work to, one within shooting range. You may need to get as close as you can, or if that's not close enough, try calling the toms to you.

Unlike elk hunting, I've had little success calling while simultaneously spotting-and-stalking turkeys. I've found this act more alerts them than calms them. They're not like elk, who can be noisy when moving through the woods. My best advice, try to go undetected during your spot-and-stalk turkey mission.

One thing that has saved me on more than one occasion is the use of the turkey tail fan when stalking in on birds. Held in front of you, the tail not only helps breakup the body's outline, it calms the birds.

Take it one step further and put a real tail fan in to a 1/4-lifesize tom decoy. The first time I tried this with the Thunder Chicken decoy, I was impressed. I called in a tom from over 300 yards away, but when he got 70 yards out, he stopped and lost interest. When he went to feeding, I hunkered down, held the decoy in front of my face and walked right at the tom. I closed the distance to within 25 yards, then rolled him. The bird never once grew nervous.

Another effective application for stalking in on a tom is busting up the flock he's glued to. When you encounter a tom, or toms, sticking tightly to a group of hens, try rushing in to separate them. This is normally considered a fall tactic, but I know of hunters who have pulled it off with regular success in the spring woods. With a stubborn flock located, storm them by surprise, pushing them into brush and woods, not an open field. After a bit the testosterone-induced tom will often start gobbling to relocate the hens. When this happens, move in, offer hen yelps and hope the tom comes to you. This approach offers the highest percentage of success when applied in small openings surrounded by trees or brush.

Late in the season I like stalking toms from behind. If I call and they don't respond, I'll circle to get in front of them. I'll offer subtle hen helps to try and pull them my way, nothing overly aggressive. Often it may take a few times of doing this, meaning the tom will walk by out of range, not coming to your call. But if you don't spook them, there's always a chance. This is an effective way to combine stalking skills with calling to fool a tom, something I've done many times over the years. The last tom I pulled this on found me traveling nearly a mile, getting in front of him three different times. Finally, he came in silent, through some of the thickest brush and timber I'd been in all day.

Spot-and-stalk hunting turkeys may not be for everyone, but if you're wanting to hone those big game hunting skills, it's one of the best ways I know of. Whether looking to intercept birds as they move to or from roosting, feeding, watering or shading areas, or if you're wanting to get aggressive and close the deal in open terrain, the choices are many.

Once you try it, it won't take long to realize the challenges of spot-and-stalk turkey hunting. It also won't take long to grow addicted to this approach once you find success. Remember, when applying this strategy, be safe, hunt smart and keep a constant eye out for other hunters.

Alternative Hunting Approaches

As with other big game throughout the West, there are many ways to go about hunting turkeys. The key in determining what approach might work best lies in figuring out where the birds are, then formulating a plan as to the best way to reach them.

In some areas I've hunted over the years, I doubt I could have killed any birds were it not for the use of a four-wheeler or some form of ATV. The birds were simply too far up the canyons or too far down the ridge line to reach on foot, unless I started walking at 2:00 a.m. In other situations, it might be best to cover ground quietly, and this can be done on foot or horseback.

Horseback hunts for turkeys are something a handful of outfitters offer, and an approach people use when hunting their own ranches. It's also a great way to access public land where walking might not be the best way to cover ground.

Hunting turkeys by horseback is a fun, quiet way to spend time in the woods, and the turkeys aren't nearly as spooked by horses as they are motorized vehicles. The hunts aren't nearly as daunting as backcountry deer or elk hunts, but the flavor and uniqueness it adds to a turkey hunt make it a favorable option for many hunters.

One of the places our family has hunted in the very northeastern corner of Wyoming, with Guy and Shanna Howell, owners of Center Of The Nation Outfitters, offers quality turkey hunting opportunities by horseback. Their whole family is into horses and it makes

Mark Kayser and his son, Cole, with a pair of toms taken on a horseback hunt with Center of The Nation Outfitters in northeastern Wyoming. Horses are a great way to cover ground, and a fun way to hunt.

perfect sense for them to offer such special hunts. Good friend and one of the country's top outdoor writers and TV hosts, Mark Kayser, has been on these horseback hunts with the Howell's and can't get enough of it. In fact, he and his son, Cole have enjoyed some great memories on the Howell Ranch.

Another quiet and efficient way to access turkey country is by mountain bike. The are many gated roads that allow walk-in or bike-in only access. Because turkeys can be spread out in these areas, it's more efficient to cover ground by bike than on foot.

When biking logging roads, keep one eye on the ground for sign, another ahead for turkeys. Often times in these forested habitats, turkeys spend a great deal of time along the roadsides, gathering not only food, but grit. Due to the nature of the habitat associated with many gated road settings, the roads themselves offer the best open areas for turkeys to live near and travel on. Don't get caught moving too quickly, overlooking important sign when biking such roads.

Ride slowly, take your time and stop often to call and listen. If birds are located within walking distance, stash the bike and keep moving. If you hear nothing, keep riding. It's far more efficient to cover 10 or 12 miles by bike than on foot, especially if turkey flocks are scattered.

142

As mentioned earlier, ATVs also have their place in the turkey hunting woods. As with any vehicle, hunt smart with ATVs. Cover only the ground you need to and when you approach a determined point, stop short of it, walk the final 100 yards or so, wait a few minutes, then throw out some locator calls.

One time a buddy and I were hunting from four-wheelers. We were doing it right, driving a distance, then walking out the ridge lines a few hundred yards before calling. While glassing distant ridges for toms, my buddy shared with me how, on a previous hunt, he'd sat in the same place and watched a hunter drive his quad as fast as he could, stop on the main logging road, stand up on the seat and call. When he didn't hear a bird gobble back after a few seconds, he kept driving. He did this until he went out of sight, apparently never getting a tom to gobble. That's the wrong way. Thing is, that valley was full of turkeys and the guy didn't even know it.

When used wisely and responsibly ATVs are a wonderful tool for hunting big country out West. Respect all private land access and locked gates. And remember, when on an ATV, toting a gun, decked out in camo', you're representing all hunters.

Something not a lot of hunters out West take the time to do is set up turkey camp. Just like deer camp or elk camp, turkey camp is a time-honored tradition in many eastern states, obviously due to the generations of hunters who've established it.

Though I've only been in a handful of true turkey camps, I can honestly say they're one of the most relaxing hunting camps you'll ever be a part of. Nice weather, little pressure and low impact hunts create a feeling of true relaxation in turkey camps.

In elk camp, when someone tags out, everyone spends all night and most of the next day packing out the bull. In turkey camp, you toss the bird over your shoulder and race to the tent, eager to share and hear stories. The work is easy in turkey camp when compared to other types of camps, which makes it a fun, happy place to be.

Then again, 99% of the time, the spring turkey woods are a fun place to be. The most important part is to make the time to get afield. Be it alone, with a partner or with a budding hunter, make the effort to spend time in the turkey woods. With growing turkey populations and increased hunting opportunities, the time to take to the turkey woods has never been better.

In addition to fun times, enjoying nature and securing some of the best eating meat in the birding world, pursuing turkeys will also hone general hunting skills. These are the skills you'll find being applied on future big game hunts, and more importantly, passing along to future generations. What you'll ultimately discover is that turkey hunting is about more than just filling a tag. It's about sharing experiences with others and establishing your own traditions for family and future hunters to be a part of. There are simply few places as special as the spring turkey woods of the West.

Chapter 4:

FALL HUNTING SEASON

Overshadowed by big game hunts, fall turkey season is a wonderful time to be afield and expand your knowledge about these great birds. Not only can the hunting be nothing short of spectacular, but the learning that takes place can be unmatched. Personally, I've learned more about the sounds turkeys make and actually calling turkeys in the fall, than in the spring. This is because the birds–especially the hens and young of the year–are very vocal, as are the toms. What better way to learn the sounds of the animals we hunt than by listening to the real thing.

There are many ways to go about hunting fall turkeys, and I've taken several over the years with both bow and gun. One of my most memorable fall hunts came, again with good friend Jody Smith. We were bowhunting in early November; the day was sunny and unusually warm. When we saw a tom in full-strut on the edge of a meadow, Jody told me to let out a loud yelp. I always have calls with me, even in the fall, so popped a diaphragm in my mouth and gave three sharp yelps. Not only did that tom gobble right back, but a five others also responded.

Moving to the edge of the brush, we set up and called some more. By this time of year the toms are in their bachelor flocks and every bird that popped into view was a tom. There were some jakes and yearling gobblers mixed in, but most were two to four year old toms.

Toms will strut and gobble in the fall, and even come to a call.

The more we offered loud yelps and aggressive purrs, the more the toms kept gobbling, and the more kept coming out of the brush. Within minutes we were treated to one of the most amazing sights I've ever witnessed in all my years of turkey hunting; 42 toms strutting and gobbling within 50 yards of us. And yes, it was November.

For several minutes they carried on, getting so wrapped-up in displaying and fighting with one another, they totally forgot about us. Eventually one bird broke away from the flock; that's when I brought my BowTech to full-draw and laced a broadhead right through him. That tom had an 11-inch beard and 1 3/4-inch spurs. Had I not seen the whole scenario myself, I'd have never believed it. Jody and I still talk about that hunt, one of the many great moments we've shared over the years.

Granted, our strutting, gobbling extravaganza was not the norm for fall hunting, but proved that anything can happen at any time in the turkey woods. It also confirmed that we should never limit our thinking and always be willing to adapt to what nature deals us.

Fall Turkey Behavior

To increase the odds of filling a fall turkey tag, it's best to understand what's going on behaviorally with turkeys this time of year. There are basically five types of turkey flocks that form in the fall and winter months. These are consistent across the board, be they Merriam's, Rio's or eastern birds.

Starting in late summer adult gobblers form their own groups, and though they are usually small, they will sometimes mingle with other groups of birds, even jakes and hens. Typically, adult toms in the 2 1/2 year and older range gather in small groups of between three and eight birds. These numbers may grow as winter progresses. Often times a social hierarchy is developed among these flocks in the fall, prior to winter's onset.

Fall bachelor flock of adult toms.

Yearling gobblers also establish their own flocks. These groups are made up of 1 1/2 year old birds, usually consisting of a half-dozen or more. Many of the birds in this group have been hanging out together since they left the family flocks. They're too young to join adult tom flocks, yet jakes won't associate with them either, for fear of getting pummeled. I've found these birds to be the most vocal and aggressive during the fall, both in how they react to calls and how often they can be seen fighting with one another. Over the years I've called in multiple flocks of yearling gobblers, sporting their five- to seven-inch beards. Usually the entire flocks comes to the call, and if there are other flocks of the same age class hanging nearby, they'll often come in, too.

Jakes also form their own flocks as fall progresses. Made up largely of three- to six-month old birds, jake flocks are established because the birds have grown and left their family flocks. Jake flocks often exceed a dozen birds and they can be quite vocal as they mill about, trying to establish dominance amongst one another. Jake flocks will usually hang out together all fall, winter and into the next spring, and stay together the following fall as yearling gobbler flocks.

146

Family flocks are the most commonly hunted when talking calling and scattering birds in the fall. They consist of hens with their young of the year, usually females (jennies), as the jakes have left the flock. Occasionally there will be young jakes in the family flock, but these are typically ones that hatched late, and as fall progresses, they usually break away. Fall family flocks often exceed two dozen birds, and are usually formed by various family units congregating around food sources. Often these family flocks will associate with other family flocks, especially on food sources, where numbers can reach 100 or more. Though these flocks may roost near one another and feed together, they usually break-off into their own family flocks throughout the day.

Hens that were unsuccessful in raising a brood will also form their own flocks. These are called broodless flocks, and usually consist of three to six birds. The largest broodless flock I've seen numbered eight, and I witnessed it in both Rio's and Merriam's. The adult hens congregate in small groups as a form of protection from predators.

Often times each of the flocks described above can be seen milling around together at a common food source. Though these congregations can number up to a couple hundred birds, within that large gathering are intricate social structures consisting of individual flocks. As these flocks go about their daily routines, there are several ways to hunt them in the fall.

In some western states that offer a season, fall turkey hunting opens in September, when it's hot and dry, and runs through December when snow covers the ground and temperatures plunge to well below zero. Within that four month timeframe a lot goes on within any given turkey population.

How turkeys behave and how their daily routines develop and are carried out depends largely on the weather and available food sources. As summer draws to a close, a large percentage of a turkey's diet consists of insects, especially grasshoppers, throughout many western states. If the ensuing fall months and early winter months are mild and grasshoppers prevalent, they may be the primary food source for turkeys well into late October or early November.

One fall I filled both of my turkey tags in late October by focusing on hunting meadows with grasshoppers in them. The crops of both birds carried more than 150 grasshoppers, each.

In November, I once took a tom that had a crop full of varied foods. In it were 114 caterpillars, 112 rose hips, 14 silk worms, 13 grasshoppers, one slug and a full cup of different grass seeds.

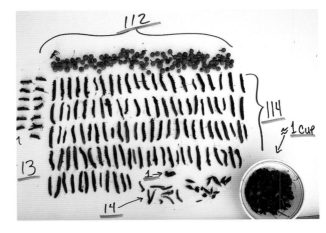

Turkeys have two goals in the fall: to stay alive and find as much food as possible. Focusing on a turkey's diet this time of year is one of the best ways to fill a tag as they are intent on consuming as much food as possible in preparation for winter. Watch for birds feeding through meadows, along timbered edges and anywhere else food exists. Be prepared to spend some serious time behind binoculars and a spotting scope, keeping careful notes on bird movement. Pay particular attention to time and place, that is, where birds are, at what specific time.

With approaching wet, cold weather, diets can quickly turn from grasshoppers to worms, grubs and vegetation. Be aware of the food sources in your region and know when they are available and prime for turkeys to be on them. By studying the crop of a bird you take, you'll know exactly what they're eating, and hopefully learn where the food is coming from. This will not only help in filling more tags that season, but for years to come as long as food sources don't dramatically shift.

Early one November season, my buddy, Bret Stuart and I were out chasing turkeys. We were having trouble finding mature toms, and we wanted to each take one with our bows. After two days and no mature toms spotted, we were about to give up when rains fell that night. The following morning we were back out, looking one last time for toms. What we found was impressive.

With that heavy, warm rain, earth worms crawled out of the ground in short grass meadows in astounding numbers. That day we watched multiple flocks of toms emerge from hiding and feed all day long in the open. Before dark we set up two blinds in two different areas, and each of us arrowed a nice tom from them the following day. It goes to show how persistence pays off, as does keeping eyes open to how food sources can quickly shift with changing weather conditions.

Food sources can change quickly in the fall, especially with a shift in weather.

In addition to keying on fall food sources, it's important to physically watch the birds as they develop daily routines and establish habitual travel routes. If the food is there, the birds will usually slip in to a routine that takes them to the same place, at roughly the same time, every day. When the food is gone, the birds will leave, but until then, they may hang out for several weeks, even months, doing the same thing day after day.

Where some birds spend winter is also where they spend the spring, and sometimes, their entire lives. Some turkeys will move great distances to find food and protection from the elements during the winter months, and if they find the conditions favorable,

Bret Stuart arrowed this dandy fall Rio after patterning a flock of toms the day prior, then setting a blind in their pathway.

will remain in the area come spring. This is good for adding genetic diversity to a local flock of birds, which will ultimately take root and then expand into neighboring valleys.

Early in my turkey hunting career, one area I hunted in the spring was full of birds. Then, a few years later, for some reason the birds left. But in the winter numerous birds were back on the private land. Though the landowners no longer allowed me to hunt in the spring,

As fall flocks grow in number, it makes for a great time to not only hunt, but to scout for spring opportunities. Note the white hen (not a true albino) in this flock.

they welcomed my presence in the fall because they were tired of the noisy, messy birds. When I explained to them that these were the same birds that were here a few springs back, but had likely just shifted their spring living area to higher in the valleys, they were surprised. Going from a couple dozen birds in the spring, to only a few in the spring, then to more than 200 birds in autumn, opened the landowners's eyes to how these birds can move and how stable their numbers really were on their 2,500 acre ranch. It also secured a hunting spot for me for the following spring.

Fall is a great time to not only hunt turkeys, but to scout for places to hunt the following spring. With bird densities high on some of these private properties, landowners can be eager to thin bird numbers in the fall, whereas convincing them to do the same in the spring can be a different story. When you explain that these birds, in their less striking winter plumage, are the same

In the fall and winter months, turkeys often congregate around livestock.

birds that occupy the area in the spring, but are likely more spread out, it can open the doors for possible spring hunting opportunities.

In a couple of the fall areas I hunt, cattle and sheep ranching are big, and turkeys often gather in these habitats in search of food. Ranchers don't like livestock ingesting turkey manure for fear of illness. When you have dozens of birds hanging around an area for months on end, it doesn't take long for large amounts of waste to accrue. These are great places to search for turkey hunting opportunities, and is a sensible way for hunters to help keep burgeoning numbers in check. It's the prime example of how turkey hunters can act as conservationists.

If your request to hunt turkeys is turned down, check back in a couple years. Often times winter flocks continue to grow, and sometimes ranchers and landowners get so overrun with birds, they call game officials for help. Game officials often refer hunters to such areas, or go in and trap them for relocation to a different place.

In areas where turkeys become overpopulated, they are often trapped and relocated.

Fall Hunting Tactics

Fall hunting seasons are in place to help keep turkey populations in-check and at optimal levels for encouraging genetic diversity and promoting healthy growth. On average, fall harvests are limited to between 5% and 10% of the total population within that state or region. Biologists closely monitor bird populations and hunter success rates, then regulate fall hunting seasons, accordingly.

As with hunting any animal, success comes down to knowing their seasonal behaviors, where they sleep, travel and what they're feeding on. It's no different for turkeys, especially fall turkeys. We've already detailed their behaviors during this time of year, and touched on food sources. The key is finding the birds, themselves.

Once turkeys have been located, it's up to you to devise a strategy to fill a tag based on what you're observing. Thanks to larger sized flocks this time of year, versus the spring, finding roosting sites is easier and offers a great starting point. Once the leaves have fallen, it becomes even easier to locate roosted birds.

Where they roost depends on habitat. I've found large fall flocks roosting in the same cottonwood trees they do in the spring, in a meandering river bottom. I've also found them in places I'd never dreamed of them being.

Usually, fall birds like roosting where they're protected from elements, but that's not always the rule. One winter while hunting the Dakotas, I found a good number of birds roosting in stands of Russian olives, no more than 20 feet off the ground, exposed to the biting cold temperatures and high winds. I've seen them roosting high atop the upper limbs of big Douglas firs on a rugged hillside, in small cedar trees on the leeward side of large barns, inside old barns, in giant pine trees, and of course, oak trees.

Bottom line, the turkeys will roost where they want; sometimes these roosting sites make sense to us, sometimes they don't. If a roosting site puzzles you, step back and evaluate the terrain. Ask yourself where the food sources are, where water is as well as what protection the site might offer from wind, rain and blowing snow.

Once a roost site is located, watch where the birds fly down, then pay close attention to their routine. Usually you'll find them eating, resting, drinking, eating some more, preening, eating again, resting, drinking, and so on. You get the idea. Their goal is to take in calories, not waste them, so they may not move far if ample food is in the area.

If you don't have the time to scout, find a roosting site and set up some trail cameras along the edges of meadows, pastures, logging roads and well-used game trails leading to the area. Once you find where the birds are moving, narrow down the timeframe they're moving through then start figuring out where to set up.

Once you've found a roosting site and patterned the birds, it's time for the hunt. As for fall hunting tactics out West

Finding food sources is a key to consistently tagging fall turkeys. This bird's crop was stuffed with grasshoppers.

there are many options, but likely the most common is spot-and-stalk. Spot-and-stalk turkey hunting is much more accepted in the fall than the spring for the simple reason hunters aren't calling birds to them. Because hunters aren't calling birds, there's no risk of calling in other hunters who might inadvertently shoot a decoy, potentially hitting a well camouflaged hunter sitting on the opposite side. In the fall, birds are flocked up, on the move and usually in sight

of the hunter, leaving virtually no room for error in deciphering between a real turkey and a decoy. In other words, spot-and-stalk hunting in the fall is very safe.

Out West, most hunters pursue big game by way of spot-and-stalk, and autumn turkeys fall right in line with that approach. Many hunters I've talked with feel there's no better practice when it comes to honing big game stalking skills than to try it on turkeys. Many of these same hunters feel it's tougher to stalk a turkey than most big game, due to their nervous nature and superior vision.

I've taken a good number of fall toms by way of spot-and-stalk, and have blown many stalks, too. What I've found to be most effective is to locate a flock, predict where they're going based scouting missions, then get ahead of them and wait for them to come to me. This can be a waiting game, as the birds often stop to feed, preen and sometimes just rest. But if you're in their line of travel, be patient, they will usually show up.

Spot-and-stalk hunting turkeys, even with a bow, can be done under the right circumstances and conditions.

Another option is to approach a flock by spotting then stalking them from behind. When doing this, use any broken terrain to help hide your movement. If there's ample cover, it's surprising how fast you can close the gap on a flock of birds. If cover is sparse, cover ground fast when birds are moving, but slow it down when they pause to rest or preen, so they don't catch your movement.

If the flock is working the edge of a field or meadow, and walking straight at them is not an option due to lack of cover, try marking their position, then loop into the trees and come out on the birds from the side. If they moved while you were in stalk mode, withdraw into the timber and try it again. This is a safe approach, for it ensures you remain well hidden during the stalk and puts you in a good position for a shot. Just be careful when reaching the edge of the opening, for large winter flocks means lots of eyeballs to contend with and if one busts you, the gig is up.

Should snow hit the ground, not only can this aid in your spot-and-stalk approach, but it can lead to tracking opportunities. On average, throughout the course of any given day of the year, a turkey will travel about four miles. This number may drop in some areas experiencing a harsh winter, or where food sources are concentrated and birds don't have to travel. But

the fact remains that turkeys are walkers, that's how they're wired.

When snow falls in your turkey hunting area, get out, find tracks and follow them. This is a great way to see where turkeys go and what food sources they're after. It's also a good way to learn about flock dynamics, where birds might stop to preen and where they go given the conditions being faced on that particular day.

As with hunting any big game animal, tracking turkeys is a skill that develops with time. The more time you spend in the woods, the more aware you become of what's happening around you. Avoid the urge to cut tracks and follow them as quickly as possible. Instead, take your time, read the sign and learn. This is how woodsmanship skills are built, and not only will these skills make you a better turkey hunter, but a better tracker of big game, too.

When following tracks, be sure to frequently pause and look ahead. Often times a flock will feed through an area, then take a 90° turn. If you're too focused on following the trail and not seeing what's ahead, you'll spook the birds, I know, I've done it.

One tip to help you learn about tracking turkeys, and make the correlation between the tracks and the size of the bird leaving them, is to watch the birds from a distance. Find a jake or an old tom, mark where they walk, then once they leave, study and

A lot can be learned about turkey movement when snow covers the ground. It's also a good time to track down a tom.

even measure their tracks. The same is true when it comes to connecting droppings to toms and hens.

Where I'm from, snow rarely frequents the fall turkey hunting grounds. But when it does snow, I try to get out and learn something. The same holds true when I find myself in other states this time of year, and a fresh skiff of snow blankets turkey country. As with hunting any animal, there's a lot that can be learned about their behavior when hunting them in fresh snow.

If the terrain is too flat or doesn't offer enough cover to pull-off a spot-and-stalk attempt, then it may be best to intercept the birds with a ground blind. Once the flock's path of travel has been patterned, try placing a pop-up blind on the edge of some brush, near the predicted path. If there's enough brush around you might be able construct a rudimentary, natural blind to sit behind. Sitting by a tree is an option, but if the birds are in the open and working your direction, the slightest movement could alert them.

Braxton and I doubled from this spot, situated along an established travel route. I scored on a hen with the bow, while Braxton took a nice tom from a bachelor flock that passed by soon after.

If you're observing a flock and their patterns aren't 100% consistent, it may be in your best interest to set up two pop up blinds. Watch the birds from a distance, see which route they're favoring, then head to that blind.

One fall I had a flock of mature toms patterned, or so I thought. I set a blind where I'd seen the birds moving, but when I sat it in the next morning, they went to the upper end of the meadow, not the lower end where I was waiting. I let the birds leave the area, then set up a second blind, this one in the upper end of the field.

The next morning I was back out there, watching the flock as they left the roost, pitching into the middle of a pasture. Not sure if they'd go high or low, I watched through binoculars and waited. The flock was moving my direction, but because they were well over a quarter-mile away, had no idea I was around. Finally, after about 45 minutes, they started veering to the high side of the field. Wasting no time, I hoofed it through the oak-studded rolling hills, using the trees and terrain as cover.

Sneaking into the blind I'd erected the day prior, it didn't take 20 minutes and the first tom appeared, followed by 11 others. The entire flock walked right by my blind without a care in the world. I went home that night with a fat tom for our upcoming Thanksgiving dinner.

Because food sources can change, and may be somewhat spread out this time of year, it might be worth watching a flock for as long as possible before making a move. Sometimes a storm exposes food

A trail camera will reveal where birds are moving and what time they're passing through. In the fall, turkeys grow very habitual.

sources overnight, and birds may veer off their regular routine to see what's available. Though this is more the exception than the rule, it does happen. If birds do stray from their routine, they usually get back on it within a few days, unless food sources along that route have been totally depleted.

Perhaps the most well-known fall hunting approach across the country is to break up a flock, then call them back together. The first few times I tried this, I thought it was a farce, then I figured out what I was doing wrong. Since then, scattering a turkey flock has become a favorite fall application.

My mistake was the fact I was breaking up flocks in the open. Not only did this put birds on-edge because they could see me too soon, but it also forced them to all fly off in the same direction, not breaking them up at all. Once I began breaking up flocks as they moved through the timber, and getting closer before making my move to displace the flock, I discovered just how effective this approach could be.

155

When breaking up a fall flock, watch the birds from a distance until they move into brush or timber. If the flock seems to be moving through cover from point A to point B, figure out how much cover they have to move through before once again hitting the open. If the birds are moving into a stand of trees to scratch for food, then they might spend a good deal of time under cover, and this is the best place to bust up the flock.

Should the flock quickly be passing through a narrow strip of trees or brush, you might have to move quickly in order to scatter them at the right time. If they're feeding

Tiffany and I broke up a family flock and took these two birds. Both were skinned for decoy mounts, and both were eaten.

into trees, your sense of urgency isn't as high. Attacking a flock from below, as they move uphill, works best, for the birds take wing sooner than running downhill.

The idea of splitting a fall turkey flock makes perfect sense, since they are dependent upon one another for safety this time of year. Because the family flocks are so maternal in their lifestyle, when they get separated they have a strong urge to reunite. They do this by calling, especially in thicker cover where they may not be able to see one another.

When you move to break up a flock, do it fast. You might ask, "Why break up a flock and not just shoot one as I run in?" For one, running with a loaded gun is dangerous and should be avoided. Then again, I know of hunters who claim that the best way to break up a flock is to burst in and shoot over their heads, rather than hollering and waving their arms. The say the gunshot is alarming and sends birds in all different directions. But the main point of busting up a flock and not shooting them is to be able to call the birds back to you, something that's not easy to accomplish this time of the year.

With a flock in sight and a break up point determined, move in like a predator. I avoid going in waving my arms, hollering, like I did early on. Instead, think of how a coyote, cougar or bobcat would attack them. They'd stealth as close as possible, then sprint, low to the ground, right into the flock, singling out a bird at the right time. When you move in for the spook, try to hit the middle of the flock so the birds scatter in all directions. If they move as flock, the mission has failed; abort and search for another flock. If they make you for a human, the attempt to call them back may be more challenging, but don't give up. Make yourself small, compact, and move fast. Cover your face and hands and anything else that may look human and stay low to the ground.

If you split the flock into multiple directions, half the job is complete. From there, sit tight and listen. After about 15 or 20 minutes, I'll start calling, unless I hear the birds start talking, first. If the country is open and the birds can see one another, they may not call, as they can reassemble by sight. That's why it's best to bust up flocks in brushy, timbered habitat.

Once a bird makes a sound, mimic it. Avoid the urge to get aggressive, as reassembling fall flocks isn't about who is the most aggressive; it's about coming together for protection. If

When busting up a flock, try doing so as the birds move uphill, into cover.

birds answer back, keep calling. A glass or aluminum slate call is great for bringing family flocks back together, as they are higher pitched and this is how most young birds sound. Mouth calls work well, too, and box calls make excellent purrs and soft clucks.

Toss out some kee-kees and soft yelps if you're the one starting things off. If the birds start answering you, give them an assembly call followed by more kee-kees and lost yelps, then start mimicking the sounds they make. The idea is to create the illusion that you're hens and poults chatting back and forth in an effort to reunite. If you're lucky, birds on both sides will start talking, and if you're in the middle of it, hold on, the encounter could be close.

A good scenario for breaking up a flock is when they're on the roost. Sneak in as close as possible early in the morning, under the cover of darkness. When it's still plenty dark, get as close as possible, then spook the birds, trying to get them to scatter in multiple directions. Often times they'll reassemble by calling as daylight approaches. I've had the best success with this when birds were spread throughout a few trees that were low to the ground.

Once the birds spook, setting up a few decoys can help bring them to you. Try placing a couple hen decoys, or a hen and jake decoy, together. Ten to 15 yards, place another hen decoy, then sit between the decoys, off in the brush or at the base of a tree. This decoy setup works in other fall calling situations, too, not just when breaking up flocks.

Spooking birds off the roost as night falls is also a great ploy. Be sure and move in late enough so the birds can't reunite. The idea is to send the flock in different directions, then return early in the morning to catch them as they reassemble by calling. I've had the best success doing this in big, timbered draws where birds often fly across canyons once spooked. Not only does this sort of habitat spread out the birds for the night, it also requires more calling in their efforts to reconnect with one another. Decoys work well here, too.

Personally, I've had poor success in consistently busting up a flock of mature toms and calling them back together. This could be due to the fact I've never hit the right situation, but I think it's more due to their lack of innate social bonds the hens, juveniles and jakes carry this time of year. Toms may take a day or two to reunite.

One thing I have had happen though, on three occasions, is that when I moved in on a flock of toms to try and bust them up, some birds fled while others tucked tight to the ground, holding just like a pheasant or chukar. The first time I witnessed this I thought maybe the tom was injured. Curious to see what was wrong, I approached the tom. His head was stretched flat on the ground in front of him, and he laid on one side of his body. When I got three steps from the tom, he erupted in a flurry of wings and feathers. It was the last thing I expected, and though I chambered a round and got a quick shot off, all I hit was a big tree as he flew behind it. The bird sailed through the trees and across the timbered draw, where he landed 200 yards away and ran up the hill. I learned a lesson that day.

The next time that happened, I was ready. I moved in on a small flock of toms, all mature birds. Three of the birds flew, one ran off, but one hunkered down behind some tall grass. I shot that bird at five yards. I've seen toms react this way in the spring, too,

and it usually occurs in areas of thick cover, where they feel safely surrounded and confident that hunkering down will save them. It's a very upland bird like instinct, one that makes sense when you think about it.

Speaking of turkeys holding tight, more states than not throughout the West allow the use of dogs when hunting fall turkeys. If you're into flushing upland birds, you owe it to yourself to try this approach at least once in your turkey hunting career.

158

My first fall turkey hunting experience with dogs came unexpectedly. A friend and I were hunting sharptails along the Yellowstone River in Montana. A snow storm came through the night prior, putting a few inches of powder on the ground.

Two dogs worked ahead of us, noses tight to the ground and in-line with a set of grouse tracks. The canines worked toward a section of tall, yellow grass that had been partially folded over by the snow. The leaning grass was still about knee-high, which created the perfect hideaway for birds.

As the German shorthairs locked on point, my buddy and I moved in close, ready for the shot. The instant I shouldered my gun, a torrent of snow erupted at my feet. Less than two steps away, snow, ice and shards of dead grass shot into the air, temporarily obscuring my view. The thundering sound of heavy wings jolted the calm, morning air to life and my pulse raced. To be honest, it flat-out shocked me.

I was expecting a grouse to jump up in front of me, but when a big tom broke out in raging fashion, it more than caught me off guard. By the time I gained my composure, the bird was behind a grove of Russian olives, coasting safely away on cupped wings.

"Pretty impressive flush, huh?" my partner smiled. He'd seen it before, as he grew up hunting this area.

Continuing forward the dogs went on point again, less than 20 yards from the last spot. This time I was ready and when another tom exploded from beneath the show, I let him have it with a payload of six shot. The tom hit the ground with a resounding thud, driving home the fact that a turkey flush is impressive all the way to the end.

As with spring turkey hunting, hunting turkeys in the fall and winter months are deep in tradition across the country. In fact, some sources reveal an even longer tradition of hunting turkeys with the aid of dogs in the fall than calling them in the spring. After all, that's where our Thanksgiving tradition came from, having wild turkey for the celebration dinner.

If anyone's ever told you they don't like hunting turkeys in the fall, rest assured, they're the ones missing out. Be it a tom you're after or a hen, both offer great sport and are excellent eating. I like taking a hen every fall or two, for once they're down I use the skin to create my own decoy, the wing bones to craft calls and of course, the family eats every bit of meat.

As mentioned earlier, breaking up a flock and calling them back together is a proven, exciting approach, but with dogs, the chance of success greatly increases. Make sure this is legal in the state(s) you're hunting. The idea is to get as close to a flock as you can without being detected, then sending the dog in for the scatter. Dogs are faster and a more realistic predator than bipedal humans, and likely resemble a coyote in its scurried rush to attempt to catch food. Once the dog scatters the birds in every direction, discretely sneak into the flush site, sit 10-15 minutes then start calling with kee-kees and lost yelps. Keep the dog tight by your seat so it doesn't alert approaching birds.

Whether using dogs to flush or jump turkeys, there's no denying how effective they can be. If you're used to flushing and shooting quail or grouse, hold on when you try this approach with a 25 pound turkey. Be warned, once you find success you'll become addicted to this hunting style.

Calling is another autumn hunting option, and one that can work well if you catch birds in the right mood. There's nothing like the sounds of turkeys in fall or winter, gathered on a roost site, ready to start their day. The variety of sounds you'll hear at this time greatly surpass any conversations heard in the spring. This is not only the best learning resource for hunters–to actually hear how turkeys sound–it's also an ideal starting point for your hunt.

Once a roost site is located, move in as close as you can without spooking them, well before daylight. If possible, try setting up where you saw the birds enter the roost from the night prior. Once a bird makes a sound, mimic it, but with a bit more feeling. Hopefully, as they pitch out of the trees they'll come right to you.

As they land, they often spread out and start feeding. This is where, if you're set up on the fringes of where they pitched down, you can use soft yelps and clucks to try and draw birds to you. This is a

Tiffany arrowed this fall bird after it was called off the roost. The bird was silent, but came right in.

common vocalization turkeys rely on to reunite once they've separated from their morning fly-down. This is also a good situation in which to use a hen decoy.

As fall flocks become established, there's a pecking order that exists within each. For this reason it's not uncommon to find a lone bird–usually a jake or young tom–wandering by himself, looking for a flock to become a member of. If you see this, waste no time trying to get in front of the bird, then set up and call. Be careful not to intimidate the lone bird, rather employ soft yelps and purrs to get his attention. These sounds of a content hen feeding are often heard in the autumn turkey woods, and sends the message that not only is food available, but that all is relaxed and no threats exist. A two note tom yelp can also be effective, catching the lone tom's curiosity.

Not only will single birds be looking for a flock to spend the winter with, but small groups of birds may be looking to join with more birds, again, to gain the security of having safety in numbers. When you see a flock of jakes, young toms or even mature toms, try issuing a series of challenge calls. Start softly, then if the bird's don't respond progress to hard yelps, clucks and even fighting purrs. Toms can be very aggressive in the fall, and often entire flocks will fight one another.

One December day, a skiff of snow covered an already frozen ground. I'd spotted a flock of about 15 jakes from atop a ridge I walked. Curious to see how they'd react, I let loose with some cutting and aggressive yelps. Almost immediately their heads turned from a dull maroon to a brilliant red and blue hue. They began gobbling, strutting and before I knew it, the whole flock started moving my direction.

Braxton took this lone tom before school one fall morning. We'd been seeing a flock of toms, but when this bird was spotted, alone, we offered some tom yelps which brought him right by the blind.

A few minutes later another flock of toms started gobbling. They approached from the backside of the ridge on which I sat; I didn't even know they were around. Within a few minutes the jakes were in front of me and soon the flock of mature toms closed in. The two flocks met, 12 yards in front of where I sat. By this time I'd quit calling, as they kept one another gobbling, yelping and sounding off with fighting purrs.

For more than 10 minutes the two flocks faced-off. Though the fighting resembled more that of a shoving match than an all-out street brawl, it was nonetheless very impressive to be a part of. It also confirmed that birds can be called in during the peak of winter. The temperatures barely broke zero in the day, dipping to more than 20-below at night.

Eventually the flock of jakes moved away, but the toms stayed put. For another 10 minutes I watched and listened, in awe. The number of sounds they made was an education, and watching them strut, pirouette and posture toward one another only drove home the fact that we, as hunters, can learn so much about the game we pursue when we're not too quick to pull the trigger. In fact, I let those birds walk away, not ready to fill my fall tag so early in the hunt.

Believe it or not, toms can even be gobbled in during the fall and winter months. Though it's a low percentage proposition, it can work. The key is catching a bird when he's in an aggressive mood, and being able to fire him up. It's a lot like calling bull elk in the middle of the day during September. There are several times I've been in the elk woods,

Spring isn't the only time toms will gobble and strut. I called this mixed flock to within 20 yards in early December in below freezing temperatures.

hunting timber where herds are bedded. Accepting of the fact I won't be able to stalk within bow range of the bulls, I start calling. My goal is to get the herd of cows and calves talking, which will eventually get the bull up and moving, curious to see what's happening. This is a forced response I'm trying to achieve, and the same can be accomplished by gobbling at toms in the fall and winter months.

Ideally, I like being able to first spot a flock of toms before issuing a gobble. This allows me to see how they react. Sometimes they toss their heads up and the colors quickly change. Other times they keep their beaks to the ground, not even acknowledging the fact they heard my gobbles.

For the toms that won't give me the satisfaction of answering back to my gobbles, I won't push it. I'll let out another gobble or two, and if they don't respond, I'll try circling in front of them, then calling again. But if only one or two toms seem interested, then it's game time.

November toms called to within 10 yards. They came in gobbling and strutting the whole way.

At this point the goal is to get that one tom to reply. Often, if he responds, the rest of the flock will often follow suit. Try getting him going with more gobbles and very aggressive purrs. Some deep, raspy, pleading yelps will also help. In the fall, tom yelps may exceed 20 or more continuous sounds,

162

so don't be timid with these sounds. Create a scene of a challenge, where fighting is about to break loose, as in the fall, toms are still trying to determine social rank. This aggressive approach will often get a flock of toms talking aggressively and heading your direction. When this happens, I'll still keep calling aggressively with gobbles, yelps and cutts. Do whatever it takes to keep them fired-up and talking.

One mid-November day I got a single tom to respond to my gobbling. His head colors transitioned, but he was the only one in the flock that seemed interested. No matter how much I gobbled, the other birds kept quiet. A few lifted their heads, but went back to scratching for food. Then I picked up the intensity and interjected fighting purrs. This piqued the curiosity of the interested tom. Finally, he gobbled, and when he did, I answered right back with a gobble of my own. He gobbled again, as did another tom in the flock.

When my target bird broke into a strutting posture, I knew it was over. Soon half the flock reacted by assuming strutting positions, while the rest picked up their heads, most of which instantly changed color. They looked around, curious, almost seemingly asking, "Okay, we'll give in, but what are we giving in to." When you gain this type of reactionary response, the odds of calling those toms in greatly increases. If they continue gobbling and start fighting amongst themselves, the flock might stay put. This is a good time to head for cover and call your way to them. Keep them riled-up with periodic calls while simultaneously cutting the distance. Such an approach, where you're calling and stalking, together, can be a great combination in the fall.

Gobblers will also briefly yelp quite often in the fall. The sequence is short, two or three notes, but it's loud, rough and powerful. This can be a good call to use if trying to locate a flock of toms. They'll often respond by yelping back in an effort to "reconnect" with the lost bird (you).

Hens do a great deal of yelping in the fall, again, with the intent of keeping track of one another as they feed or to locate each other or their poults should they wander off. The lost yelp of a hen is much different than that of mature toms. Hens will string out their lost yelp sequence by joining together 12 to 15 notes, sometimes more. It's a distinct, pleading yelp and if you hear hens issuing such sounds, answer back with the same number of notes trying to match her intensity. If you can get hens talking to you with such a call, you have a good chance of calling them in, or moving in on them while you keep calling.

Fall turkey hunting is a thrill, offering some of the best opportunities out there to learn about the birds themselves, as well as hone hunting skills. Not much is written about the how-to aspects of fall turkey hunting, let alone the allure and cultural depth it carries. Once you get a taste of it, you'll see why hunters who yearn for fall turkey season make sure to pick up tags the minute they're available.

When planning a fall turkey hunt, be sure to do so well ahead of time. Not all western states had

Braxton scored on this hen one Christmas morning. We skinned the bird for a mount and had fresh turkey for Christmas dinner.

fall seasons at the time of this writing, while others were continually growing their fall hunting opportunities, county by county, year by year. Some states allot a set number of tags, and once they're sold out, that's it. Some are issued on a lottery. Plan ahead and you'll be fine. I often plan my fall turkey hunting in other states around big game hunts. In other words, I may not travel to Montana to hunt turkeys in the fall, but if I'm there on a deer or elk hunt, why not pick up a turkey tag?

Just because toms aren't sporting their spring plumage, gobbling and strutting all day long doesn't mean they're any less worthy of a quarry because of what the calendar says. Fall is a special time to be in the turkey woods, and it's always a gratifying feeling to sit down at the dinner table and take that first slice of Thanksgiving turkey, knowing it was taken from the woods, not the store.

Chapter 5:

YOUTH TURKEY HUNTING

The first turkey hunt I took my oldest son, Braxton, on was when he was four years old. It rained, was cold, and we heard only a few gobbles. Still, I let him work the box call and was happy we chose to hunt out of a blind that morning.

I elected to hunt from a blind for two reasons: First, heavy fog was forecasted and that usually means rain in the valley we hunted. Second, Braxton was young, and I don't know of a kid that age who can sit still for any length of time.

With us in the blind that morning we had a thermos of hot chocolate, some snacks he's never allowed to eat at home and hand-warmers. Though none of these things were necessary, they served their purpose of making the overall experience more fun for Braxton. We left without firing a shot that morning, but we did hear some toms in the distance, their thundering gobbles carrying through the valley in classic fashion. From that point on, Braxton was hooked on turkey hunting despite not seeing a single bird.

When Braxton was six, he was invited back east to film a youth turkey hunting show. He, myself and the camera hopped on a plane for an October turkey hunt. On day two of the hunt, Braxton took his very first turkey, a bearded hen. What's even more gratifying, he shot the bird at 11 yards with his bow.

On that trip, just as with Braxton's first turkey adventure where we didn't get a bird, everything was set up to help make it fun for him. If there's one thing I learned through 12 years of being a public school teacher, it's that the attention span of kids is generally short, and you have to work efficiently and in a multi-tasking fashion if you want to keep their minds engaged. Hunting with kids is no different, it's just that the classroom is outside.

The Setup

The most important part of youth turkey hunting to pay attention to is the setup. Not only does this apply to youth who are actually hunting, but non-hunting youth who may be spending a day in the woods with an adult. In fact, this actually applies to turkey hunters of all ages, for of all the turkey guides I've ever talked with around the West, they all agree that the number one thing that spooks an incoming turkey is the inability of a hunter to sit still.

Turkeys have some of the best eyesight in the animal kingdom, and if they catch any movement, the gig is up. Knowing this, it's critical to take the time to set up so movement can be masked. Without a doubt, a ground blind is the best tool for hiding a hunter, no matter what their age.

Today's pop up blinds are easy to carry, quick to set up and offer multiple shooting windows. Be sure the walls of whatever blind you get are black on the inside, as it's the dark shade inside the blind that conceals you.

To keep things comfortable inside the blind, take a couple stools. Be sure the stools are quiet when moving around in them. Often times hunters have to shift body position at the last second to get a shot, and a noisy, squeaky chair will tip-off a tom. As mentioned earlier, I prefer a milk crate with a padded cushion, as it's quiet and makes for easy movement, but a youth may desire something with back support.

166

When setting up the blind, take the time to clean the ground inside. Remove any twigs, rocks or dry leaves that could potentially lead to unwanted noise. I like putting a carpet down to keep things quiet and clean.

Also, be sure all the windows are closed, except for the shooting window(s). If needing to look around the blind for birds that may approach from a different angle, open the flaps ever-so-slightly and look through the mesh, so the birds won't see your movement. It's important to have as much shade inside the blind as possible, and absolutely no backlighting that will give away motion.

When it comes to youth, the next most important tool to have inside a ground blind is a set of shooting sticks. For young hunters, raising a shotgun can be awkward and heavy. To remedy this, get shooting sticks that will allow the gun to comfortably rest and easily swing on approaching birds.

My favorite shooting sticks for youth turkey hunters are Bog-Pod's three legged style. They are sturdy, easy to adjust, low-profile and the 360° rotating head easily pivots. If the hunting youth is small of stature or not very strong, then attach an Xtreme Shooting Rest to the top of the Bog-Pod. This will allow the entire gun to be slid into shooting position upon entering the blind, meaning all the hunter has to do is move the gun ever so slightly to track an approaching tom. Movement is minimal with this setup and allows kids to focus on the bird, not struggling with lifting and aiming their gun.

The next best setup for a youth hunter is in front of a fat tree. Choose a tree that's wide enough at the base to breakup the body's outline. Avoid the temptation to stick a youth behind a tree, or worse yet, behind some brush that may seem like a good blind. When situated behind trees and brush, youth see this as an invitation to move around; it's also next to impossible to get a shot without having to move, and keen eyed birds will bust you every time.

When setting up in front of a tree, be sure to have the youth in a face mask and gloves. It's vital to cover the face and hands, the two body parts that move the most in this situation. If a mask won't work, try camo' face paint–youth usually love putting on "war paint." A cushion to sit on will keep the shooter comfortable, and those tripod shooting sticks are perfect for getting the gun into shooting position and keeping it there, before a turkey even comes into sight.

If the tree is big enough, the accompanying adult can situate next to the youth. If the tree is too small, the adult can get to the side, or somewhat behind it, looking over the youth's shoulder. The key is not moving once a bird pops into sight. Remember, hens might approach first, and you don't want to spook them since a tom will likely be following. Get comfortable, utilize a padded cushion and be ready to sit stone-still for several minutes should the need arise.

On my most memorable youth hunting experience, all went as planned, but the toms took their time approaching. I was with Braxton on his first spring turkey hunt in Oregon. It was day two of the hunt, and right off the bat we got a tom gobbling at our locator calls.

The lone tom was across a canyon, on the edge of a small meadow more than a mile away. The bird was so far it could not be seen with the naked eye, but binoculars revealed his exact location. When we switched to aggressive cutting calls, the tom fired-back with every sound we made. He was so far off, when watching him through binoculars, by the time his gobbles reached our ears his outstretched neck had already retracted into his puffed-up body.

Soon the tom started moving our direction, and picked up another eager tom along the way. I gave the tom about a 2% chance of reaching us, given the fact he had to cross 100 yards of open meadow, two livestock fences, a big creek in the bottom of a canyon that required him to take flight, and more than a quarter-mile of thick Douglas fir timber. The final 150 yards would force the tom to ascend a steep hill that had recently been logged and negotiate thick brush covering any trails that may have once been carved into the land.

As the aggressive toms drew near, we kept calling so as to keep their interest peaked. The birds were out of sight, but we could hear them, so Braxton worked his box call with fervor. The hot toms double and triple gobbled at every sound. It took several minutes, but the toms finally appeared at the bottom of the logged unit.

We sat at the crest of the ridge, decoy already in-place. Braxton and I both nestled against a pair of thick maple trees, side-by-side, a padded cushion under our backsides. Braxton had his gun loaded, the barrel resting in the V of his Bog-Pod shooting sticks.

After 20 minutes of sitting in the same place, virtually motionless, the toms finally appeared. The first one came up the ridge and popped out less than 10 yards, directly behind us. His gobbles were deafening, and we could clearly hear him stacking his feathers, spitting and drumming. We dared not move.

Then, finally, the second tom materialized on the far side of the decoy. Braxton made a perfect shot and was elated to tie his tag on the 22 pound tom sporting a 10-inch beard.

The hunt was longer than usual as the toms had so much ground to cover. The fact we had everything in place for Braxton to comfortably sit still, made the difference. Having his gun on the sticks, in shooting position, meant movement was minimal, almost non-existent. Had Braxton not had his gun on the sticks, I'm sure the bird behind us would have busted him when he went to shoot the tom in front of us. Our planning paid off and Braxton was as excited as he'd ever been in the turkey woods. The fact we were fortunate to catch it all on film for one of our TV shows made the experience that much more special.

Three generations of turkey hunters. Braxton and my dad, Jerry, scored on these two birds, while I ended up tagging one later in the hunt. This is what turkey hunting is all about.

The Accessories

Above all else you want the youth hunter to have fun in the turkey woods. This means planning ahead and predicting situations you may find yourself facing. When hunting from a blind, take a fun book for them to quietly read. This can help them pass the time if and when there's a lull in the action.

When hunting with youth, let them work calls. This is how learning takes place.

Having easy-to-use turkey calls is a great way to get youth involved in the hunt, keeping their mind engaged. Box calls, push-button calls and slates are easy to use, and the sounds don't have to be perfect to get a tom to gobble. Nothing will motivate a youth hunter to focus more quickly on the hunt than getting a gobble response from a call they, themselves, generate. Once that gobbling tom pops into view, chances are high you've just hooked a youth on turkey hunting, for life.

Early morning spring hunts and those throughout the fall can be chilly. We never go into a hunt without hand-warmers. My boys love them, and even if they're not necessary, hand-warmers make it fun for the kids and gives them something to do. Such attention-getting hunting accessories–ones that kids only get to use in the field–can have a big impact on their desire to follow along on future hunts.

The same is true for having that thermos of hot cocoa and snacks. Our family eats no candy bars or other sweets at home, so when the boys have a chance to snack on something fun, that's a motivator. Give them the snack during downtime, or when you sense they are losing interest in the hunt. The goal is to keep things positive and fun, remembering that the attention span of youth is not to the level of adults.

When hunting in bug-laden areas we always have a ThermaCELL mosquito repellent unit. This unit not only keeps biting bugs away, but kids love operating them. Again, it gives them something to do and it does make the hunt more comfortable.

Hunting masks, binoculars and clothes that fit are important for youth hunters. Kids love putting on masks, and a favorite of my two sons' is the Quick-Camo cap that has a built-in facemask. All they have to do is lift the cap from their head and let the mask drop.

Kids also like looking at things, and having a set of lightweight binoculars has made a big difference in many of the youth hunts I've been a part of. The great thing about binos' is they allow kids to focus on aspects of the hunt rather than let their mind wander. Whether watching turkeys at a distance, deer feeding on the edge of a meadow, geese flying overhead or anything else that grabs their attention, binos' are a great learning tool and keep minds engaged. One thing to note about binoculars, if you turn them upside-down and look from one of the big ends into the small end, they convert to a microscope. My boys love looking at tiny bugs, flowers, cuts on their hands and anything else that looks cool under high power magnification. It's a great learning tool and keeps their mind engaged.

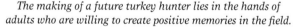

The making of a future turkey hunter lies in the hands of adults who are willing to create positive memories in the field.

WESTERN TURKEY HUNTING

Kids also enjoy working with decoys. When hunting from a blind or in front of trees, decoys serve a very important purpose of keeping a turkey's attention focused away from the hunter. Decoys are also one of the most effective tools there is when it comes to bringing a tom into shooting range.

Not only are decoys valuable tools of the hunt, they are great educational props to help teach youth about turkey behavior. It's the perfect situation where entertainment and learning simultaneously take place, and any time you can combine those two elements, focused progress is made in developing a future turkey hunter.

I make it a point to have a variety of decoys on-hand, whereby making it more interesting for youth. Be it a single feeding hen, a submissive hen, jake, strutting tom or a combination thereof, I make certain to involve the kids in the decision making process as to what decoys we'll use that day, and why.

Taking it a step further, have a youth help you stuff a real hen turkey, whereby creating your own, homemade, mounted decoy. One fall, Braxton shot a hen turkey (legal where we were hunting). We skinned the bird and ate every bit of meat, then prepared the skin for taxidermy work. After getting all the necessary parts to complete our mount, we mounted the bird, together. In spring seasons that followed, Braxton and other hunters took a good number of strutting toms off that mounted hen. Talk about having a vested interest in your decoy; it meant the world to Braxton that he took a hen, mounted it, and later took a mature tom from his creation. The mount doesn't have to be award-winning, just natural looking enough to fool a turkey, and that doesn't take much.

If looking to hunt hens in the fall, to eat and create a decoy from their skin, make sure it's legal where you're hunting. It's easy to identify a hen versus a tom or even a jake as fall progresses. Hen's take on a winter plumage that includes more buffed coloration on the outer edges of the body feathers. The feathers going up the back of the neck and head also become more pronounced on a hen. Toms and jakes will turn darker in appearance, and though their heads may not be as brightly lit-up as in spring, the lack of feathers on the neck and the presence of minor caruncles will help identify them.

Note the difference in fall plumage between a tom (left) and hen.

As for clothes, make sure they fit and that the fashion-conscious kids of today like the looks and feel of them. Pants that drag the ground not only make noise but absorb water, making for potentially wet and cold legs. There's more youth camo' clothing on the market today than ever before, and it's worth the investment to outfit kids with their own clothes that properly fit. Make a big deal of it, giving kids ownership of their newly acquired hunting gear. The same goes for boots; make sure they fit well, and on those rainy days, have waterproof rubber boots available.

The Learning

Perhaps the best thing to grab the attention of kids and truly engage their mind is teaching them all you can about turkeys, and nature, while in the woods. Take time to teach them about any sign you come across while in the field. When you find turkey tracks in the mud, talk about it. Show them the difference between tom and hen tracks. If you see where turkeys have walked across a grass field, knocking off the morning dew, show them where the turkeys likely roosted or came from, where they're going and why.

When you find a turkey feather laying on the ground, talk about it. Explain why the feather may have fallen out and what part of the body it came from. If it's a feather laced with iridescent colors, take time to hold it at different angles to the light and admire its beauty, whereby giving you the opportunity to tell why these colors are important to other turkeys. If it's a hen feather, explain why that's important to finding a tom. If it's a primary wing feather from a tom, share what that has to do with the breeding process.

When you find droppings, explain the difference between those of hens (coiled up) and toms (J shaped). Point out the shape differences and again, tell why this is important information to know when it comes to learning about animals you're hunting.

Should you stumble across an egg that's been prematurely dropped along a trail, talk about it. Point out that the mother was likely a one-year old hen who wasn't sure what her body was telling her, thus not being able to make it to the nest in time to deposit the egg. If you find a nest, don't disturb it, but talk about the laying and incubation process, even the lifecycle of the turkey and where it all starts.

Dust bath sites are important for turkeys when it comes to hygiene. Teach why the dust is necessary to de-louse their bodies and also keep them cool on hot days, and why these are good places to focus hunting efforts around.

When youth are afield, the learning never stops.

Turkey trails and roost trees are also great teaching tools to help kids learn about turkey behavior. When you hear turkeys making sounds, explain what they are and what they mean. In the turkey's never ending quest to keep a full crop, take time to look at the variety of food sources in your area. From various seeds to berries, insects and more, show kids what foods turkeys rely on and share their nutritional value. When you do kill a bird, break open the crop and look closely at the variety of food the bird had been eating–kids love this.

Don't overlook the value that comes with learning about non-turkey related aspects when afield. Gun safety can always be taught and is quite different in an actual hunting situation than on the range.

My youngest son, Kazden, is enthralled with insects and birds. If we're seeing lots of cool bugs and birds, he could care less if we get a turkey. The key is recognizing a child's interests and capitalizing on them. Take time to explore things that interest them, be it bugs, plants or pond life.

When you run across snakes, lizards, interesting plants and more, take time to educate kids. There's no greater teaching tool than the real thing, and it means far more

to them to see it in person rather than on TV or in a book.

One of the toughest things for adults when hunting with kids is knowing when to call it quits for the day. Be cognizant of when it's time to give in. No matter how much you want to push and keep hunting, it may not be in the best interest of the youth to do so. Pushing them too hard can have negative repercussions, I know, I've done it more than I care to admit. Keep it fun for the kids, hopefully to the point they'll yearn to return to the woods.

If it gets too cold or rainy, you may have to end your hunt sooner than planned. If the terrain is tough to negotiate, keep the kids in mind. Should the action be slow, pay attention to the youth's level of interest and either divert it by teaching them something special, or get out of the woods.

At the same time, if a kid wants to go hunting, even though it may not be the best time for you, do it. Even if it's just for a little while and you know the chances of finding a turkey are slim, make an effort to get out. The child may not care about killing a turkey or seeing you take one, they may simply be looking to spend quality time with a parent, away from distractions.

When Braxton was four he awakened me from a nap. "Dad," he whispered, nudging my shoulder, "the sun is out, can we go turkey hunting? You said that when the sun came out we'd go turkey hunting."

There were only two days left in the spring season and hunting conditions were tough. I'd already filled two tags, and didn't really care if I filled my third and final one. The fact I'd had an emergency appendectomy two days prior could have had something to do with my lack of motivation.

Painfully, my body still in recovery mode, I sat up and looked outside. It was sunny. Then I looked into my son's eyes, he was looking to me for approval, a questioning expression filling his face. "Let's do it!" I smiled.

Braxton was elated and couldn't get his camo' clothes on quick enough. Never mind the fact that it was the middle of the day, nor that we were going to an area close to home that had seen loads of hunting pressure over the past five weeks. "We'll be home in a couple hours," I told Tiffany with a smile and kiss goodbye.

Soon Braxton and I were afield, slowly walking shaded logging roads and creekbeds where turkeys might be hanging out at 2:00 in the afternoon. Immediately Braxton wanted to start calling, so I handed him a crow call, then a box call. Educating him on what sounds to make, when, was an important lesson that day, despite the fact no toms responded.

Sitting to rest my sore body, Braxton was more than content playing in a creek and dismantling spider webs with his light saber (stick). After a bit, we started walking back to the truck. With less than 200 yards to go, that's when it happened.

Though Braxton couldn't see them, a flock of 11 turkeys were feeding in the grassy field in front of us. Braxton was not tall enough, and the green grass the turkeys were in was too high, hiding the flock from his view–I could barely see their heads.

Fortunately we were still in the heavily shaded timber, and the flock was feeding right toward us. We'd gotten lucky, intercepting the flock as they moved out of a creek bottom, quickly feeding across the meadow, picking grass seeds from the maturing stocks. The best part, they were headed to the shaded timber in which we stood.

Sitting down in front of a big Douglas fir tree, Braxton to my left, we waited. It didn't take long and the first bird crossed the logging road, 25 yards in front of us. Nine other birds followed, but most were jakes with a couple odd hens. Then the last bird stepped on to the road, his brilliantly colored body seeming to light up the dark shadows of the forest. The shot was simple.

Braxton was thrilled beyond words; I was speechless. The last thing I honestly expected to see that day was a turkey, let alone kill one. All of the conditions were against us and my body was in pain, but because my boy wanted to go hunting, we went. Had we not taken a tom that day, Braxton still would have been pleased, for he got to spend time in the woods with his dad. In this situation, a filled tag just made the experience that much sweeter.

174

Prior to any hunt, preparation at home can also help make a child's time afield more enjoyable. Take the youth through what might happen on the hunt, so they know what to expect. Let them try on all their clothing at home and make sure everything fits. If they'll be using face paint, let them play with it at home. If sitting on cushions or in low-profile chairs, let kids try them for themselves to see what they like best. Encourage them to do their own calling, which will result in a lot of teaching taking place at home, weeks, even months prior to setting afield. This helps build anticipation.

When youth are interested, get afield. Having experienced an emergency appendectomy two days prior, turkey hunting wasn't foremost on my mind, but the end result says it all.

One thing both of my boys liked doing when they were young was watching turkey hunting shows. Every time a turkey appeared, they shot it with their toy guns. I took it one step further and took a laser pointer, showing them where to aim on the birds. Kazden loved that and ended up taping the laser pointer to his gun. We had fun and it was a valuable learning situation.

When sighting in the shotgun, make it fun and comfortable. For youth, start with suppressed loads so they don't worry about the recoil. Letting them shoot from a Caldwell Lead Sled will get them used to the loud "bang," and eliminate kick. When ready to shoot off-hand, slipping a recoil-reducing pad over the butt end of the stock will help absorb the kick, allowing kids to focus on the shot, not flinching to avoid pain. Let them fill and shoot their own water balloons. There are also some great turkey targets on the market, ones that instantly show where the pattern hits. Kids love this stuff, and it's a great opportunity to have fun, together.

When it came time for Kazden's first spring turkey hunt, he couldn't wait to shoot his 20 gauge. Finally, after all that practicing on targets, he got to pull the trigger on a live bird. He made a great shot and things ended on a positive note. But the experience wasn't over.

Following his hunt, Kazden, myself and our buddy, Jody Smith, went to Arlene's Cafe in Elkton, OR, where we ordered-up a big breakfast. Jody stepped into the kitchen, coming out with a grin on his face. He shot me a wink, and I didn't question it. Soon the waitress came out and presented Kazden with a big pancake crafted into the shape of a turkey. It was a thoughtful gesture, one Kazden will never forget. As a father, I'll never forget it either, for it bonded a youngster with other adults who loved hunting, and exemplified how turkey hunting is about so much more than killing a bird.

When afield with a child, should something go wrong–like spooking a bird–don't worry about it, and whatever you do, don't blame a youngster, even if it is their fault. Instead, use the moment to enlighten the kid as to what likely happened, taking the opportunity to educate them about hunting and animal behavior. Convey the fact that there are more turkeys out there, then keep trying. Remember, our goal is to shape a future hunter, not turn them away from our great sport.

Kazden's famous turkey pancake, one we'll never forget.

By preparing ahead of time, the chances of offering youth hunters a positive experience greatly increase. Make it fun, keep it interesting and above all else, be aware of kids' needs when in the field. The number one goal is to have fun. Second is to keep kids wanting more. When you get right down to it, bagging a turkey is surprisingly low on the priority list when it comes to developing the skills of future hunters. That's because there's so much more to hunting than simply filling a tag.

Kieli (left) and Taylor Stults with a pair of spring gobblers taken with their dad, Doug. This is how future generations of hunters develop.

176

Chapter 6:

CONCLUSION

With any form or hunting comes a continual learning curve and nowhere is this more true than in the turkey woods of the West. As if the birds aren't cagey enough, throw them in to a habitat that's unforgiving, mentally and physically daunting, and it's safe to suggest that hunting turkeys throughout the West could be the toughest hunt of its kind anywhere in North America.

A few days of chasing toms in the wide open West, where oxygen can be out of comfort's reach more times than not, isn't easy. Move further West, to the Coast Range of Washington, Oregon and California, and dense brush and big timber enter the game. While hunters in the eastern states may have a smaller playing field, and are forced to employ tactics in confined areas, western hunters often face the challenge of having too much land to cover, with much of it being overwhelmingly vast and rugged.

No matter where we hunt them, the more we learn about turkeys, their behaviors and how they survive in and adapt to the habitats they call home, the more knowledgable we'll become as hunters. Of course, education leads to success as long as wise application prevails. The great thing about turkey hunting, if you make a mistake, you can get back on your feet, learn from the experience and move on; there's always another bird to pursue.

For turkey hunters, not only is our growth of knowledge perpetual, but so is how we go about hunting these birds. The fact that new gear allows and encourages hunters to employ ever-changing strategies raises the excitement of turkey hunting to another level. There aren't many animals hunters get to apply something new on–be it with gear or tactical approaches–year after year, thanks to technological advancements and an increased understanding of animal behavior.

From that first turkey I shot while hunting with my dad back in the mid-1980s in our home state of Oregon, to the many exciting hunts I've since had throughout the West, one of the biggest impressions turkey hunting has left on me is how it fosters sportsmanship. This has been true not only for myself and my family, but for nearly all the turkey hunters I've had the honer of associating with over the years.

Face it, the spring woods is a fun place to be. The weather is usually nice, song birds are calling, flowers blooming and people's spirits are lifted. Fill the woods with echoes of gobbling toms and life just gets better.

Some of the hardest working, most dedicated, most enthusiastic hunters I've met, hold the wild turkey in high esteem. Though these people love their deer and elk hunting, along with their predator and other bird hunting, when it comes to pursuing turkeys in the midst of spring, the wild turkey ranks high on their list of favorites.

I've seen grown men trembling in anticipation for the hunt, some unable to bring their bow to full draw when a thundering tom strutted into range. Perhaps this excitement is a result of the uncertainty turkey hunting carries. We know the chances of success are usually good when we enter the turkey woods, but we're never sure how the hunt will unfold. Then, just when we think we have the birds figured out, they do the total opposite and we're left scratching our heads, trying to figure out what went wrong.

Keane Lohmiller, one of the most dedicated, enthusiastic turkey fenatics I've had the honor of hunting with. It's positive people like this who make turkey hunting so special.

For me, as a father and mentor, both the spring and fall turkey woods have been a great platform to spend quality time with my family. It's also opened doors for some priceless learning opportunities. In the spring we've spent time watching Canada geese on their nest, Roosevelt elk giving birth, bears feeding in the same meadows we hunted turkeys and deer fawns stumbling about as they entered the world. In the fall, we've heard bugling bull elk and witnessed impressive waterfowl migrations. During the winter months we've watched big mule deer move from the high country in mass numbers, blacktails rutting and whitetails foraging in the snow. Each of these special experiences were possible, thanks to turkey hunting.

178

Whether you live in the West or are looking to travel to any number of the western states in search of turkey, don't overlook the other hunting and fishing opportunities that come with it. In the spring it's easy to combine a turkey and bear hunt in many places. Some of my most memorable Merriam's turkey hunts have taken place in Idaho, where I've taken some nice bears on the same trip. The same holds true for Oregon and parts of Washington.

If heading to northern California, don't overlook the world-class hog hunting that takes place during turkey season. California not only has pigs, but excellent salmon and steelhead fishing in many parts; as do Washington, Oregon and

A California double. There are many great hunting and fishing opportunities that overlap with turkey seasons throughout the West.

Idaho. Trout and bass fishing opportunities exist in just about every western state turkeys live in, and make for another great spring bonus.

If looking to take the family on a luxurious turkey hunting getaway, look to Hawaii. Hawaii has some of the best turkey hunting in the country and can be teamed with sheep, goat and boar hunts, just to mention a few. Of course, Hawaii also offers great ocean fishing. One of the last trips we went on, our son's couldn't get in enough snorkeling time, and loved diving with the manta rays at night.

James Guthrie with a Spanish goat and Chad Schearer with a plump Rio, taken in Hawaii.

As for traveling hunters in the fall, turkeys are usually pursued as secondary quarry on higher priority big game hunts. Amid many western states, wherever you're chasing deer, elk or bear, turkeys usually aren't far. And don't forget the fall fishing opportunities which are many, especially for trout, as well as salmon and steelhead in the Pacific Northwest.

One of the most memorable fall hunts with my dad found us with Jody Smith, again. Dad tagged a whopper of a tom right off the bat, and I wasn't far behind. Smith then suggested we go after pheasant in a nearby field, and Dad and I each scored on a plump ringneck. Then Smith tossed out the idea of jump shooting valley quail. We won't talk about the ones I missed, but we came away with a brace of birds. On the way back to the truck, we picked up a pair of snipe. We went duck hunting that afternoon. Talk about a mixed bag adventure, and it all started with the turkey.

Turkey hunting takes us to many great places, and as sportsman it's good to know and take advantage of these additional hunting and fishing opportunities that often go overlooked. It's also a great blessing to be able to include the family on such outings.

To this day, one our most memorable family turkey hunting adventures found us in the northeast corner of Wyoming, chasing Merriam's. Only Tiffany and I had tags, and though the boys were too young to hunt, they accompanied us into the field. Both boys learned about calling turkeys, saw lots of birds and built basic woodsmanship skills. But what they really loved was the high-volume prairie dog hunting that followed. Find what interests your children, other family members or turkey hunting friends and plan your next turkey hunt, accordingly.

Coyote hunting can also be good during the spring, especially late in the turkey season. Folks out West

It's not uncommon for coyotes to stalk your turkey decoy. Be ready, out West anything can happen.

are always eager to thin coyote populations, due to their impact on deer and elk herds. I know of one landowner who granted a hunter permission to hunt turkeys if he promised to shoot all the coyotes he saw. There are instances every spring where coyotes stalk in on the turkey decoy; be ready, you never know what will happen.

When tags are filled and trucks turned toward home, the hunt is over but the memories will forever live on. Be sure and preserve those memories with plenty of photos. With the advancement and ease of video, it's simpler than ever to capture those precious moments for all to enjoy.

Turkeys, themselves, can also be preserved, commemorating the thrills of the hunt. You don't have to get every turkey lifesize mounted to keep the memories alive. You can save a beard, make a tail fan and more, and at little or no cost.

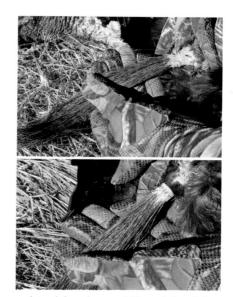

A tom's beard can quickly and cleanly be removed by firmly grasping it (top), and pulling it off the body.

To save a beard, simply grab it and pull firmly against the body; the beard will pop right out–there's no need for cutting. Dab the end in some borax and let dry for a few

There are many ways to display a tail fan, beard and spurs.

days. Pin the beard to a shelf, secure it to the inside of the shotgun shell you took the bird with or hang it from a plaque with the tail fan. There are many options when it comes to creatively displaying a beard.

The tail fan is also easy to preserve. Simply cut the tail above the anus, keeping all quills and a portion of the tail coverts, in tact. From the backside, take a sharp knife and remove the muscle and fat from around and between the quills. Do the same from the front and undersides, being sure to keep the feathers in place. Pin to a board, cover all fleshy parts with borax, pin strips of cardboard across the tail feathers to keep them flat and even, then let dry for a week or so. Once dry, slip the fan into a display plaque, or simply glue a downy feather or two atop any exposed, dried flesh. The fan can also be used as, or in a decoy, as previously mentioned.

If wanting to preserve some of the gorgeous back feathers of your tom, along with the fanned tail, it's easy. Hang the bird by the neck. Make a horizontal cut across the back of the neck, below the caruncles, connecting the two natural "Vs" or valleys of feathers that run down each side of the bird. Cut down both sides of the bird staying above the wings. Start skinning your way down the back and toward the tail, keeping about a four-inch wide strip of skin in-tact. Once to the tail, cut it off at the base as explained above, keeping it attached to the back-skin. Remove all flesh and fat from the back-skin and tail. Lay on a board, feathers down, pin in place and cover in borax. Rub borax into all crevices. In a couple weeks the skin and tail should be dried and ready to display as you wish.

The backskin and tail fan make a beautiful display.

The spurs can also be saved, in one of two ways. The most common is to take a fine-bladed hacksaw, severing the leg bone above and below where the spur attaches on. Take a piece of wire and push out the marrow and rinse clean. Let air dry and the spur can be placed on a lanyard, necklace, displayed with a tail fan mount, framed and more.

The other option to removing spurs is taking a razor blade and cutting all the way around the base of the spur, where it attaches to the leg bone. The dark colored spur is actually the outer sheath that attaches to a sharp bone (spur) protruding from the leg bone. Be sure and cut deep enough to break through the skin and any tendons. Once a deep cut has been made completely around the spur, take a piece of rubber tubing or small hose, place between the jaws of pliers, clamp down on the spur and work the spur sheath free from the bone. The rubber tubing protects the sheath from being scratched and provides a solid grip, as the spur is smooth and slippery. The pliers are necessary to break the seal holding the sheath to the bone. When done you're left with a clean spur that can be filled with epoxy to make jewelry or used in ornamental displays.

There's really no limit to the way turkey spurs and other parts can be preserved and displayed. You can buy mounting kits or craft your own. You can even frame parts in various ways. However you choose to go about it, preserving the memories is fun.

Sitting back, admiring preserved trophies and photos, reliving the hunt through memories, not only takes us back to the adventure, but allows for much deeper reflection. For some of us, our minds might wander back thousands of years, curious as to how Native American hunters outwitted these birds with rudimentary handmade calls and weapons. For others, we might reflect upon the generations of turkey hunters who preceded us, people who paved the way to escalate turkey hunting to the level it is today.

For still others–particularly those like myself who live out West–we find ourselves being thankful. Thankful to wildlife agencies, volunteer groups and hunters for putting in

Photos are some of the best ways to preserve memories of the hunt.

the time and effort to bring turkey populations back from the brink of demise, to the point where it's an honor to hunt them.

For me, as is the case with many people, I find myself greatly appreciative of the fact we as Americans have the freedom to purchase over-the-counter tags and go hunting. When I was a kid, we had no turkeys to hunt. Today we can take five turkeys a year in the area I live. For many of you, the situation is similar.

As you enter the turkey woods, take in all of the sights and experiences you encounter. Then ask yourself, "Would I have witnessed these events were it not for turkey hunting?"

Turkey hunting takes us places we otherwise may not venture. Be it to other states or a few minute's drive from our home, the allure of turkey hunting is addicting and contagious. Once you get a taste of it, you'll know what I mean.

The more time you spend hunting turkeys, the deeper your appreciation for them will grow. Head afield, have fun, maintain an open mind and keep moving forward. Never take what we have for granted. The turkey woods are a magical place. We're privileged to pursue these grand birds in so many beautiful places throughout not only the West, but across much of North America.

Appendix I:
FIELD TO TABLE

I'll admit that the first wild turkey I sank my teeth into was nothing like those fat, round, plump birds we feasted on at Thanksgiving and Christmas. But I'll be darned if I was going to admit it to anyone. By golly, I killed, cleaned and packed out that bird, and I was going to eat every bit of it.

Subsequent birds I took over the years went into the smoker, where, even by my standards of today, yielded some of the best jerky out there. Once married, I realized that some of the tough birds I ate early in my bird hunting days had nothing to do with the birds, themselves, rather how they were prepared.

Today, thanks to the fine cooking efforts of my wife, Tiffany, turkey truly is one of our favorite wild game meats. We kill and eat several wild turkeys a year and never tire of it. As with any bird, however, the quality of the end product has a direct correlation to how the bird is taken care of in the field. It pains me to hear people say they hate eating wild turkey because it's too tough or doesn't taste good.

Honestly, we prefer wild turkey over hormone-induced, fatty, domestically raised birds, and once you get it down, you will, too. Stay with me here, as the following section on field care is lengthy. This is because the more I talk with turkey hunters, the more I realize they simply are not aware of how to best take care of a bird to optimize it's flavor. It's all excellent eating meat and none should go to waste.

Here are many options, described in detail, as to how to take care of your bird once it's dead.

The Importance Of Field Care
The best turkeys can be destroyed by inadequate handling in the field. Improper bleeding, delay or carelessness in gutting and failure to quickly cool meat can all make a major difference in the flavor and texture of the end product. By following a few simple guidelines, the quality of the meat will come through in the final preparation. Think of how much work went in to the hunt and give your downed turkey the deluxe treatment it deserves.

Due to their light bone structure and thin intestinal walls, birds need to be bled and gutted as quickly as possible after being shot. Allowing air to circulate in the body cavity will greatly increase the quality of meat. Birds don't have much fat so their body heat is held in their internal organs (unlike big game that holds much of their body heat in muscle tissues), which explains why quickly cleaning them is so important.

Keep a bottle of water handy, or rely on a stream to rinse the body cavity and get it quickly cooling. Doing this will eliminate a surprising amount of the "gamey" taste turkeys often get blamed for, when really, it's the mishandling by hunters which is at fault.

I shy away from using a vest or bag to store and transport a turkey in while afield, as this retains too much of their body heat. Instead, use a game strap to carry your turkey, or simply grab it by the head or feet and toss the bird over your shoulder. Once birds are taken, be sure to keep them cool and dry, keeping in mind that turkeys are big bodied and retain a lot of heat once dead.

For birds that are gut shot, the best advice is to quickly remove the internal organs. Bird meat can easily be tainted by a gut shot wound, and a quick inspection after the shot usually leaves no question as to the point of impact. When head shot, turkey often flop on the ground and routinely break their wings and sometimes a leg. When this happens, inspect the bird to make sure no broken bones punctured the internal organs. If they have, immediately gut the bird.

Proper field care is a must in order to optimize the eating quality of your turkey.

Once the internal organs are removed, give the body cavity a thorough rinsing and let air-cool. If hunting with a buddy who has a tag left to fill, hang your bird in the shade with the body cavity opened and keep hunting; don't toss it in the back of the truck. If you've planned ahead, having a cooler full of ice will help. Simply place the tom in the cooler, filling the body cavity with ice. It takes a big cooler to hold a tom, but cooling it quickly will yield the best eating meat.

Because birds are so fragile compared to big game, it's a good idea to cook them quickly after being taken or appropriately age them (more on this, below). Make every effort possible to keep them cold until ready to cook, or freeze.

Bleeding A Turkey

Some turkey hunters opt for bleeding their birds prior to field dressing them. Bleeding a bird is simply done by cutting the throat and letting the head hang downward until the bleeding stops.

Bleeding a bird will optimize it's overall flavor. If you don't want to mess with blood potentially getting everywhere, gutting a bird will have the same effect as bleeding it, which I prefer and recommend. Be sure to remove all internal organs, including heart, liver and lungs, in order for proper bleeding to occur.

If wanting to eat the gizzard, heart and/or liver, get them on ice or refrigerated as soon as possible. These organs are best when consumed soon after the kill, as they don't require any aging time.

Gutting A Turkey

Gutting a turkey is easy, and is best done when they are still warm. Not only will gutting warm birds make organ removal easier, it allows the bird to completely bleed out and cool down, which will yield a much better tasting meat.

With a small knife, begin by making a shallow incision from the vent (anus) straight up to the edge of the breast bone. There's no need to pluck the bird first, as turkeys have sparse feathers in this region of the body, making it easy to see the skin, thus where the incision should be made.

Next, reach inside the body cavity, grab a handful of internal organs and gently pull them out, being careful not to puncture or tear the thin-walled intestines. Be sure to remove all internal organs (stomach, intestines, gizzard, liver, heart, lungs and windpipe), completely. Note that the lungs of all birds lays tight against their back, by the back portion of the rib cage. It's crucial to remove every piece of lung, for these organs quickly rot and can taint the taste of your birds.

If you have trouble getting a finger underneath the lungs to pull them out, use the tip of your knife to get under the subcutaneous sheath that holds the lungs in place. From there, either continue peeling the lungs away from the ribs and spine with the knife, or your fingers. Once the lungs are free from both sides of the rib cage, all the way to the spine, they can be extracted in one piece. Should remnants of lung be wedged between the ribs, use the tip of the knife blade to pick them free.

Be sure the trachea and esophagus are also removed, as these quickly spoil in big birds like a turkey. You'll likely need to wrap the trachea and esophagus around your fingers or hand and give a firm yank. Removing the trachea and esophagus not only ensures proper, thorough bleeding, it allows air to more freely move throughout the entire body cavity, cooling the meat.

When finished gutting the bird, rinse the body cavity and allow air to reach it so it can begin cooling. Once you get a turkey down, it only takes a matter of seconds to gut a bird–it's that easy.

186

How To Pluck A Turkey

Plucking a turkey sounds easy, and it can be, but it can also be time consuming. Turkeys are the exception to the easy plucking of upland birds, which is why most people wet pluck or skin them.

So, why pluck birds, not just skin them? Because game birds have so little fat in their muscles, when cooked they can become dry. Cooking birds with the skin on helps retain moisture and flavor.

When plucking a turkey, be careful not to grab handfuls of feathers and start yanking, as this could rip the skin. Once a bird skin rips, it's challenging to finish plucking it with the skin intact.

To dry-pluck a turkey, grasp it by the neck with one hand, grab a few feathers with fingers of the other hand and start pulling in a downward motion, toward the tail. Pulling with the quills allows the feathers to more easily slip out of the follicle in the skin and also helps prevent the skin from ripping.

Work around the bird ensuring all feathers are removed. Note that it is easier to pluck a turkey with the wings removed.

Remove the wings of birds by either cutting at the wrist joint (where the radius and ulna meet) or breaking along the wing shaft. Remember, bird bones are hollow and the bones of the wings, in particular, are very strong. If wings are broken, either intentionally or upon being shot or making impact with the ground, be sure all sharp fragments are removed before cooking or serving.

It's a good idea to keep the feet attached to a bird while plucking, as this provides something to hold on to as you rotate and move the carcass around for thorough plucking. With all the feathers removed, you'll see small, downy feathers still intact. These are so small they are nearly impossible to pluck out one by one, but should be removed.

Rather than spending time plucking these tiny, fine feathers, try singeing them with a torch. A quick pass with a flame will burn the feathers, giving you a clean, fully plucked bird. Rarely do we eat the skin of a game bird so if there are a few feathers or a bit of stubble, it comes off with the skin prior to eating.

Birds are easiest to pluck while still warm, but should only be plucked right away if they can be immediately refrigerated. Gutting birds in the field and leaving the feathers on is a good way to transport them, whereby protecting the meat from bruising and dirt. Plucking is most efficiently done back at camp or home.

Wet-Plucking A Turkey

Dry-plucking a turkey can be challenging and require lots of time, which is why many hunters prefer wet-plucking their bird. When wet-plucking a bird, bring a large pot of water to a boil, noting that it takes a big pot to dunk a turkey in. Be sure there is enough water to fully submerge the turkey. This is best done outside in an open space. While the water is reaching a boil, remove the wings from the turkey and pluck out the tail feathers. Note that some turkey hunters believe bringing the water to a boil is too hot and will dip their bird once the water temperature reaches 140°.

Once the water reaches a boil, grab the bird by the feet and completely submerge it. Grab the feet rather than the head, as once rigor mortis sets in, they provide better leverage to submerge the carcass. Hold the bird under water for seven seconds, no longer. Submerging it for too long will result in the meat starting to cook and the skin more easily ripping when plucking the feathers.

Remove the bird, then grab it by the head (wearing thick rubber gloves helps, as the head is hot) and start plucking. Pull the feathers in a downward motion, toward the tail, as pulling against the way they grow will tear the skin. Having a trash can nearby to drop the plucked feathers into helps quickly move the process along.

Waxing A Turkey

Plucking birds by way of waxing them is something waterfowlers have been doing for years, but it also works on turkeys. In fact, some commercial turkey farms have greatly cut their overhead costs by plucking birds via waxing, versus wet- or dry-plucking methods. This is because it's a fast process. Remember, turkeys have over 5,000 feathers; that's a lot of plucking.

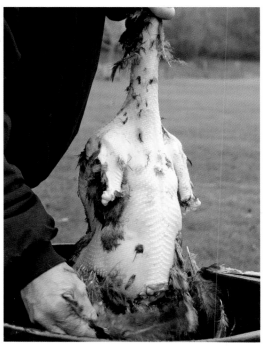

Wet plucking is just one way to prepare a turkey.

There are two types of wax that can be used in plucking turkeys: paraffin wax and duck wax. Paraffin wax, like that used in candle making and home canning, can be purchased online or from supply companies. Duck wax is what serious waterfowlers prefer, as it sticks to the feathers in larger, easier to peel pieces than the paraffin. Duck wax can be purchased online or in select sporting goods stores in five or 10-pound lots.

Outside, in an open area, heat a pot of water to about 160°F. Do not bring the water to a boil and do not get the water too hot or it will not allow the wax to evenly buildup on the surface. As the water heats up, add your wax, allowing it to melt and rise to the surface. When the wax melts, it should be 1/4- to 1/2-inch thick on the surface. If it's not thick enough, either cool the water or add more wax. A good rule of thumb ratio is 25% wax and 75% water.

Prior to waxing your bird, remove the wings close to the bird's body, then dry-pluck the tail feathers and other large body feathers. Holding the turkey by the feet, dip and gently move it around in the melted wax. The objective is to allow about 1/2-inch or so of wax to buildup on the bird. Once evenly covered in wax, remove the turkey and let cool until the wax is hardened, which usually takes about 10 minutes.

Once hardened, peel the wax in a downward motion, toward the tail-end. Wax and feathers will come off, together. When done peeling you can put the wax back in the hot water and allow to re-melt. Skim feathers off the top and re-dip the carcass as needed. Repeat dipping, cooling and peeling process until all feathers and down are removed. This gives a clean, sleek appearance many people prefer.

When finished, the wax can be re-melted and feathers skimmed off the top. Let the water cool and the wax harden, storing it for future use.

Skinning A Turkey

If not plucking a turkey, skinning it is another option. This is a great option when there isn't time for plucking. There are numerous cooking methods that work on skinned turkeys. Skinned birds can be used whole or they can be breasted out. If breasting-out a bird, remove thighs and legs and cook separately. Many recipes suggest cooking breast meat separately from leg and thigh meat due to the differences in fat content and cooking time.

Birds should only be skinned if they can be immediately refrigerated or placed in a cold ice chest. Skinning is much faster than plucking, but because the protective skin has been removed, these birds cannot be aged under refrigeration for more than a day or two.

To skin a bird, pick up where you left off when gutting it. Simply continue making the cut from the anus, all the way up the breast bone to the base of the neck. Continue peeling the skin down the sides of each breast, all the way to the wings. If the wings haven't already been removed, now is a good time to sever them at the wrist or shoulder joint.

Continue peeling the skin off the carcass, working your way around the back and tail section. Peel the skin down each leg, much like how you would unroll a sock, and sever each leg at the knee joint.

With the skin now loose from the legs, back and breast, work the skin around the shoulders, all the way to the neck. Sever the neck at desired point.

Breasting A Turkey

If looking to breast out your turkey, that's simple and quick. Peel away the skin from both sides of the breast, as described above, all the way down to the base of the wings and the back of the rib cage. Next, take a sharp fillet knife and slice into the breast, keeping the blade firmly running against the keel as you cut. Continue filleting the meat away from the keel and breast bone until removed from the bone. Sever the chunk of breast meat where it attaches to the shoulder, at the base of the wing, and repeat on the other side.

Be sure and remove the legs and thighs of your turkey, as not only is it required by law, but it also yields excellent eating meat. Simply peel away the skin from these parts, cut the foot off at the knee and remove the leg from the body by cutting through the ball-and-socket joint. Legs and thighs, separate of the breast, are great eating, as you'll find in recipes that follow.

Aging Turkey

Aging meat is something big game hunters regularly practice, and many bird hunters do it, too. Aging your turkey allows the muscles to breakdown and is especially effective on older toms.

Opinions on how best to age a turkey run the gamut. There are those that adhere to the motto "fresh birds are the best birds" and others that wouldn't think of eating a bird before it had aged at least four days. Differences on aging temperatures and whether or not birds should be gutted prior to aging exist as well.

We have had delicious birds, both fresh and aged, and find that it comes down to time and personal preference. It is important to note that wild turkey can be aged right after it is killed or aged after it has been frozen. When aging a turkey, follow the guidelines below to attain the best eating meat.

Aging Guidelines

- Only head-shot birds should be aged without skinning.
- Skinned birds should not age more than 24 hours.
- Place birds on a rack, or hang by head or feet, for proper ventilation.
- Age boneless breast uncovered, up to 4 days (remove hardened outer layer prior to cooking).
- Juvenile birds need no aging time.
- Dry-pluck birds that have hung for longer than 3 days.

Preparing A Turkey To Cook

Once a turkey has been cleaned, plucked or skinned and maybe aged, it is ready to cook. The next step is preparing it for the recipe or cooking method. Whole birds are easy as they can be roasted, bagged, grilled or smoked. Cooking turkeys whole however, may not always be the best approach.

With wild turkeys, their lack of fat predisposes them to drying out quickly. If birds have been skinned, something often needs to be added to help replace that protection (bacon, spice paste, crust, etc.). Also keep in mind that breast meat cooks faster than leg and thigh meat and may be ruined with the whole-bird cooking method. One remedy is to fillet the breast meat off and continue cooking the leg and thigh meat, but this may impact your presentation. Moist-heat cooking methods (braising, steaming, poaching, Dutch oven, oven bag, etc.) help greatly when cooking whole birds. Smoking these birds is also beneficial as the meat cooks in the smoker but can be removed from the bones and added or cooked into another recipe that will then rehydrate it.

Another way to prepare turkeys, bone-in, is to cook the breast meat separate from the thigh and leg meat. Once separated, they tend to take about the same amount of cooking time.

A versatile and quick way to prepare turkeys for cooking is to skin and cut the meat in cubes, slices or small chunks. Meat prepared in this way can be stir-fried, stewed, sauteed, poached or fried.

Grinding or dicing game bird meat makes for even more versatility as it can be made into nuggets or meatballs; mixed with ground pork, beef or chicken; or simply treated like any ground filling for tacos, spaghetti, gravy, casseroles or sandwich spreads.

Deboning game birds takes the guesswork out of cooking. Without bones, meat cooks evenly and can be stuffed with a variety of flavors and moisture-rich fats.

Because turkeys, by nature of the harvest, can carry a shot pellet or two in their flesh, the more they are handled, cut up and inspected, the less likely someone will need to visit the dentist after their meal.

Butchering A Turkey

Prior to cooking any turkey, breaking them down into body parts can separate some of the finer eating breast or thigh meat from the more sinuous legs and boney parts used in stock. Remember, it is law to retrieve all edible body parts of a wild turkey. People who cut out the breast and toss the rest of the carcass are in violation of state laws because they are discarding edible leg and thigh meat, parts that eat well if properly prepared.

There are a couple options when it comes to breaking down birds prior to cooking them, and the more time you spend doing it, the more you'll discover what suits your personal needs. Typically, turkeys are broken down once they've been skinned, as it's challenging to keep the skin in-tact when cutting birds into parts.

One skinned, take the carcass and lay it on its back. Push down on the legs, forcing them away from the body, until the ball-and-socket joint separate. With a sharp knife, cut though the muscles at the hip joint, keeping as much of the upper thigh and lower back muscles as you'd like.

The thigh meat can be separated from the drumstick, too. Separating the tasty thigh from the tougher, more sinuous drumstick allows you to cook them independently of one another.

The entire breast bone and keel can be separated from the spine, ribs and neck, with both sides of the breast meat intact. To do this, simply pull the ribs away from the breast, separating the ribs. Next, cut the breast away from the wings, at the shoulder joint.

Once this process is complete, you're left with a whole breast (the meat still attached to both sides of the keel), a pair of legs and thighs, and a backbone with ribs and neck attached. The spine, neck and ribs make for excellent stock.

Grinding A Turkey

As with wild game meat, we never mix any kind of fat into the grinding process of our turkeys. If adding another meat is desired, we do that right before cooking, not before freezing the meat. When cooking ground turkey, use plenty of olive oil in the pan to prevent the meat from sticking and drying out. Do not overcook the delicate meat.

Despite their size, turkeys have a soft textured meat. A fine chop/dice may be all that is needed for the meat to resemble ground meat. A few pulses in a food processor or mini-chopper can also accomplish "grinding" the meat.

Deboning A Turkey

Deboning an entire turkey sounds more intimidating than it really is. In fact, the deboning process is easy, it just takes time.

Deboning a turkey is just like deboning a fish or big game animal. As long as you keep reminding yourself that the objective of deboning is to remove the muscles from the bone, you'll be fine.

Place the skinned turkey carcass on it's breast, backbone facing you and parallel to the counter. With a sharp knife begin carving your way down one side of the bird, separating the meat from the muscle (fillet one side of the bird at a time). Work all the way from the neck, down to the thigh meat. The purpose is to cut and peel the meat away from the bone, working around the side of the bird and eventually to the front.

When cutting around the wing area, make as few slices as possible to get the muscles away from the boney structures. When cutting around the legs, a section of leg muscle may need to be cut so you can free the rest of the sinuous muscles from the bone.

Once you've filleted the back, wing and leg muscles, continue to the breast. Be sure to keep the knife blade riding against the breast bone in order to retain as much meat as possible. Continue filleting up the breast bone and keel, stopping when you reach the cartilaginous ridge. From there, flip the bird back on its breast and repeat the filleting process for the other side.

As you cut through the second breast, be careful not to separate the meat as you work toward the breast bone and keel. Keep the cuts close to the bone, ensuring both filleted halves remain intact. The final cut is made down the ridge of the breast bone, ensuring that all the meat remains connected in one piece.

The deboning process does take a while, so be patient. The more of these you do, the faster you'll get at it, and the more cooking opportunities you'll have at your fingertips.

Wondering what to do with a deboned bird? Try combining game birds you have available, to create Turkpheasquail (see recipe page 199).

The cooking options don't stop with the meat you've just removed. The entire skeleton can now be used to make a tasty stock. With this method, absolutely nothing goes to waste.

Soaking Solutions: Marinades & Brines

Marinades and brines help flavor, tenderize and protect game birds during the cooking process. Flavors are endless and can be combined in many ways to please all tastes. Acids in these liquids help to break-down the proteins in meats making them more tender as well as enhancing the flavor. Oil added to marinades helps prevent moisture loss in cooking and also protects meat if cooking with dry-cooking methods such as grilling.

Acids include vinegars, citrus, wine, spirits, tomato, fruit juices and yogurt. Flavors include herbs, spices, garlic, ginger, honey, soy sauce and hot sauce, to name a few. Any oil will work in a marinade but stronger flavored oils such as sesame or walnut oil will help add flavor as well.

Depending on how much meat is soaking, marinade time usually varies from 30 minutes to overnight. If looking to soak birds for better texture, try an overnight soak in one of the soaking solutions below. Double or triple suggestions in order to soak larger portions or whole birds.

Soaking Solution Ingredients
- Buttermilk
- Strong brewed coffee (cooled)
- Tomato juice or Bloody Mary mix
- 1 cup apple juice + 1 cup chicken broth
- 2 cups milk + 2 tablespoons vinegar or lemon juice
- 2 cups water + 1/2 teaspoon salt + 1/2 teaspoon baking soda
- 1 cup water + 1/2 cup vinegar + onion stuffed in body cavity

Other "taming" flavors include oranges, ginger, sauerkraut, onions, celery, BBQ sauce and curries.

Thermometers

When cooking wild turkey, use an internal cooking thermometer. With this lean, delicate meat, just a degree or two of overcooking can drastically impact the end result.

USDA recommends all birds cooking to 165°. We usually aim for 150°-155° as birds do continue to cook after they are removed from the heat source. When using ground or stuffed turkey, play it safe and cook until meat reaches 165°. Some birds taste better cooked to "falling-off-the-bone" while others get stronger flavored and become tougher. Leg and thigh meat cooks up quite differently from breast meat so for best results, we recommend different preparations. Take notes, experiment and perfect your skills through trial and error.

Appendix II:
FAVORITE RECIPES

Wild turkey is one of our family's favorite eating meats. If taken care of properly, from the field to the kitchen, you're in a good position to discover just how good the meat can be.

Following are some of our favorite recipes that Tiffany has developed over the years. For more recipes, check out our popular book, Cooking Game Birds at www.scotthaugen. com or www.tiffanyhaugen.com.

Turkey Cutlets

Make this meal quickly by using a favorite prepared spaghetti sauce for the marinara sauce or make the marinara sauce from scratch. Cutlets can be pounded and tenderized ahead of time and kept covered in the refrigerator between sheets of waxed paper.

- 1-2 pounds turkey cutlets
- 2 teaspoons meat tenderizer (optional)
- 2 teaspoons granulated garlic
- 1/3 cup lemon juice
- 2 eggs, well beaten
- 1 tablespoon cold water

- 1 cup Italian bread crumbs
- 1/3 cup parmesan cheese, finely grated
- 1 teaspoon fresh ground black pepper
- 3 tablespoons olive oil
- Mozzarella cheese, thinly sliced
- Marinara Sauce

Slice turkey breast into 1/2" cutlets. Between two layers of waxed paper, pound cutlets to 1/4". Sprinkle cutlets with meat tenderizer and granulated garlic.

Prepare three shallow dishes for the three step process. In the first dish, squeeze lemon juice. In the second dish, beat the eggs with water. In the third dish place bread crumbs, parmesan cheese and black pepper. Place pounded cutlets in lemon juice.

In a large skillet, heat olive oil on medium-high heat. One at a time, take cutlets from lemon juice, coat with egg mixture, press into bread crumbs to completely coat and add to hot oil. Fry cutlets, 3-4 minutes per side. Immediately top cutlet with mozzarella cheese. Top or serve with warm marinara sauce on the side.

Rosemary Brown Sugar Steaks

Talk about a game "tamer," this full-flavored marinade enhances anything from wild turkey to antelope to bear. An older bird can marinate in this for up to 36 hours. Younger birds will benefit from a 6-12 hour soak.

- 1 1/2 pounds turkey breast, steaks

Sweet Rosemary Marinade:
- 1/4 cup real maple syrup
- 1/4 cup soy sauce
- 1/4 cup Worcestershire sauce
- 1/4 cup cider vinegar
- 1/4 cup brown sugar
- 1/4 cup olive oil
- 3-4 cloves garlic, crushed
- 3 sprigs rosemary

Cut turkey into 1/2" steaks. In a large bowl, mix marinade ingredients until thoroughly combined. Marinate turkey breast steaks 6-24 hours, refrigerated. Let meat sit at room temperature 30 minutes before cooking. On a hot, well-lubricated grill, cook only until grill marks appear, 2-3 minutes per side. Steaks are thin and lean so they will grill quickly. Steaks can also be fried in olive oil on medium-high heat in a large skillet, 5-6 minutes per side.

Mexican Slow-Cooked Turkey

We've smoked, roasted, braised and stewed wild turkey legs and thighs. Many recipes, countless methods and one way to cook this flavorful dark meat still stands above them all–slow-cooking. Because turkeys spend most of their time running around on the ground, their legs and thighs are sinuous. Unless you want to spend a lot of time separating out all the meat from the tendons and ligaments, throw this part of the bird into the crock pot. The meat stays moist, absorbs flavors and becomes incredibly tender when cooked "low & slow."

- 2-4 turkey thighs & legs
- 1 onion, diced
- 1 tomato, chopped
- 1-2 jalapeno peppers, diced
- 1 4.5-ounce can green chilies, diced
- 1 6-ounce can tomato paste

- 1 cup white wine or beer
- 2 tablespoons chili powder
- 2 teaspoons cumin
- 1 teaspoon salt

In a medium bowl mix all ingredients. Place turkey meat in slow cooker/crock pot. Cover with vegetable/spice mixture. Cook on "HIGH" heat 4-5 hours or until meat falls from bone. Remove bones, tendons and ligaments (careful, some are quite small) and use meat for burritos, tacos, enchiladas, etc.

Honey Mustard Planked Turkey Breast

Hands-down, our family favorite for wild turkey. This is the recipe to turn to when someone complains they don't like wild turkey–it's guaranteed to change their mind!

- 1 boneless wild turkey breast (approximately 1 pound)
- 3-4 strips of raw bacon
- 1 alder or cedar plank soaked 1-2 hours in water

Honey Mustard Marinade:

- 2 tablespoons Dijon mustard
- 2 tablespoons rum
- 2 tablespoons honey
- 1 tablespoon olive oil
- 1 teaspoon coriander
- 1/2 teaspoon meat tenderizer (optional)

In a small bowl, mix all marinade ingredients until thoroughly combined. Place turkey breast in a sealable bag or casserole dish and cover with marinade. Marinate 6-24 hours, refrigerated. Place turkey breast on a prepared plank. Cover with sliced bacon. Grill or bake in a preheated, 375° oven, 30-45 minutes or until meat thermometer reads 150°-160°. For more information on plank cooking go to www.tiffanyhaugen.com.

Bag-Roasted Turkey

Oven bags are a fantastic invention and work well with many meats. With the right amount of liquid, oven bags clearly help keep wild birds from drying out while roasting. When roasting a turkey, plan to put the carcass directly into a pot for turkey stock/broth; you won't be disappointed. Any unused veggies, stuffing and/or pan drippings help flavor the stock/broth as well.

- 1 whole or cut-up turkey, cleaned & dressed (skin on or off)
- 4 tablespoons bacon grease or olive oil
- 1 cup onions, chopped
- 2 cups celery, chopped
- 1 1/2 cups turkey/chicken stock

- 1 1/2 cups white wine
- 1/2 tablespoon salt
- 1/4 tablespoon pepper

- 1 large oven-safe roasting bag

In a medium bowl, combine onion, celery and bacon grease or olive oil. Stuff turkey with mixture. Rub salt and pepper outside of turkey. Place turkey inside roasting bag. Pour stock and wine into bag and secure bag. Place 3-4, 2" slits in the top of the bag. Roast in a preheated, 325° oven, 1 1/2 hours or until the breast reaches an internal temperature of 150°-160°. Remove from oven and keep oven bag closed. Let turkey sit 10-15 minutes before carving. Discard onion and celery.

Deep Fried Turkey

Deep frying a wild turkey is a great way to quickly cook the bird without drying out the meat. Although it takes a lot of oil to cook it, the result is a super flavorful, moist bird. The oil is not absorbed by the meat, so it is not oily or greasy tasting.

- 1 whole turkey, cleaned & dressed (skin on)
- 4 tablespoons Cajun seasoning
- 5 gallons peanut oil (see note)
- Long handled tongs
- Deep-fry or candy thermometer

Weigh turkey to determine deep-frying time. Dry turkey thoroughly with a clean dish towel and coat with 2 tablespoons Cajun seasoning. Pour peanut oil into a 10 gallon pot. On a propane cooker, bring oil to 375°. Using long handled tongs, carefully submerge turkey in the hot oil. Fry for 4 minutes per pound or until internal thermometer reads 150°-160°. Remove turkey from hot oil and place on a carving surface. Sprinkle with remaining Cajun seasoning and let sit 15-20 minutes before carving.

Note: To determine exactly how much oil is needed, fill frying pot with water first. Place unseasoned turkey in a clean plastic trash bag. Immerse bag in water letting excess water spill over the edges. Remove water 4"-5" below the pot. Lift turkey out of the water and note the water level. Discard water and thoroughly dry pot. Fill pot with oil to the last water level noted; that's the amount of oil needed to cook your bird with.

Turkpheasquail

This recipe carries a "wow-factor" people will be talking about for years, thanks to both the beauty and unique flavors. Any bird combinations can be used so be creative with your catch. The challenge in this recipe lies in fully deboning the game birds but it is well worth the effort.

- 1 wild turkey, deboned
- 1 pheasant, deboned
- 1 quail, deboned
- 1 1/2 pounds country pork sausage
- 1 onion

- 2 carrots
- 2 celery stalks
- 2 sprigs rosemary
- 1/4 cup olive oil
- Seasoning rub of choice

After deboning birds, lay each bird out butterfly style, skin-side down. Sprinkle seasoning over turkey and evenly distribute half of the sausage in a thin layer on top of the turkey. Lay pheasant, skin-side down over the sausage layer. Place remaining sausage on top of the pheasant. Place quail, skin-side down over the sausage layer.

Starting with the leg area of the turkey, roll up toward breast area. Pull both sides of the turkey in, like closing a book. Place roasting pan on top of the turkey and turn the whole thing over so the "seam" is down.

Place onion, carrots, celery and rosemary in the pan around the birds. Coat turkey with a light layer of olive oil. Sprinkle on additional seasoning rub.

Roast in a pre-heated 325° oven, 2 1/2 - 3 hours or until internal temperature reads 165°. Baste with pan drippings every 20-30 minutes. (Check temperature in several places to ensure a proper reading throughout.) Let Turkpheasquail rest 30 minutes before carving/slicing. Turkpheasquail can also be braised, grilled or smoke-cooked.

Note: Many combinations of upland game birds and waterfowl can be used in this recipe. Bird breasts can be used in place of the whole, deboned birds (with the exception of the turkey, it must be used whole).

Turkey Stock

- Turkey carcass
- 3 onions, skin on
- 6 carrots
- 5 celery stalks
- 6-8 cloves garlic
- 1-2 teaspoons salt

Place turkey carcass in a large stock pot. Fill with water, leaving at least 2" of space at the top. Quarter onions, chop carrots and celery into large chunks. Add remaining ingredients and bring to a boil. Turn heat to low, simmering 6-8 hours. Strain stock, discarding all bones and vegetables. Stock is ready to use or freeze. For a quick turkey soup, bring broth to a boil, add desired diced vegetables and 12-16-ounces of pasta. Cook pasta to desired texture. Salt and pepper to taste.

Honey-Orange Turkey Jerky

- 2-3 pounds wild turkey breast, sliced to jerky size
- 3 cups water
- 1/2 cup orange juice
- 1/4 cup white sugar
- 1/4 cup honey
- 1/4 cup Morton's Tender Quick or curing salt
- 1/2 tablespoon granulated onion
- 1/2 tablespoon garlic powder
- 1 teaspoon liquid smoke (optional)
- 1 teaspoon white pepper (optional)

In a large ceramic or glass bowl, mix all brine ingredients with a wire whisk until salt and sugar are dissolved. Add meat, mix thoroughly, and put a plate on top to be sure all meat remains submerged. Soak 8-10 hours, stirring occasionally. Drain brine and remove meat. Do not rinse meat. If additional pepper flavor is desired, sprinkle white pepper or other seasonings on meat at this time. Pat dry or place on racks and let air dry for up to 1 hour. Follow smoking directions on your smoker. Cooking times vary greatly and depend on make and model of smoker and outside weather conditions. Try to keep the temperature of the smoker between 150° and 200°. Check for doneness after 3 hours. Larger cuts of jerky can be finished on a baking sheet in the oven at 165°, check every 15 minutes. When jerky is done, refrigerate or freeze (vacuum sealing works best) if storing for an extended period of time.

A

Aging Turkey Meat, 189-190
Anatomy, 17-20
Archery, 59-67
ATV Hunts, 143

B

Behavioral Progressions (Spring), 112-115
Behavioral Progressions (Fall), 145-150
Binoculars, 68
Biology & Behavior, 10-48
Bleeding a Turkey, 185
Bow Poundage, 66
Bows, 59-67
Bow Shot Placement, 62-66
Box Calls, 70-74
Breaking Up Flocks, 156-158
Breasting Turkey, 189
Broadheads, 60, 66
Butchering, 190-191

C

Calling Fall Turkeys, 160-164
Calling Spring Turkeys, 123-127
Calls, 69-92
Color Phases, 27-28
Communication, 28-44
Cooking Turkey, 193-201
Cutts, 34-35

D

Deboning Turkey, 191
Decoys, 92-100
Diaphragm Calls, 74-78
Diet, 44-48, 117-118, 147-148
Dogs, 158-160

E

Eastern Turkey, 26-27

F

Facemask, 109
Fall Turkey Behavior, 145-150
Fall Hunting, 144-164
Fall Tactics, 151-164
Field Care, 184-192
Fly-Down Cackle, 37-38

G

Gear, 49-111
Gobble, 39-43
Gobbler Call, 86
Ground Blinds, 60, 61, 95, 101-105, 154, 166-167
Gutting Turkey, 186

H

Hand Warmers, 109
Heated Clothing, 109
Hen Yelp, 30-32
Horseback Hunts, 141-142
Hunt Hot Days (Spring), 135-138

I

Internal Anatomy, 66

K

Kee-Kee, 38-39
Knee Gun Rest, 108
Knee Pads, 107

L

Lifecycle, 11-16
Locator Calls, 91-92
LoopRope, 111

M

Marinades & Brines, 192
Merriam's, 25-26
Mountain Bike Hunts, 142
Mouth Calls, 74-78

O

Optics, 67-68

P

Pattern Birds (Spring), 121-123
Patterning Shotguns, 56-58
Plucking Turkey, 187
Pot Calls, 78-85
Private Lands, 118-120
Purr, 32-34
Push-Pull Calls, 85
Putts, 35-36

R

Rain (Spring), 127-129
Rangefinders, 109
Reading Signs (Spring), 116-118
Recipes, 193-201
Rio Grande, 23-24
Roosting, 151

S

Seats, 108
Senses, 21-22
Shock Gobbling, 90-92
Shooting Sticks, 59, 167
Shotgun Chokes, 53-55
Shotguns, 50-59
Shotgun Sights, 58-59, 80
Shotgun Sling, 109
Shot Size, 56-57
Skinning Turkey, 189
Slate Calls, 78-85
Spit & Drum, 43-44
Spring Turkey Behavior, 112-115
Spring Hunting, 112-143
Spot & Stalk (Fall), 152-154
Spot & Stalk (Spring), 138-140
Spotting Scope, 68
Stools, 108
Strikers, 79-83

T

Tall Grass (Spring), 133-135
Targets (3D), 61-62
ThermaCell Heated Insoles, 107
ThermaCell Mosquito Repellant, 106-107
Trail Cameras, 155
Tree Call, 36
Tree Stands, 61, 101-104
Trophy Preservation, 181-183
Turkey Recipes, 193-201
Turkey Vest, 108, 110

W

Waxing Turkey, 188
Western Turkeys, 23-27
Wet-Plucking Turkey, 187-188
Wind (Spring), 130-133
Wingbone Calls, 88-90
Wing Calls, 87-88

Y

Youth Accessories, 169-172
Youth Field Education, 172-176
Youth Hunting, 165-176
Youth Setups, 166-168

SCOTT HAUGEN is a full-time television host, author and speaker. Former teachers for 12 years, Scott and his wife, Tiffany, now make their living from the outdoors and enjoy every minute of their blessed lifestyle.

Scott annually spends more than 200 days a year in the field, and his greatest reward, be it through television, writing or seminars, is sharing what he's learned with others. The Haugen's live in western Oregon's Cascade foothills.

For more information, visit www.scotthaugen.com.

Other Popular Books by Scott and Tiffany Haugen
(For more information or to order go to www.scotthaugen.com)

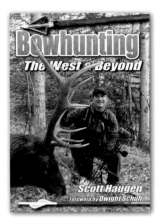

Bowhunting the West & Beyond
by Scott Haugen

Join noted author and TV host, Scott Haugen, on some of his most exciting bowhunts throughout the West and abroad. In addition to thrilling adventures, you'll learn valuable tips sure to improve your bowhunting skills.

Thanks to a lifetime of hunting experience, a formal education and serious dedication, Scott Haugen is able to make his living from the outdoors. His passion is sharing what he learns.

In these pages, over 50 thrilling hunts come to life, with many record-class animals being taken. Whether you're a newcomer or veteran to bowhunting, this book has something for everyone. 6 x 9 inches, 256 pages, all-color.

SB: $20.00

ISBN-13: 978-0-9819423-2-2
UPC: 0-81127-00292-4

Life in the Scope
by Scott Haugen

From the Rocky Mountains to the Pacific Ocean, from Alaska to Mexico, Haugen experienced some of the most exciting hunts the West has to offer. Join Scott on 25 of his most memorable big-game rifle hunts for elk, deer, bear and more.

While many of these hunts culminated with record-class animals, the stories brought to life in these pages reveal much more. Feel what it's like to endure the pain, heartache and jubilation of Western big-game hunting. Learn what drives this avid hunter and what it's like to catch the action on film for award-winning television.

This book is more than the retelling of hunting stories, it's about a way of life. 6 x 9 inches, 180 pages, all-color.

SB: $14.99

ISBN-13: 978-0-9819423-1-5
UPC: 0-81127-00291-7

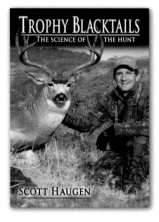

Trophy Blacktails
by Scott Haugen

When it comes to Western big-game hunting, blacktail deer are in a class by themselves. Never before has there been such a book written on the behavior of blacktail deer and how to hunt them. This comprehensive work will take you deep inside the secretive lifestyle of blacktail deer, revealing information that will help make you a more successful hunter.

From year-round deer behavior to advanced hunting tactics, the author shares facts and experiences that have worked for he and his family for several generations. Scott Haugen has been fortunate to hunt many corners of the globe, for some of the world's most prestigious big game, and rates trophy Columbia blacktail among the most challenging to consistently attain – this book tells why! 6 x 9 inches, 192 pages b/w, color insert.

SB: $19.99

ISBN-13: 978-0-9819423-0-8
UPC: 0-81127-00290-0

Cooking Game Birds

by Scott & Tiffany Haugen

This book guides readers from the field to the table, offering helpful tips on how to best preserve and prepare waterfowl, wild turkey and upland birds. From veteran to novice, everyone can find success in this cookbook which offers more than 150 delicious recipes. The time-tested, creative, recipes found within these pages feature minimal ingredients, color photographs and easy-to-follow instructions. 6 x 9 inches, 152 pages, all-color.

Spiral SB: $20.00 **ISBN-13: 978-0-98194-233-9**
UPC: 0-81127-00327-9

Cooking Big Game

by Scott & Tiffany Haugen

More than 100 recipes designed specifically for cooking wild game. Including recipes for stir fries, pizza, pasta, burgers, pot pies, curries, stews & soups, jerky, marinades, rubs & stock, and more, you are sure to find new and delicious ways to prepare your wild game. 6 x 9 inches, 136 pages, all-color.

Spiral SB: $19.95 **ISBN-13: 978-1-57188-407-7**
UPC: 0-81127-00241-2

Scott & Tiffany Haugen

Grill It! Plank It! Wrap It! Smoke It!

by Tiffany Haugen

The latest in Tiffany Haugen's exciting line of cookbooks, this book is geared toward anyone who enjoys food infused with the smoky essence of wood. Packed with flavorful, healthy, family-friendly recipes and creative techniques, this all-in-one book shares all that you need to know about grilling, plank and wrap cooking, and smoking foods. Each cooking style includes appetizers, vegetables, meats, seafood, and desserts. Marinades, rubs, salsas, and sauces are also featured. This is the first book to combine these three styles of cooking into one convenient and attractive book. Keep it on your shelf, flip to any page, and you will find recipes that please even the pickiest of eaters. 6 x 9 inches, 156 pages, all-color.

Spiral SB: $19.95 **ISBN-13: 978-1-57188-416-9**
UPC: 0-81127-00250-4